Measuring Cuban Economic Performance

Special Publication
Institute of Latin American Studies
The University of Texas at Austin

MEASURING CUBAN ECONOMIC PERFORMANCE

By Jorge F. Pérez-López

University of Texas Press, Austin

Library of Congress Cataloging in Publication Data

Pérez-López, Jorge F.
  Measuring Cuban economic performance.

  (Special publication/ Institute of Latin American Studies)
  Bibliography: p.
  Includes index.
  1. Cuba—Economic conditions—1959-   . 2. National income—Cuba—Accounting. 3. Gross national product—Cuba. I. Title. II. Series: Special
publication (University of Texas at Austin. Institute of Latin American Studies)
HC152.5.P47   1986   339.37291   86-24907

First Edition, 1987
Requests for permission to reproduce material from this work should be sent
to:

Permissions
University of Texas Press
P.O. Box 7819
Austin, Texas 78713-7819

To my parents, René G. and Marta J. Pérez-López

Contents

Preface   xi

Introduction   1

1. Physical Output Data   7

2. Value-Added Weights   33

3. Product/Services Weights   83

4. Results   97

5. Comparisons with Other Measures   117

6. Conclusions   127

Appendix A. Physical Output Data   129

Appendix B. United Nations International Standard Industrial Classification of All Economic Activities   165

Appendix C. Estimating Total Agricultural Output from *Acopio* Data   173

Appendix D. Stability of Shares of GSP Components across Valuation Methodologies   177

Appendix E. Activity Index Aggregation Formulae   181

Abbreviations   183

Notes   185

Bibliography   193

Index   199

Tables

1. Collectivization in Cuba   10
2. Land under State Control   11
3. Correlation between Cuban Classification of Economic Activities (CAE) and International Standard Industrial Classification (ISIC) of All Economic Activities   12
4. Physical Output Series for Branches of Industrial Sector   21
5. Nonmonetary Activity Series for Service Sectors   22
6. Production and *Acopio* of Agricultural Products   25
7. Production of Selected Agricultural Products   30
8. Physical Output Series for Branches of Agricultural Sector   31
9. Gross Value Added in Productive Activities   34
10. Comparison of GVO and Value Added, 1962 and 1963   36
11. Value Added by Selected Branches of Industry, 1963   38
12. Wage Bill of Civilian State Employees   40
13. State Civilian Employment by Economic Activity   42
14. Economically Active Population in 1970, by Economic Activity   44
15. State and Private Civilian Employment   46
16. Economically Active Population in 1970, by Occupational Category   48
17. Employment in 1979, by Occupational Category   53
18. Economically Active Population in 1970 and Employment in 1979, by Occupational Category   54
19. Capital Stock of State Industrial Sector circa 1963, Valued at Acquisition Prices, by Type   55
20. Total Value of State Investment   56
21. State Investment, by Sector   57
22. Gross Investment, by Sector   58
23. Total Value of State Investment, by Sector   59
24. Gross Investment, by Type   60
25. Gross Investment in Nonproductive Sectors, by Sector and Use   61
26. Composition of Value Added in 1964   62
27. GVO and Value Added in 1974   63
28. Estimated GSP and GVO for Productive Sectors, 1974   63
29. Statistical Detail for Selected Economic Sectors   64
30. Branch Contribution to Output of Selected Economic Sectors   66
31. Disaggregated Estimates of GSP and GVO for Productive Sectors, 1974   68

32. Output Measures for Banking and Insurance Services, 1974   69
33. State Budget Allocations for Financing of Nonproductive Activities   70
34. GVO of Nonproductive Sphere in 1974 and Estimated GVO for Selected Nonproductive Activities   72
35. Purchases of Labor and Capital Inputs per 100 Pesos of Output   73
36. GVO and Value Added in 1953   75
37. Estimated Value-Added Weights, 1974   77
38. Labor Requirements per Peso of Output   80
39. Official Cuban Consumer Prices, 1977   85
40. Official Cuban Consumer Prices, December 1981   87
41. Official Cuban Consumer Prices, 1977–1981   88
42. Prices of Selected Goods in Different Markets, 1977–1978   90
43. Proxy Prices, 1973–1974   94
44. Calculated Activity Indexes for Goods-producing Sectors   98
45. Calculated Activity Indexes for Services Sectors   106
46. Estimated Output Indicators for Cuba, 1965–1982   111
47. Official Output Indicators for Cuba, 1965–1982   118
48. Cuban Output Indicators, 1965–1981, Based on Brundenius's Estimates   119
49. Average Annual Growth Rates for Selected Indicators of Cuban Economic Activity   120
A-1. Branch/Sector Codes   131
A-2. Cuban Economic Indicators   132
C-1. Private Production of Rice Distributed between *Acopio* and Self-Consumption   174
C-2. Private Production of Beans Distributed between *Acopio* and Self-Consumption   175
D-1. GSP Based on Complete Circulation and Enterprise Exit Valuation   178
D-2. Calculated $r_{i,t}$ for 1975 and 1976 and Estimated for 1974   179

Charts

 1. Output of Goods-producing Sectors   102
 2. Output of Productive and Nonproductive Services Sectors   105
 3. Output of Investment and Consumer Goods Sectors   112
 4. Output of Investment and Consumer Goods and Services Sectors   114
 5. Estimated Cuban Output Indicators   115
 6. Measures of Cuban Industrial Output   121
 7. Measures of Cuban Agricultural Output   122
 8. Measures of Cuban Material Product   123
 9. Measures of Cuban Global Social Product   124
10. Measures of Cuban Gross Domestic Product   125

Preface

This book describes in considerable detail the application to Cuba of a methodology that produces indexes of economic performance roughly comparable to those produced by Western nations. It then relies on the constructed measures to analyze patterns of real economic growth in Cuba during the period 1965-1982.

The original study (for the period 1965-1980) was carried out as part of a contract awarded to Wharton Econometric Forecasting Associates (WEFA) by the External Research Program of the Department of State. Views and conclusions contained in the study should not be interpreted as representing the opinion or policy of the United States government, however.

I am grateful to a number of current and former WEFA staff members for their assistance at several stages of the study: Daniel Bond, the project director, for his overall guidance and expert advice on several thorny conceptual questions; Charles Movit for his excellent work in developing and executing the index calculation modules; Vladimir Klimenko for his painstaking work in constructing and verifying the accuracy of the data base; and Peggy Dunn and her staff for typing and production of the study.

I am also indebted to numerous colleagues for data, comments, and expert advice. First and foremost, I am grateful to Carmelo Mesa-Lago for making available to me several Cuban official statistical publications that were essential in the construction of the data base underlying the index calculations; he also read an early draft of the study and made a number of constructive comments. Similarly, I am indebted to Jorge Salazar-Carrillo and to Antonio Jorge, of Florida International University, for permitting me to use the specification price data for Guatemala available to them and for giving me their views on the Cuban price system, and to Paul Marer, of Indiana University, for his efforts to educate me on some conceptual issues dealing with the construction of activity indexes. Kathleen Pérez-López made an important contribution to the statistical work in Appendix D.

In updating (to 1982) and making some revisions to the study, I had the good fortune of working with Albert Alexander and Lloyd Dugan of

Deloitte, Haskins and Sells. I am grateful to them for their assistance and for several valuable suggestions to streamline the calculations. Needless to say, I remain responsible for any errors and inconsistencies that others did not find.

Measuring Cuban Economic Performance

Introduction

In attempting to assess economic growth in revolutionary Cuba, analysts are faced with two formidable challenges: (1) official macroeconomic indicators published by the Cuban government are scarce, and those that are available are not always consistent because of frequent changes in the calculation methodology; and (2) official macroeconomic indicators are not compatible with those produced by market economies because of differences in national income concepts. The scarcity and inconsistency of macroeconomic indicators make it difficult to analyze the performance of the Cuban economy over time. The lack of international comparability of the official macroeconomic data precludes direct comparison of Cuban economic performance with that of other nations.

At the start of the 1960s, the Cuban government began to pursue a socialist development path and made significant changes in economic organization, including the adoption of central planning. These changes resulted in the disruption of the national statistical data collection and processing system and the introduction of the material balances system (more compatible with central planning) as the basic national income accounting system. Thus, for most economic series, a gap exists for the period 1959–61 and, beginning with 1962, available macroeconomic data follow the methodology of the Material Product System (MPS), which differs significantly from the System of National Accounts (SNA) methodology used by prerevolutionary Cuba and by market economies.[1]

The MPS uses a different concept of national income than does the SNA. The focus in the MPS is on measuring value added in the production of material goods and in the provision of the limited group of services directly required to produce and distribute these goods.[2] Sectors of the economy engaged in material production are industry (manufacturing and mining), agriculture, and construction; services associated with material production are freight transportation, communications, and wholesale and retail trade. Material production and supportive services sectors make up the productive sphere. Aggregate measures of economic activity under the MPS, such as the Gross Material Product (GMP), the Net Material Product (NMP), and the Global Social Product (GSP), refer exclusively to the output of the productive sphere and therefore exclude the contribution to national income of the so-called nonproductive sphere, which is made up of public and private services such as education, health, culture, housing, passenger transportation, government administration, and defense. However, the value of these nonproductive or nonmaterial services (NMS) are included in the SNA aggregate measures of economic activity generally available for market economies, such as the Gross Domestic Product (GDP), the Gross National Product (GNP) or the Net National Product (NNP).

Conceptually, national income statistics of centrally planned economies (CPEs) and of market economies could be made comparable if information on the component accounts were available. The Statistical Office of the United Nations has developed a methodology for converting national income data from MPS to SNA, and vice versa. This methodology can be applied to bridge the two systems, provided very detailed data on the underlying economic activities are available.[3] In May 1982, Cuba's Comité Estatal de Estadísticas (State Statistics Committee, CEE) and the United Nations Economic Commission for Latin America (ECLA) cosponsored a seminar held in Havana on the differences between the MPS and the SNA and approaches to converting from one system to the other. One of the documents prepared by ECLA for the meeting was an MPS/SNA conversion methodology for Cuba.[4] Also for discussion at the meeting, the CEE prepared a paper that reported the results of applying the ECLA conversion methodology to economic data for 1974 to arrive at an estimate of Cuban GDP for that year.[5] In this paper, CEE released data on the Cuban economy that had never before, and have not since, been made public. To be sure, the Cuban MPS/SNA conversion exercise provides important insights into the level of national income and its structure, but it does very little to assist us in assessing Cuban economic growth, since the conversion was carried out for only one year.[6]

Because the detailed data required to carry out a full-blown MPS/SNA conversion generally are not available, other methods have been developed to estimate GDP for CPEs. The so-called scaling-up method estimates GDP for these nations by adding to GMP the value of NMS and making some other adjustments.[7] In practice, however, the scaling-up procedure cannot be applied to Cuba, since complete and *consistent* time series data on GMP are not available and data on the value of NMS are only available for one year.[8]

Cuba has released data on GMP only for 1962–75 and 1977–78; over these periods, the methodology used by Cuban statistical agencies for calculating macroeconomic indicators has undergone several changes with regard to price and output valuation bases, which puts into question the consistency of the published GMP data. Thus, for 1962–66, official macroeconomic indicators were reported on the basis of constant prices (of 1965), whereas those available since 1966 are given at current prices. During the period 1970–76, output was valued using the *"circulación completa"* (complete circulation) methodology, equivalent to the gross turnover valuation method. Beginning in 1977, the valuation methodology was shifted to *"a salida de empresa"* (enterprise exit), equivalent to the enterprise valuation method. The change in valuation methodology can have a significant impact on the macroeconomic indicators. Thus, for 1975 and 1976, the only two years for which GSP data on both valuation methodologies are available, the shift from complete circulation to enterprise exit methodologies resulted in a decline in GSP of 12 and 11 percent, respectively.[9] The value of NMS has only been made available for 1974, in the context of the MPS/SNA conversion exercise.

Another methodology that has been used to estimate levels of GDP per capita in dollars for CPEs is the physical indicators (PI) approach, developed by Janossy and Ehrlich.[10] The basis for this approach is the empirically observable relationship between levels of physical (that is, nonmonetary) indicators of consumption or production and overall levels of economic output, consumption, or income, both between countries and over time. The method posits that the observed relationship between the level of one or more physical indicators (for example, energy consumption per capita) and the level of overall economic activity for an economy (for example, GDP per capita) at time t approximates the relationship between these same variables in other economies also at time t. Assuming that these relationships are stable across countries with different economic systems, the estimated relationship between the level of one or more physical indicators and GDP per capita for a group of reference countries for which both measures are available (for example, countries that use the SNA) can be used to estimate GDP per capita for a target country that does not publish such a measure but that does publish data on physical indicators (for example, a country that uses the MPS). If the relationships are estimated for a group of reference countries using GDP per capita data in dollars as the dependent variable, then estimates of GDP per capita in dollars can be made for a target country.

An attempt to use the PI approach to estimate Cuban GDP per capita in dollars for several benchmark years (1965, 1970, 1975, 1977) has yielded mixed results.[11] Although Carmelo Mesa-Lago and I found that some of the results (either benchmark estimates of GDP per capita or implied growth rates) were reasonable in light of analyses of the performance of the economy of revolutionary Cuba, others were not. We question the applicability of the PI method to estimate GDP per capita for Cuba and for developing countries more generally.

The PI approach was developed as a method to estimate GDP per capita for Hungary; most applications have focused on Eastern Europe and the Soviet Union, areas characterized by industrialized and stable economies and rarely affected by severe year-to-year economic swings. In monoculture-type economies such as Cuba's, where one or a few commodities subject to highly volatile price behavior contribute disproportionately to national product, fluctuations in commodity prices in the world market can have significant influence on short-term economic performance. These external shocks may not be reflected in the behavior of consumption-oriented physical indicators or may be reflected only after a lag. For example, a dramatic drop in the world market price of sugar sharply curtailed Cuba's economic growth from 1975 to 1977; this is reflected in a significant decline in growth rates of official macroeconomic indicators. However, estimates of Cuban GDP per capita based on the behavior of more stable physical indicators fail to register the recession provoked in Cuba by the drop in sugar prices.[12]

A third approach constructs estimates of GDP growth rates for CPEs from the "bottom-up," that is, from changes in nonmonetary measures of activity in a large number of economic categories aggregated using information on factor cost prices and on value added. This method, pioneered by Bergson,[13] has been used extensively to estimate growth rates of CPEs and other economies.[14] Constructing growth rate estimates following the bottom-up approach requires that

(1) output or activity indexes be compiled for a fairly large number of individual products and services;
(2) these product or service indexes then be aggregated into branch/sector indexes using a set of base year weights (typically factor cost prices) that reflect the relative importance of each product or service within branches or sectors of the economy; and
(3) these branch/sector indexes be combined into an overall index of national economic production using base year weights (typically value-added weights) that reflect the contribution of each branch/sector to GDP.

Although this approach is generally preferred by Western analysts, since it minimizes the distortions associated with value data, it is not without limitations. It is often argued that these indexes tend to underestimate growth patterns because they fail to take into account quality changes (improvements) in existing products as well as the behavior of new, and more dynamic, products.

I have used the "bottom-up" approach to prepare a set of constant-price indexes of Cuban economic activity from 1965 to 1982 at the level of branches and sectors of the economy and the overall economy (GDP). In so doing, I have been faced with a number of problems—inadequate product selection, scanty information on value added, lack of appropriate price data, unexplained changes in official statistical series. I have been able to deal satisfactorily with some, and less so with respect to others. Analyses of these problems and approach to addressing them are reported below.

This report consists of five chapters. The first reviews available data on physical output and presents the set of nonmonetary activity series that have been identified. The second chapter deals with the issue of obtaining value-added weights for the indexes at the level of branches/sectors of the economy, and the third does the same with respect to the system of weights associated with individual products/services. Chapter 4 presents the constructed indexes. In the last chapter, the behavior of the constructed indexes is compared to that of selected official indicators and independent estimates.

1. Physical Output Data

The primary sources of official Cuban economic data are the annual statistical yearbooks, which have been published beginning with 1964. Issues for 1964–71 appeared under the title *Boletín estadístico de Cuba (BE)*;[1] with the issue for 1972, the title was changed to *Anuario estadístico de Cuba (AEC)*.[2] Although the *AEC* is the primary source of economic data released officially by the Cuban government, on occasion special publications of the Comité Estatal de Estadísticas (State Statistics Committee, CEE)[3] or of the Banco Nacional de Cuba (Cuban National Bank, BNC)[4] may throw light on specific issues. In addition, data on the Cuban economy, presumably obtained from official sources, are released in the annual statistical yearbook of the Council for Mutual Economic Assistance (CMEA)[5] or in publications of the United Nations and its specialized agencies.[6]

Over the years, the quantity (if not the quality) of statistical data published by the Cuban government has increased steadily,[7] particularly since the CEE was created in late 1976. The emphasis has been on increasing the level of disaggregation of the data and shortening publication time lags. These trends have not extended to macroeconomic indicators, however, so that data on important aspects of the Cuban economy, such as inflation, capital stocks, income distribution, and foreign aid received, continue to be totally unavailable or not available as time series. Moreover, available indicators of Cuban economic performance—global social product and, for the 1960s, also gross material product and net material product—are highly aggregated and lack consistency because of numerous methodological changes.

The most recent Cuban statistical yearbook (for 1982) contains data on output of over two hundred industrial products and over fifty agricultural commodities, as well as numerous physical indicators of activity in the service sectors roughly for the period 1976–82. (Data for 1982 are given as preliminary and, in some cases, are missing.) Time series extending back to 1965 were compiled using earlier issues of the yearbook and other official

Cuban sources noted above. These physical (that is, nonmonetary) output series were the basis for my calculation of economic activity indexes.

The physical output series generally refers exclusively to activities in the state sector. For industry as well as for service sectors, production in the state sector is essentially the same as total production, given that the factors of production are under state control. This is not the case for agriculture, however, where privately owned land continues to exist alongside the state sector. The following paragraphs review briefly the collectivization process in Cuba and its bearing on the physical output data used in the study.

The Role of the State

Prior to the revolutionary takeover of 1 January 1959, the Cuban economy was predominantly capitalistic. With some notable exceptions (for example, railroads), the means of production were owned by either domestic or foreign individuals and corporations.

Soon after coming into power, the revolutionary government issued a series of law-decrees that permitted confiscation of property and funds controlled by the deposed dictator Batista and his collaborators. In February 1959, the Ministry for the Recovery of Misappropriated Goods (Ministerio de Recuperación de Bienes Malversados) was created and given the mandate of nationalizing property belonging to individuals or firms alleged to have benefited from ties with the previous regime. Under these provisions the state took control of several sugar mills; construction companies; agricultural enterprises; factories; hospitals; firms engaged in maritime, railroad and air transportation; and other services. With the exception of the construction sector, the amount of property nationalized was not significant; according to an estimate, firms nationalized under the misappropriated goods statutes accounted for only about 1.4 percent of GDP.[8]

The first Agrarian Reform Law, promulgated on 17 May 1959, had as its objective the elimination of latifundia and the distribution of land to those who worked it.[9] The law established an upper limit of thirty *caballerías* (approximately four hundred hectares) on landholding by any individual, with some exceptions for sugar and rice plantations and cattle ranches with productivity well above the national average. Landholdings beyond the upper limit were to be expropriated with compensation, divided, and distributed to landless peasants. Indeed, from 1959 to 1961 land was distributed to some 101,805 tenants, share-croppers, and squatters.[10] However, large farms that were expropriated were not divided up, but instead were organized into state-controlled production cooperatives along the lines of the Soviet *kolkhozy*.

Using the pretexts that business executives were mismanaging their firms as a form of economic sabotage or that labor-management conflicts existed, the government began in the second half of 1959 to take control of numerous key industries, including those owned by foreign investors.[11] It nationalized enterprises in the chemical petroleum refining, textiles, and metal products industries, among others. In June 1960, subsidiaries of three foreign oil companies (Esso, Texaco, and Shell), which refused to process Soviet crude oil owned by the Cuban state, were "intervened" by the government. When the U.S. government responded in early July by virtually eliminating the Cuban sugar quota for 1960, Cuba retaliated by passing Law 851, which authorized the nationalization of all American-owned property in Cuba.[12] Pursuant to this law, Resolution No. 1, of 6 August 1960, authorized the takeover of the largest U.S.-owned investments (36 sugar mills, the telephone and electricity companies, the oil refineries).[13] The combined result of these actions was that by August 1960 the state had gained overwhelming control of the economy: 40 percent of the land, 37.6 percent of the sugar industry, key public services (electricity, telephone), and a significant portion of the industrial sector, including almost 50 percent of the fourteen industrial enterprises with more than five hundred workers.[14]

Law 890, of 13 October 1960, which permitted nationalization of the remaining investments owned by U.S. citizens, those controlled by other foreign nationals, and key enterprises owned by Cuban citizens, virtually sealed the fate of private enterprise in Cuba.[15] Under authority of Law 890, the state took control of the banking system, insurance companies, 382 large corporations, including 105 sugar mills, 89 manufacturing enterprises, 13 department stores, and 47 warehouses. According to estimates (table 1), by 1961 the Cuban government had absolute control over wholesale and foreign trade, banking, and education, and commanding control over industrial, construction, and transportation activities. Only in agriculture (37 percent) and retail trade (52 percent) was state control less than overwhelming.[16]

This was a transitory situation, however. On 3 October 1963, the so-called Second Agrarian Reform Law was promulgated.[17] According to the legislation, the government nationalized landholdings exceeding five caballerías (approximately sixty-seven hectares); as a result, the state's share of the agricultural sector almost doubled, from 37 to 40 percent in 1961 to 70 percent in 1963. Earlier, in December 1962, large- and medium-sized firms engaged in retail sales of clothing, footwear, and hardware had been nationalized and placed under the direction of the Domestic Trade Ministry (approximately 23 percent of retail enterprises were affected by this action). Subsequently, in March 1968, a revolutionary offensive aimed at fighting "selfishness and individualism and [at eradicating] parasitism" was launched.[18] It resulted in the nationalization of 55,636 small private businesses (including corner grocery stores, butcher shops, poultry and fish stores, vegetable and fruit stands, laundries, dry cleaners, barber shops, photo

Table 1. Collectivization in Cuba

Sector	% under State Control		
	1961	1963	1968
Agriculture	37	70	70
Industry	85	95	100
Construction	80	98	100
Transportation	92	95	100*
Retail trade	52	75	100
Wholesale & foreign trade	100	100	100
Banking	100	100	100
Education	100	100	100

Sources: Carmelo Mesa-Lago, "Ideological Radicalization and Economic Policy in Cuba," *Studies in Comparative International Development 5*, no. 10 (1969-70):204. The same table (without sources) is given in José Acosta, "Cuba: de la neocolonia a la construcción del socialismo," *Economía y Desarrollo*, no. 20 (November-December 1973):79.
*Excludes a limited number of private workers in cargo-handling activities.

shops, lodging and boardinghouses, shoe and auto repair shops, bars, restaurants and snack shops, as well as those engaged in the sale of garments, shoes, hats, furniture, books, flowers, hardware, and electrical appliances). In addition, the remaining small businesses manufacturing handicrafts, plastic, leather, rubber, wood, metal and chemical products, textiles, perfumes, and tobacco were also absorbed into the state sector.[19] As is clear from table 1, by 1968 agriculture was the only sector of the Cuban economy where vestiges of the private sector were still present.

Though no sweeping legislation affecting ownership in the agricultural sector has been passed since the Second Agrarian Reform Law of 1963, the proportion of land under state control has increased steadily (table 2). Several factors are responsible for this trend. The state has acquired land on the retirement or death of farmers (land can only be handed down to descendants who will work it directly)[20] or as a result of abandonment by farmers migrating to the cities.[21] The First Congress of the Cuban Communist party, held in December 1975, called for "superior forms of production" in the private agricultural sector, where the "superior forms" are attained either through integration of privately held land into state farms

Table 2. Land under State Control (percentages)

Year	All	Agricultural Land	Nonagricultural Land
1972	85.3	82.2	93.2
1973	86.4	83.4	93.6
1974	84.1	80.2	93.2
1975	86.5	83.4	93.9
1976	90.8	87.9	96.7

Sources: 1972: *Anuario estadístico de Cuba 1975*, p. 54.
1973-76: *Anuario estadístico de Cuba 1980*, p. 66.

or by organization of private farmers into production cooperatives.[22] This party resolution has given rise to the progressive voluntary incorporation of private farmers into agricultural production cooperatives; between 1977 and 1980, 1,035 such cooperatives with over twenty-nine thousand members were created.[23]

Industry and Service Sectors

Physical or nonmonetary activity measures for industry and for service sectors for the period 1965–82 are given in Appendix A. The definitions of economic sectors as well as branches correspond to the official Cuban economic classification system, the Clasificador de Actividades Económicas (Classification of Economic Activities, CAE), the same system used by CEE to report data in the most recent issues of the *Anuario estadístico de Cuba*. Table 3 correlates the categories of the CAE and the United Nations International Standard Industrial Classification of All Economic Activities (ISIC); additional information on the structure of the ISIC is given in Appendix B.

For the industrial sector, time series on output of over 180 individual products have been gathered. In table 4, the distribution of physical output series by branches within the industrial sector is given. Though these series refer exclusively to production by the state sector, in effect they can be considered as total production, given the very high control exercised by the state over the industrial sector since the early 1960s.

For service sectors, whether productive or nonproductive, forty-one nonmonetary activity time series have also been collected and reported in Appendix A. The number of series gathered for each of the service sectors and branches is given in table 5. As is the case with the industrial sector,

Table 3.   Correlation between Cuban Classification of Economic Activities (CAE) and International Standard Industrial Classification (ISIC) of All Economic Activities

Sector	Branch	Description	Major Group	Description
		Productive Sphere		
01		*Industry*		
	01.01	Electricity	4101	Electric light & power
	01.02	Fuel	2200	Crude petroleum & natural gas production
			2909	Mining & quarrying not elsewhere classified (n.e.c.)
			3530	Petroleum refineries
			4102	Gas manufacture & distribution
	01.03	Ferrous mining & metallurgy		
			2301	Iron ore mining
			3710	Iron & steel basic industries
	01.04	Nonferrous mining & metallurgy		
			2302	Nonferrous ore, mining
			3720	Nonferrous metal basic industries
	01.05	Nonelectrical machinery	3821	Manufacture of engines & turbines
			3822	Manufacture of agricultural machinery & equipment
			3823	Manufacture of metal & woodworking machinery
			3824	Manufacture of special industrial machinery & equipment, except metal & woodworking machinery
			3825	Manufacture of office, computing & accounting machinery
			3829	Machinery & equipment except electrical n.e.c.
			3841	Shipbuilding & repair
			3842	Manufacture of railroad equipment
			3843	Manufacture of motor vehicle
	01.05	Nonelectrical machinery	3844	Manufacture of motor-cycles & bicycles
			3845	Manufacture of aircraft
			3852	Manufacture of photographic & optical goods

Table 3—Continued

CAE Classification			ISIC Classification	
Sector	Branch	Description	Major Group	Description

01 (continued)

			3853	Manufacture of watches & clocks
			9513	Repair of motor vehicles & motorcycles
			9519	Other repair shops n.e.c.
	01.06	Electronics	3825	Manufacture of office, computing & accounting machinery
			383	Manufacture of electrical machinery, apparatus, appliances & supplies
			3831	Manufacture of electrical industrial machinery & apparatus
			9512	Electrical repair shops
	01.07	Metal products	381	Manufacture of fabricated metal products, except machinery & equipment
			3811	Manufacture of cutlery, hand tools & general hardware
			3812	Manufacture of furniture & fixtures primarily of metals
			3813	Manufacture of structural metal products
			3819	Manufacture of fabricated metal products, except machinery & equipment n.e.c.
	01.08	Chemicals	2902	Chemical & fertilizer mineral mining
			2903	Salt mining
			3511	Manufacture of basic industrial chemicals, except fertilizers
			3512	Manufacture of fertilizers & pesticides
	01.08	Chemicals	3513	Manufacture of synthetic resins, plastic materials & man-made fibers, except glass
			3521	Manufacture of paint, varnishes & lacquers

Table 3—Continued

CAE Classification			ISIC Classification	
Sector	Branch	Description	Major Group	Description

01 (continued)

			3522	Manufacture of drugs & medicines
			3523	Manufacture of soap & cleaning preparations, perfumes, cosmetics & other toilet preparations
			3529	Manufacture of chemical products n.e.c.
			3551	Tire & tube industries
			3559	Manufacture of rubber products n.e.c.
			3560	Manufacture of plastic products n.e.c.
	01.09	Paper & cellulose	3411	Manufacture of pulp, paper & paperboard
			3412	Manufacture of containers & boxes of paper & paperboard
			3419	Manufacture of pulp, paper & paperboard articles n.e.c.
	01.10	Printing	3420	Printing, publishing & allied industries
	01.11	Wood products	1220	Logging
			3311	Sawmills, planing & other wood mills
			3312	Manufacture of wooden & cane containers & small caneware
			3319	Manufacture of wood & cork products n.e.c.
			3320	Manufacture of furniture & fixtures, except primarily of steel
	01.12	Construction materials	2909	Mining & quarrying n.e.c.
			3540	Manufacture of miscellaneous products of petroleum & coal
			3691	Manufacture of structural clay products
			3692	Manufacture of cement, lime & plaster

Table 3—Continued

CAE Classification			ISIC Classification	
Sector	Branch	Description	Major Group	Description

01 (continued)

			3699	Manufacture of nonmetallic mineral products n.e.c.
	01.13	Glass & ceramics	2901	Stone quarrying, clay & sand pits
			3610	Manufacture of pottery, china & earthenware
			3620	Manufacture of glass & glass products
	01.14	Textiles	3211	Spinning, weaving & finishing textiles
			3213	Knitting mills
			3214	Manufacture of carpets & rugs
			3215	Cordage, rope & twine industries
			3219	Manufacture of textiles n.e.c.
	01.15	Apparel	3212	Manufacture of made-up textile goods, except wearing apparel
			3220	Manufacture of wearing apparel, except footwear
			9520	Laundries, laundry services & cleaning & dyeing plants
	01.16	Leather products	3220	Manufacture of wearing apparel, except footwear
			323	Manufacture of leather and products of leather, leather substitutes & fur, except footwear
			3233	Manufacture of products of leather & leather substitutes, except footwear & wearing apparel
			3240	Manufacture of footwear except vulcanized or molded rubber or plastic footwear
	01.17	Sugar	3118	Sugar factories & refineries
	01.18	Processed foods	3111	Slaughtering, preparing & preserving meat

Table 3—Continued

CAE Classification			ISIC Classification	
Sector	Branch	Description	Major Group	Description

01 (continued)

			3112	Manufacture of dairy products
			3113	Canning & preserving of fruits & vegetables
			3115	Manufacture of vegetable & animal oils & fats
			3116	Grain mill products
			3117	Manufacture of bakery products
			3119	Manufacture of cocoa, chocolate & sugar confectionery
			3121	Manufacture of food products n.e.c.
			7192	Storage & warehousing
	01.19	Fishing	1301	Ocean & coastal fishing
			3114	Canning, preserving & processing of fish, crustacea & similar products
	01.20	Beverages & tobacco	3131	Distilling, rectifying & blending spirits
			3132	Wine industries
			3133	Malt liquors & malt
			3134	Soft drinks & carbonated water industry
			3140	Tobacco manufactures
	01.21	Other industrial activities	3122	Manufacture of prepared animal feeds
			3699	Manufacture of nonmetallic mineral products n.e.c.
			390	Other manufacturing industries
			3901	Manufacture of jewelry & related articles
			3903	Manufacture of sporting & athletic goods
			3909	Manufacturing industries n.e.c.
			4200	Waterworks & supply

Table 3—Continued

CAE Classification			ISIC Classification	
Sector	Branch	Description	Major Group	Description

01 (continued)				
			9520	Laundries, laundry services & cleaning & dyeing plants
02		*Construction*		
	02.01	Building & assembly	5000	Construction
	02.02	Geological exploration, prospecting & geodesy	5000	Construction
	02.03	Project engineering & design	8324	Engineering, architectural & technical services
03		*Agriculture*		
	03.01	Sugar agriculture	1110	Agricultural & livestock production
	03.02	Nonsugar agriculture	1110	Agricultural & livestock production
	03.03	Livestock	1110	Agricultural and livestock production
			1302	Fishing n.e.c.
	03.04	Irrigation & drainage	1120	Agricultural services
	03.05	Agricultural services	1120	Agricultural services
			9332	Veterinary services
04		*Forestry*	1210	Forestry
05		*Transportation*		
	05.01	Railroad	7111	Railway transport
	05.02	Motor	7112	Urban, suburban & interurban highway passenger transport
	05.03	Road administration	7116	Supporting services to land transport
	05.04	Maritime	7121	Ocean & coastal water transport
			7122	Inland water transport
			7123	Supporting services to water transport
	05.05	Air	7131	Air transport carriers
			7132	Supporting services to air transport
	05.06	Cargo handling	7123	Supporting services to water transport
			7191	Services incidental to transport

Table 3—Continued

CAE Classification			ISIC Classification	
Sector	Branch	Description	Major Group	Description

05 (continued)				
	05.07	Other transpor- tation activities	7112	Urban, suburban & interurban highway passenger transport
06		*Communications*	720	Communications
07		*Trade*		
	07.01	Domestic trade	6100 6200	Wholesale trade Retail trade
	07.02	Restaurants & food services	6300	Restaurants, cafes & other eating & drinking places
	07.03	Foreign trade	6100	Wholesale trade
	07.04	Material procurement	6100	Wholesale trade
	07.05	*Acopio* of agri- cultural products	6100	Wholesale trade
	07.06	Recycling of raw materials	6100	Wholesale trade
08		*Other productive activities*		
	08.01	Technical services	8324	Engineering, architectural & technical services
	08.02	Data processing	8323	Data processing & tab- ulating services
	08.03	Other productive activities	3240	Printing, publishing & allied services
			3832	Manufacture of radio, tele- vision & communication equipment & apparatus
			8325	Advertising services
			9411	Motion picture production
		Nonproductive sphere		
09		*Personal & community services*		
	09.01	Housing adminis- tration	8310	Real estate
	09.02	Lodging services	6320	Hotels, rooming houses camps & other lodging places
	09.03	Community ad- ministration	4200	Waterworks & supply
			9200	Sanitary & similar services
	09.04	Personal services	9591	Barber & beauty shops

Table 3—Continued

CAE Classification			ISIC Classification	
Sector	Branch	Description	Major Group	Description

09 (continued)				
			9592	Photographic studios, including commercial photography
			9599	Personal services n.e.c.
10		*Science & technology*		
	10.01	Scientific-technical research	9320	Research & scientific institutes
	10.02	Other scientific-technical activities	9320	Research & scientific institutes
			9420	Libraries, museums, botanical & zoological gardens & other cultural services n.e.c.
11		*Education*	9310	Education services
12		*Culture & art*	9412	Motion picture distribution & projection
			9413	Radio & television broadcasting
			9414	Theatrical producers & entertainment services
			9420	Libraries, museums, botanical gardens & other cultural services n.e.c.
13		*Public health, social security, sports, and tourism*	7191	Services incidental to transport
			9331	Medical, dental & other health services
			9340	Welfare institutions
			9490	Amusement & recreational services n.e.c.
14		*Finance & insurance*	810	Financial institutions
			820	Insurance
15		*Administration*	832	Business services, except machinery & equipment rentals & leasing
			9100	Public administration & defense
16		*Other nonproductive activities*	9350	Business, professional & labor associations
			9391	Religious organizations

Table 3—Continued

CAE Classification			ISIC Classification	
Sector	Branch	Description	Major Group	Description

16 (continued)

			9399	Social & related community services n.e.c.
			9600	International & other extraterritorial bodies

Sources: United Nations, Economic Commission for Latin America (ECLA), *Comparabilidad de los sistemas de cuentas nacionales y de producto material en América Latina*, pp. 150-154; and United Nations Statistical Office, *International Standard Industrial Classification of All Economic Activities*, pp. 27-40.

Table 4.   **Physical Output Series for Branches of Industrial Sector**

Activity	No. of Series
Electricity	1
Fuel	9
Ferrous mining & metallurgy	10
Nonferrous mining & metallurgy	5
Nonelectrical machinery	10
Electronics	8
Metal products	8
Chemicals	31
Paper & cellulose	10
Printing	5
Wood products	4
Construction materials	12
Glass & ceramics	5
Textiles	5
Apparel	11
Leather products	4
Sugar	4
Processed foods	28
Fishing	1
Beverages & tobacco	11
Other	3
Total	185

Source: Appendix A.

activity series for the service sectors are deemed to be representative of total (state plus private) activity.

I have identified twenty-three activity series referring to productive services. Thus Appendix A reports eight series related to activity in the construction sector, nine in transportation, and five in communications. However, for the trade sector, which includes retail, wholesale, and foreign trade activities, I have been unable to obtain *nonmonetary* activity indicators. Time series on total sales at the retail and wholesale levels are available and so is a series on foreign trade turnover, but all three of these series are in value terms and are potentially affected by valuation changes, inflation, and other distortions that I seek to avoid in my measures.

In the absence of appropriate data, I have used employment in trade activities as a proxy for output of the trade sector. The implicit assumption is that the labor/output ratio for this sector remains relatively constant over time so that changes in employment can be used to approximate changes in output. Even if this assumption were to hold, however, other problems arise because the available employment data (1) have gaps and (2) apparently have not been collected using the same methodology over the period 1965–80.[24]

Given the importance of the trade sector (see chapter 2), I have investigated the possibility of constructing activity indexes at constant prices for retail or wholesale trade that could be combined with a foreign trade series (calculated from available trade data) to reflect activity in this sector.

Table 5.   Nonmonetary Activity Series for Service Sectors

Sphere/Sector	No. of Series
Productive Sphere	23
Construction	8
Transportation	9
Railroad	2
Motor	2
Maritime	2
Air	2
Cargo handling	1
Communications	5
Trade	1
Nonproductive Sphere	18
Housing & community services	2
Education & public health	7
Social security, welfare, cultural and scientific activities	7
Public administration	1
Defense & internal order	0
Other nonproductive activities	1

Source: Appendix A.

Data on physical quantities for a wide range of products entering retail and wholesale trade, which could be the basis for activity indexes, are available, but I have been unable to obtain data that could be used to develop weights. I am aware of national consumer expenditure surveys carried out since 1974 by the Instituto Cubano de Investigaciones y Orientación de la Demanda Interna (Institute for Research and Orientation of Domestic Demand, ICIODI).[25] The expenditure patterns obtained in these surveys, had they been available, could have served as the basis for developing weights for indexes of activity for the domestic trade sector.[26]

Similarly substantial difficulties in identifying activity indicators for nonproductive services have been encountered. The CAE-ISIC correlation in table 3 as well as the description of activities corresponding to each of the ISIC groups and subgroups have been useful in defining the scope of each of the nonproductive services categories. For example, I was able to determine that lodging services are considered part of "housing and community services," and therefore a series related to tourists lodged was identified as a potential activity indicator for this sector. Although, as noted in table 5, data on eighteen indicators related to activities in the nonproductive sphere have been gathered, the bulk are concentrated in two sectors: (1) education and public health; and (2) social security, welfare, cultural, and scientific activities. For the remaining nonproductive services sectors (housing and community services, public administration, defense and internal order, other nonproductive activities), I have relied heavily on employment data, subject to the same limitations mentioned above.

Agriculture

It is clear from table 1 and the earlier discussion that agriculture was the only economic sector in which private ownership played a significant role during the period 1965–82. Thus, an economic activity index for agriculture should take into account production by private farmers.

Data on state production for a large number of agricultural commodities and livestock products are readily available, but not so data on production by private farmers, except for the portion sold to the state. An exception is sugarcane, for which total production data are readily available. For other commodities and livestock products, I have explored the possibility of adjusting available data (on state production plus private output sold to the state) to estimate overall production; as discussed below, I do not feel that it is possible to make such adjustments with the data currently available.

The "Acopio" System

Early in 1959, the state began to purchase corn from farmers in the eastern region to be used as animal feed.[27] Later, the system was expanded to cover other products (rice, beans) and areas. By 1962 a national *"acopio"* (procurement) system covering all agricultural products was in operation. Under the system, which remains in effect, farmers are required to sell certain production volumes to the state at fixed prices. Fulfillment of these quotas is a condition for private farmers to continue to receive agricultural services, fertilizer, and other inputs from the state. Output in excess of the *acopio* quota is used by farmers for self-consumption, for barter or black market sales, or, in recent times, for sale in government-sanctioned "free peasant markets." Presumably, all agricultural output of state enterprises enters into the *acopio* system, since family plots originally available to state farmers were abolished just prior to the 1968 revolutionary offensive.

Time series data on *acopio* for over fifty agricultural commodities are available in Cuban statistical yearbooks. Also available for each product is a breakdown of the contribution to total *acopio* by the state sector and by private farmers. As table 6 indicates, the contribution by private farmers to *acopio* varies widely, depending on the product. For example, in 1980 private farmers produced 6.5 percent of the rice, 57.9 percent of the papayas, and 87.7 percent of the peppers procured by the state. Further, there is considerable year-to-year variation in the contribution by the state and private sectors to *acopio*, though there is an overall tendency for the share provided by the private sector to decline over time. Again referring to rice, private farmers contributed 2.5 percent of *acopio* in 1970 and 7.2 percent in 1976, and for papayas, the contribution by the private sector ranged from nearly 91 percent in 1970 to 52 percent in 1979.

Total Production

As noted above, systematic data on total agricultural production (including private farms' output outside *acopio*) for most agricultural commodities and livestock products are not available. Thus, analyses of Cuban agricultural performance heretofore have been based on *acopio* data.[28] Use of these data instead of total production data may or may not influence the results, depending on whether *acopio* is a reasonable proxy for total production.

In the *Anuario estadístico de Cuba 1980*, CEE for the first time published a table containing total production data for twenty important commodities for 1970 and 1974–80.[29] The title of the table as well as two notes make it clear that the data refer to state and private production and, further, that production for self-consumption is included (the production data are reproduced in table 6). Interestingly, since the mid-1970s, Cuba has been reporting to the CMEA Statistical Office data on total production for selected agricultural commodities; *Statisticheskii ezhegodnik*, the CMEA statistical yearbook, has published time series for the 1970s for a handful of agricultural commodities (table 7). I have no explanation for why

**Table 6.   Production and *Acopio* of Agricultural Products
(thousands of metric tons)**

| Crop/Year | Production | Acopio | | | | |
		Total	State	Private	Private/ Total (%)	*Acopio* Production (%)
Rice						
1970	365.9	290.0	283.7	7.2	2.5	79.5
1974	436.6	309.3	293.5	15.8	5.1	70.8
1975	446.7	338.0	316.1	21.9	6.5	75.7
1976	451.1	335.1	310.9	24.2	7.2	74.3
1977	455.8	334.2	313.3	20.9	6.3	73.3
1978	457.5	344.1	324.5	19.6	5.7	75.2
1979	425.1	311.8	294.4	17.4	5.6	73.3
1980	477.8	352.2	329.3	22.9	6.5	73.7
Corn (threshed)						
1970	15.3	3.4	2.2	1.2	35.3	22.2
1974	20.4	4.7	2.2	2.5	53.2	23.0
1975	20.5	3.2	1.5	1.7	53.1	15.6
1976	14.3	4.1	2.3	1.8	43.9	26.7
1977	16.3	1.8	0.8	1.0	55.6	11.0
1978	16.2	2.4	0.9	1.5	62.5	14.8
1979	16.6	2.2	1.1	1.1	50.0	13.0
1980	33.6	1.9	0.3	1.6	84.2	5.7
Beans						
1970	1.9	5.0	2.5	2.5	50.0	263.2
1974	1.7	3.1	1.1	2.0	64.5	182.4
1975	2.8	4.8	1.8	3.0	62.5	171.4
1976	2.4	3.1	1.3	1.8	58.1	129.2
1977	3.2	2.4	1.0	1.4	58.3	75.0
1978	4.3	2.4	0.9	1.5	62.5	55.8
1979	4.4	2.5	0.9	1.6	64.0	56.8
1980	9.7	4.7	2.8	1.9	40.4	48.5
Tomatoes						
1970	53.2	62.4	40.6	41.8	34.9	117.3
1974	168.4	183.5	105.4	78.1	42.6	109.0
1975	168.8	184.1	96.9	87.2	47.4	109.1
1976	173.5	193.9	94.1	99.8	51.5	111.8
1977	160.3	145.8	68.1	77.7	53.3	91.0
1978	139.5	131.8	54.0	77.8	59.0	94.5
1979	163.9	157.3	75.6	81.7	51.9	96.0
1980	206.9	217.6	92.2	125.4	57.6	105.2

Table 6—Continued

Acopio

Crop/Year	Production	Total	State	Private	Private/ Total (%)	*Acopio* Production (%)
Onions						
1970	5.7	11.9	3.3	8.6	72.3	208.8
1974	9.9	10.0	4.0	6.0	60.0	101.0
1975	9.3	9.5	3.0	6.5	68.4	102.2
1976	14.7	15.0	5.8	9.2	61.3	102.0
1977	9.3	8.6	3.5	5.1	59.3	92.5
1978	8.2	7.8	2.3	5.5	70.5	95.1
1979	10.0	9.4	3.3	6.1	64.9	94.0
1980	9.6	9.6	3.1	6.5	67.7	100.0
Peppers						
1970	--	10.9	3.3	7.6	69.7	--
1974	16.2	22.3	2.7	19.6	87.9	137.7
1975	20.5	24.4	3.5	20.9	85.7	119.0
1976	24.2	29.4	2.6	26.8	91.2	121.5
1977	27.3	20.6	1.0	19.6	95.1	75.5
1978	30.7	31.1	2.4	28.7	92.3	101.3
1979	30.8	29.8	2.6	27.2	91.3	96.8
1980	44.9	44.6	5.5	39.1	87.7	99.3
Potatoes						
1970	77.5	77.3	41.6	35.7	46.2	99.7
1974	87.7	87.8	59.8	28.0	31.9	100.1
1975	120.9	116.7	79.9	36.8	31.5	96.5
1976	149.4	145.1	100.8	44.3	30.5	97.1
1977	154.9	137.0	98.2	38.8	28.3	88.4
1978	198.3	173.7	133.7	40.0	23.0	87.6
1979	200.8	172.2	139.3	32.9	19.1	85.8
1980	239.4	208.5	168.2	40.3	19.3	87.1
Sweet potatoes						
1970	18.7	22.0	14.0	8.0	36.4	117.6
1974	74.2	83.6	50.8	32.,8	39.2	112.7
1975	82.1	89.9	55.0	34.9	38.8	109.5
1976	70.9	78.6	47.0	31.6	40.2	110.9
1977	67.6	61.6	39.4	22.2	36.0	91.1
1978	64.8	54.3	30.2	24.1	44.4	83.8
1979	94.6	79.2	54.9	24.3	30.7	83.7
1980	228.1	195.2	137.1	58.1	29.8	85.6

Table 6—Continued

Acopio

Crop/Year	Production	Total	State	Private	Private/ Total (%)	*Acopio* Production (%)
Malanga						
1970	9.4	12.0	5.3	6.7	55.8	127.7
1974	21.0	25.5	5.5	20.0	78.4	121.4
1975	29.8	32.5	9.0	23.5	72.3	109.1
1976	43.7	45.2	11.0	34.2	75.7	103.4
1977	85.8	59.3	29.8	29.5	49.7	69.1
1978	217.4	117.4	82.5	34.9	29.7	54.0
1979	196.0	102.2	64.4	37.8	37.0	52.1
1980	161.4	87.1	67.3	29.8	30.7	60.2
Oranges (sweet)						
1970	69.5	122.3	69.5	52.8	43.2	176.0
1974	98.3	109.4	60.2	49.2	45.0	111.3
1975	121.2	126.5	73.7	52.8	41.7	104.4
1976	119.9	124.0	80.8	43.2	34.8	103.4
1977	159.7	131.7	89.0	42.7	32.4	82.5
1978	185.7	141.4	92.8	48.6	34.4	76.1
1979	185.1	136.1	87.4	48.7	35.8	73.5
1980	298.0	193.7	144.4	49.3	25.5	65.0
Lemons						
1970	5.2	8.1	5.4	2.7	33.3	155.8
1974	12.4	16.6	11.7	4.9	29.5	133.9
1975	11.7	14.0	10.5	3.5	25.0	119.7
1976	12.1	14.6	10.8	3.8	26.0	120.7
1977	14.0	13.9	10.3	3.6	25.9	99.3
1978	13.3	12.1	9.8	2.3	19.0	91.0
1979	19.4	15.0	12.2	2.8	18.7	77.3
1980	25.2	21.5	18.3	3.2	14.9	85.3
Plaintains						
1970	30.8	40.6	28.5	12.1	29.8	131.8
1974	76.3	102.2	64.3	37.9	37.1	133.9
1975	81.4	95.2	69.8	25.4	26.7	117.0
1976	90.1	107.0	76.3	30.7	28.7	118.8
1977	85.5	81.1	58.5	22.6	27.9	94.9
1978	98.2	91.4	54.7	36.7	40.2	93.1
1979	84.2	76.6	43.4	33.2	43.3	91.0
1980	88.9	82.2	46.9	35.3	42.9	92.5

Table 6—Continued

Crop/Year	Production	Acopio Total	State	Private	Private/ Total (%)	Acopio Production (%)
Bananas						
1970	42.7	47.2	38.7	8.5	18.0	110.5
1974	69.4	85.0	59.4	25.6	30.1	122.5
1975	101.4	109.9	83.7	26.2	23.8	108.4
1976	121.3	131.3	96.4	34.9	26.6	108.2
1977	134.5	133.7	96.4	37.3	27.9	99.4
1978	149.7	149.1	104.3	44.8	30.0	99.6
1979	146.8	137.8	96.6	41.2	29.9	93.9
1980	144.5	137.6	97.7	39.9	29.0	95.2
Papayas						
1970	0.8	8.6	0.8	7.8	90.7	1075.0
1974	21.2	45.1	14.9	30.2	67.0	212.7
1975	26.8	51.1	17.6	33.5	65.6	190.7
1976	31.6	75.0	16.0	59.0	78.7	237.3
1977	65.5	61.9	15.7	46.2	74.6	94.5
1978	52.8	49.5	14.1	35.4	71.5	93.8
1979	23.2	24.2	11.7	12.5	51.7	104.3
1980	38.1	38.7	16.3	22.4	57.9	101.6
Mangoes						
1970	2.6	9.1	2.6	6.5	71.4	350.0
1974	25.5	60.1	13.5	46.6	77.5	235.7
1975	33.2	48.9	12.2	36.7	75.1	147.3
1976	28.6	46.2	13.9	32.3	69.9	161.5
1977	46.3	52.2	14.4	37.8	72.4	112.7
1978	19.0	19.3	5.6	13.7	71.0	101.6
1979	65.8	68.8	20.5	48.3	70.2	104.6
1980	59.1	61.6	19.1	42.5	69.0	104.2
Guavas						
1970	6.4	14.1	6.4	7.7	54.6	220.3
1974	13.3	23.3	8.9	14.4	61.8	175.2
1975	17.8	24.4	9.1	15.3	62.7	137.1
1976	20.4	30.4	12.1	18.3	60.2	149.0
1977	23.8	28.8	10.8	18.0	62.5	121.0
1978	31.6	31.6	15.0	16.6	52.5	100.0
1979	41.3	43.5	22.3	21.2	48.7	105.3
1980	45.6	45.7	25.8	19.9	43.5	100.2

Table 6—Continued

Acopio

Crop/Year	Production	Total	State	Private	Private/ Total (%)	*Acopio* Production (%)
Dark tobacco						
1970	27.5	27.6	2.9	24.7	89.5	100.4
1974	39.4	39.4	6.4	33.0	83.8	100.0
1975	37.8	36.9	5.7	31.2	84.6	97.6
1976	45.7	44.8	7.0	37.8	84.4	98.0
1977	37.7	36.6	5.9	30.7	83.9	97.1
1978	36.3	35.7	6.7	29.0	81.2	98.3
1979	28.0	28.4	6.7	21.7	76.4	101.4
1980	6.7	5.3	2.4	2.9	54.7	79.1
Light tobacco						
1970	4.2	4.2	1.9	2.3	54.8	100.0
1974	5.3	5.3	2.1	3.2	60.4	100.0
1975	4.5	4.5	1.7	2.8	62.2	100.0
1976	6.0	6.0	2.4	3.6	60.0	100.0
1977	5.6	5.5	2.0	3.5	63.6	98.2
1978	5.0	4.7	1.9	2.8	59.6	94.0
1979	4.6	4.6	1.8	2.8	60.9	100.0
1980	1.5	1.4	0.8	0.6	42.9	93.3
Coffee						
1970	19.7	--	--	–	--	--
1974	28.8	28.8	12.1	16.7	58.0	100.0
1975	20.1	17.5	7.9	9.6	54.9	87.1
1976	27.2	19.0	9.9	9.1	47.9	69.9
1977	16.8	15.7	8.6	7.1	45.2	93.5
1978	14.8	13.4	6.6	6.8	50.7	90.5
1979	25.7	22.3	11.7	10.6	47.5	86.8
1980	23.8	20.6	11.8	8.8	42.7	86.6
Cocoa						
1970	1.3	1.3	0.1	1.2	92.3	100.0
1974	1.4	1.3	0.2	1.1	84.6	92.9
1975	1.3	1.3	0.3	1.0	76.9	100.0
1976	1.4	1.5	0.4	1.1	83.3	107.1
1977	1.2	1.3	0.3	1.0	76.9	108.3
1978	2.2	1.6	0.4	1.2	75.0	72.7
1979	2.6	1.4	0.4	1.0	71.4	53.8
1980	1.4	1.4	0.4	1.0	71.4	100.0

Sources: Anuario estadístico de Cuba 1980, tables V.15 and IX.14; and *Anuario estadístico de Cuba 1976,* table V.38.

Table 7.   Production of Selected Agricultural Products (thousands of metric tons)

Production

Crop	1970	1971	1972	1973	1974	1975
Grains	379.0	376.0	336.0	352.0	459.0	470.0
Rice						447.0
Corn	11.6	18.2	16.3	17.3	20.8	20.4
Beans	1.8	7.9	2.3	1.7	1.7	2.8
Oil-producing crops				0.4	0.5	0.9
Vegetables	87.2	130.0	145.0	233.0	341.0	402.0
Potatoes	46.0	46.8	72.0	53.7	87.7	121.0
Tobacco	31.7	24.6	39.6	43.5	44.7	42.3
Fruit*	224.0	229.0	375.0	411.0	438.0	512.0
Citrus						191.0

	1976	1977	1978	1979	1980
Grains	468.0	476.0	478.0	447.0	511.0
Rice	451.0	456.0	451.0	425.0	478.0
Corn	14.3	16.3	16.2	16.5	23.5
Beans	2.4	3.2	4.3	4.4	9.7
Oil-producing crops	1.4	0.6			
Vegetables	380.0	326.0	327.0	342.0	446.0
Potatoes	149.0	155.0	198.0	201.0	243.0
Tobacco	51.6	43.3	41.0	32.6	8.1
Fruit*	692.0	652.0	710.0	718.0	900.0
Citrus	216.0	226.0	282.0	285.0	441.0

Source: *Statisicheskii ezhegodnik 1976, 1980.*
*Including coffee and cocoa beans.

Cuba withheld until the 1980 *Anuario* publication of production data presumably being provided periodically to the CMEA Statistical Office. Further, I cannot satisfactorily explain some differences in the Cuban and CMEA data for 1970, or the Cuban source's emphasis that, for 1970, production by private farmers has been estimated, but there is no such lack of caveat in the data published by CMEA.

Table 6 also presents the ratio of *acopio* to total production for the products for which official Cuban production and *acopio* data are available. Examination of the behavior of this ratio is important, since conceptually it could be used to adjust the available *acopio* data to obtain estimates of production. Two types of adjustment might be possible. First, since production data are only available for selected years (1970 and 1974–82) in the period 1965–82, estimates of production for the remaining years could be made based on the observed relationship between *acopio* and production data. Second, recognizing that production data are available only for a subset of the products for which *acopio* data are reported, estimates of production for other products could be made based on *acopio*/production ratios and some additional information on the importance of the private sector in the production of specific products.

A cursory examination of the *acopio*/production ratios in table 6 raises serious questions about the reliability of the production data and suggests that adjustment of the *acopio* data is not feasible with the data available at this time. For rice, for example, the data are well behaved; the *acopio*/production ratio hovers around 75 percent, suggesting that production for the missing years could probably be estimated by adjusting *acopio* data upward by about 25 percent. For beans, however, serious problems with the production data are apparent. For 1970 and 1974–76, reported total production data are lower than *acopio*, an impossibility, given that *acopio* is a proper subset of total production, the difference being the portion of production retained by private farmers. In Appendix C, I elaborate on the relationships between total production, *acopio*, and private farmers' production and illustrate how the share of private production destined for *acopio* and self-consumption could be calculated. I also discuss how the relationship between the rates of change over time in total production, *acopio*, and state production could be estimated if sufficient time series observations were available.

Thus, in the activity indexes for the agricultural sector I have relied on *acopio* data (with the exception of the series for the sugar and forestry branches.) As noted in table 8, forty-three time series indicative of activity in the agricultural sector have been identified. The series are reproduced in Appendix A.

Table 8.   Physical Output Series for Branches of Agricultural Sector

Branch	No. of Series
Total	43
Sugar	1
Nonsugar	34
Livestock	6
Forestry	2
Agricultural services	0

Source: Appendix C.

2. Value-Added Weights

The most commonly used source of weights for aggregating output indexes is value-added data. As will be discussed below, appropriate value-added data are not readily available for Cuba. Relying heavily on gross value of output (GVO) data for 1974 released by the Cuban government in a special publication, on an input-output table for the industrial sector for 1963, and on several other sources, I have estimated a set of value-added weights for around 1974. Thus, although I refer to 1974 as the base period for the indexes, it would be more accurate to say that the base period refers to the mid-1970s. The available value-added data, the estimated value-added weights, and the procedure used in developing the value-added estimates are discussed in detail below.

Official Value-Added Data

To the best of my knowledge, the Cuban revolutionary government has not released comprehensive data on either gross or net value added for any year. Highly aggregated fragmentary data for selected productive sectors or branches for 1961–63, and for 1963 alone, were published in two semiofficial reports that appeared in the mid-1960s.

In 1965 ECLA published in its *Economic Survey of Latin America* a lengthy article on the Cuban economy containing many data for the period 1959–63.[1] According to ECLA, the study was based on official data obtained directly from JUCEPLAN. Although shortly after the publication of this article ECLA revised a significant portion of the data (apparently it had used certain production goals as real production and the goals proved to be too high),[2] nevertheless, the 1965 ECLA report stands out as an important source, since at the time it was published virtually no official economic data were available.[3]

Data on gross value added in productive sectors as reported in the ECLA study are given in table 9. According to a footnote to the study, the data refer to net material product, that is, "the total value added in the processing of

**Table 9.   Gross Value Added in Productive Activities
(million pesos at current prices)**

Activity	1961	1962	1963
All productive activities	2731.6	2992.6	3244.2
Industry	954.2	1002.4	1030.4
Mining	26.1	43.7	35.9
Metallurgy & metal transforming	62.4	64.4	68.1
Building materials	40.0	36.5	38.9
Petroleum & petroleum products	78.7	94.3	95.0
Chemicals	82.6	106.5	111.8
Textiles & leather products	119.2	126.5	146.8
Sugar	143.4	99.9	90.6
Food	153.2	155.9	144.5
Beverages & tobacco	152.7	149.4	161.1
Electricity	55.1	58.6	61.6
Other	40.8	66.7	76.1
Agriculture	730.5	700.8	683.0
Sugar	264.5	204.8	186.2
Nonsugar	247.3	266.4	261.9
Livestock	178.1	175.9	196.4
Forestry	29.0	38.3	32.7
Fishing	11.6	15.4	15.8
Construction	196.5	207.2	207.0
Transport & communications	256.4	229.7	236.5
Trade	594.0	799.4	1,031.3
Other	--	53.1	56.0

Source: ECLA, "The Cuban Economy in the Period 1959-63," tables 257, 274, 282.

goods and services during the year, expressed in market prices."[4] Actually, as the same footnote explains, JUCEPLAN only provided value-added figures for 1961; the reported figures for 1962 and 1963 were estimated by ECLA on the basis of the 1961 value-added coefficients and GVO data for 1962–63.[5]

In table 10, I have attempted to relate value-added and GVO data to develop a set of value-added/GVO coefficients for the material product sectors. Unfortunately, GVO data are not available for 1961 and therefore I was only able to obtain value-added/GVO coefficients for 1962–63. Since the value-added data are reported in current prices, it was necessary to estimate GVO at current prices. This was done using GSP at current prices and the percentage distribution of GSP according to economic sectors and branches. (Since the latter data refer to the distribution of GSP at *constant 1965 prices*, it has been implicitly assumed that the *constant-price* distribution reasonably reflects the *current-price* distribution.)

The official Cuban submission to a symposium on Latin American industrialization held in March 1966 also contains information on value added.[6] The data presented in this report, which relate only to selected branches of industry and to one year (1963), are given in table 11. Comparison of data in table 11 and data for 1963 in table 9 suggest a very close correspondence in the total value added by industry (1030.4 million pesos versus 1035.8 million pesos), but it is not possible to make comparisons at disaggregated levels, because different classification systems are used in the two. For the latter reason it is not possible to relate the value-added data in table 11 to GVO data in table 9.

It is quite clear that the value-added data reported in tables 9 and 11 are neither sufficiently comprehensive nor detailed enough to provide a set of weights for the construction of the activity indexes: no information is given on value added by nonproductive activities; branch data (particularly in the industrial sector) are not sufficiently disaggregated; and the data may contain some errors.[7] Thus, although value-added data in tables 9, 10, and 11 provide valuable information, it is necessary to turn to other sources to develop a suitable weighting scheme.

Estimating Value-Added Weights from Returns to Factors Data

In the absence of published data, it may be possible to estimate value added using information on the payments to the major factors of production: labor (wages and salaries), capital (return to capital, profit, depreciation), and land (rent). Since Cuba has regularly published data on wages (the wage bill) and on employment, the possibility of using those data as the basis for developing value-added weights deserved careful consideration.

Table 12 presents available information on the wage bill of civilian state employees for the period 1962–82. Systematic information on the wage bill of nonstate civilian workers (small farmers, self-employed workers and the like) or of the military is not available. Table 13 presents data on state civilian employment corresponding to the wage bill data in table 12; employment data for 1967–70 are not available. It should be noted that neither the wage bill nor the employment series is continuous; rather, each is three different, unconnected subseries for 1962–66, 1967–76 (1971–76 for employment), and 1977–82. The subseries for 1962–66 and for 1977–79 appear to be compatible with one another, as they report either wages or employment according to economic activity, whereas the subseries for 1967–76 (1971–76 for employment) appears to be based on enterprise employment and differs from the others. The level of detail at which state employment and wage bill data are available varies according to the subseries; there is a tendency for product detail to decline over time, with no detail beyond the major economic sectors available in the most recent subseries (1977–82).

Table 10. Comparison of GVO and Value Added, 1962 and 1963 (million pesos at current prices)

Activity	1962			1963		
	GVO	Value Added	Value Added as % of GVO	GVO	Value Added	Value Added as % of GVO
All productive activities	5,167.9	2,992.6	57.9	5,634.0	3,244.2	57.6
Industry	2,331.3	1,002.4	43.0	2,529.5	1,030.4	45.6
Mining	56.9	43.7	76.8	56.3	35.9	63.8
Metallurgy & metal transforming	108.6	64.4	59.3	118.3	68.1	57.6
Building materials	129.2	36.5	28.3	146.5	38.9	26.6
Petroleum & petroleum products	237.8	94.3	39.7	253.5	95.0	37.5
Chemicals	196.4	106.5	54.2	219.7	118.8	50.9
Textiles & leather products	232.6	126.5	54.5	281.7	146.8	52.1
Sugar	351.8	99.9	27.6	332.4	90.6	27.3
Food	532.4	155.9	29.3	574.7	144.5	25.1

Beverages & tobacco	237.8	149.4	62.8	270.4	161.1	59.6
Electricity	67.2	58.6	87.2	78.9	61.6	78.1
Other	170.6	66.7	39.1	197.2	68.1	34.5
Agriculture	800.1	700.8	87.6	845.1	683.0	80.8
Sugar agriculture	230.9	204.8	88.7	225.7	186.2	82.5
Nonsugar agriculture	274.1	266.4	97.2	283.6	261.9	92.3
Livestock	268.8	175.9	65.4	312.6	186.4	59.6
Forestry	10.5	38.3	--	5.8	32.7	--
Fishing	15.8	15.4	97.5	17.4	15.8	90.8
Construction	315.3	207.2	65.7	326.8	207.0	63.3
Transport & communications	284.3	229.7	80.8	326.8	236.5	72.4
Trade	1,426.6	799.4	56.0	1,588.8	1,031.3	64.9
Other	10.3	53.1	--	16.9	56.0	--

Sources: GVO estimated using GSP in current prices from United Nations, *Statistical Bulletin*, various issues distribution of GSP by sectors and branches from *Boletín estadístico de Cuba 1970*, p. 32; the value of agricultura services has been redistributed among the other five branches. Value added from table 9.

Table 11.   Value Added by Selected Branches of Industry, 1963
(million pesos at current prices)

Industrial Branch	Value Added
Total	1,035.8
Food, beverages & tobacco	485.4
Textiles	52.1
Apparel & footwear	74.3
Wood products	30.5
Paper & paper products	29.2
Printing & publishing	21.7
Leather products	7.1
Rubber products	22.0
Chemicals & petroleum products	198.2
Nonmetallic minerals	30.6
Basic metals	15.6
Metal products	49.1
Other manufactured products	20.0

Source: "El desarrollo industrial de Cuba," Cuba Socialista, pt.
2, 6, no. 57 (May 1966): table 10, p. 98.

The most disaggregated data available on civilian (state and private) economically active population by economic activity come from the 1970 population and housing census (table 14). Limited data are available on employment in the private sector, but not so on the private sector wage bill. BNC estimates of private sector employment for 1962, 1964, 1966, and 1971–77 are given in table 15; a breakdown of the data by economic sector is not available. However, the 1970 census does provide information on economically active population in the private sector by economic activity in that year (table 16). More recent data relating to private sector employment in 1979 are available from the 1979 demographic survey (table 17). It is clear from table 18 that by 1979 the state sector accounted for the vast majority of civilian employment, with agriculture (private farmers) and transportation (private taxi and truck drivers) the only two sectors in which the participation of the private sector was not negligible. In view of the overwhelming importance of the state sector in employment, it can be argued that the wage bill of civilian state employees can be reasonably used as a proxy for value-added by labor.[8]

With reference to returns to nonlabor factors of production, the situation is quite different. To the best of my knowledge, there are no data on returns to capital or land inputs. In addition, there are no data that would permit the estimation of the magnitude of such returns. Theoretically, returns to capital and land inputs could be constructed from data on capital and land stocks, net additions to stocks (investment), and a rate of return. Unfortunately, as discussed below, data on these variables are not available either.

The official Cuban report on industrialization mentioned earlier contains the most detailed information available on capital stock.[9] These data, which are reproduced in table 19, probably refer to capital stock around 1963 for the state industrial sector and, of course, do not refer to nonindustrial productive activities (agriculture, construction, and so on) or to the nonproductive sphere. I am not aware of any other body of data on capital stock that is more comprehensive (that is, that includes capital stock of the nonindustrial productive sector or of the nonproductive sectors) or that reflects a more recent vintage.

With reference to changes in capital stock (or investment), the data availability problems are similarly acute. A reasonably reliable time series on state investment at current prices for the period 1962–82 can be pieced together from several Cuban sources (table 20). Data on the distribution of investment by economic sectors or on use of investment remain weak, despite the recent availability of key information.

Until recently, annual data on the distribution of state investment by economic sectors were only available for the period 1962–66 (table 21). Investment data by sectors of the productive and nonproductive spheres for 1970 and for 1976–82 have been published in official statistical publications (table 22). For some time the *CMEA Statistical Yearbook* has included data on overall state investment and investment by sector not available from Cuban sources until 1982. Thus, the 1979 and 1980 editions of the CMEA yearbook contain data on Cuban state investment and investment in the productive and nonproductive spheres for 1960, 1965, 1970, and 1975–79 (table 23). (Unfortunately, the 1981 issue of the *CMEA Statistical Yearbook* does not contain any Cuban investment data beyond what appeared in earlier volumes.) There are discrepancies in the data reported in Cuban and CMEA publications, with official Cuban data indicating higher levels of investment. These differences might result from disparities in the definitions used in the two sources, but this cannot be confirmed.

In 1982, data breaking global investment data for selected years (1970, 1975, 1980, and 1981) into expenditures in construction and assembly, purchases of capital goods, and other expenditures, were released for the first time; subsequently, similar data for some of the intervening years have also been published (table 24). The *Anuario estadístico de Cuba 1982* includes data on both the distribution of investment by user (that is, economic sector and branch) and use (that is, type of investment) for productive sphere investments from 1975 to 1982. However, similar data

Table 12. Wage Bill of Civilian State Employees (million pesos)

Activity	1962	1963	1964	1965	1966	1967	1968	1969	1970	1971	1972
Total	1675.9	1934.2	2172.1	2312.7	2429.4	2448.9	2694.8	2729.6	2848.0	2905.5	3094.4
Productive	1320.0	1497.5	1707.5	1813.6	1910.3	1896.2	2033.4	2061.9	2169.0	2195.2	2321.9
Agriculture*	283.2	285.2	392.3	450.9	476.3	717.5	796.2	776.3	835.2	798.4	828.4
Industry	518.3	576.2	616.3	643.2	667.1	575.4	592.9	609.1	627.7	644.4	686.4
Construction	176.8	164.8	188.9	205.4	212.8	244.7	247.3	243.5	241.6	223.5	264.5
Transportation	138.1	158.0	161.2	163.7	167.0	198.6	221.1	240.0	246.0	280.3	278.7
Communications	23.6	24.3	22.5	22.7	21.5	—	—	—	—	30.8	34.6
Trade	180.0	284.9	319.3	316.3	353.0	160.0	175.9	193.0	218.5	217.8	229.3
Other productive activities	0.0	4.1	7.0	11.4	12.6	—	—	—	—	—	—
Nonproductive	355.9	436.7	464.6	499.1	519.1	552.7	661.4	667.7	679.0	710.3	772.5
Community services & housing	20.2	28.2	29.9	30.4	26.8	—	—	—	—	—	—
Science & technology	—	7.6	19.6	20.8	24.0	—	—	—	—	—	—
Education	123.7	161.1	159.3	175.7	187.2	—	—	—	—	—	—
Culture & art	28.4	29.9	34.2	33.3	24.5	—	—	—	—	—	—
Public health	67.7	86.1	104.3	103.1	106.3	—	—	—	—	—	—
Finance & insurance	110.2	117.8	109.6	111.7	102.2	—	—	—	—	—	—
Administration	—	—	—	—	—	—	—	—	—	—	—
Other nonproductive activities	5.7	6.0	7.7	24.1	48.1	—	—	—	—	—	—

Activity	1973	1974	1975	1976	1977	1978	1979	1980	1981	1982
Total	3400.9	3615.5	3922.2	4166.6	4311.6	4590.7	4763.9	4850.8	5748.6	6088.7
Productive	2553.0	2675.4	2870.4	3043.1	3205.3	3356.9	3447.7	3466.5	4127.2	4318.6
Agriculture*	948.9	981.4	1056.9	1094.5	851.8	892.0	908.6	983.1	1229.2	1272.0
Industry	726.4	758.8								1325.2
Construction	304.9	330.3	391.7	446.0	524.1	587.6	614.0	538.3	597.0	584.2
Transportation	288.8	303.1	319.2	350.6	330.1	338.0	361.9	371.8	434.4	445.0
Communication	36.3	38.3	39.7	41.6	35.5	36.6	37.9	38.2	44.5	47.5
Trade	247.7	263.5	263.4	271.7	439.7	463.2	476.0	486.4	564.5	614.0
Other productive activities	—	—	—	—	9.9	14.3				30.7
Nonproductive	847.9	940.1	1051.8	1123.3	1106.3	1223.8	1316.2	1384.3	1621.4	1770.1
Community services & housing	—	—	—	—	88.7	134.8	149.0	152.4	164.7	159.8
Science & technology	—	—	—	—	63.0	36.1	39.7	40.8	45.7	51.3
Education	—	—	—	—	431.1	491.3	529.3	580.8	675.5	729.7
Culture & art	—	—	—	—	51.3	43.1	56.9	61.7	69.4	94.0
Public health	—	—	—	—	182.6	199.4	206.7	225.1	270.2	310.0
Finance & insurance	—	—	—	—	16.7	18.0	19.7	21.7	25.2	29.4
Administration	—	—	—	—	262.5	266.9	281.5	275.8	322.5	339.8
Other nonproductive activities	—	—	—	—	10.4	34.2	33.4	26.0	48.2	56.1

Sources: **1962-66:** *Boletín estadístico, 1970,* p. 35; **1967-70:** *Boletín estadístico, 1971,* pp. 51-54; **1971:** *Anuario de Cuba, 1975,* p. 44; **1972-76:** *Anuario estadístico de Cuba, 1976,* p. 51; **1977:** *Anuario estadístico de Cuba, 1979,* p. 57; **1978:** *Anuario estadístico de Cuba,* p. 57; **1979:** *Anuario estadístico de Cuba, 1980,* p. 57; **1980-82:** *Anuario estadístico de Cuba, 1982,* p. 117. *Notes:* Columns may not add to totals because of unreported or overreported residuals. Dashes=no information.
*Includes forestry.

Table 13. State Civilian Employment by Economic Activity (thousands of civilian employees)

Activity	1962	1963	1964	1965	1966	1971	1972	1973	1974
Total	1083.3	1238.1	1368.6	1452.1	1517.3	2081.9	2125.9	2245.7	2313.3
Productive	874.4	980.7	1098.4	1162.8	1215.6	1520.0	1572.3	1658.6	1695.2
Agriculture*	297.0	305.3	386.2	433.0	449.9	603.6	636.9	670.3	674.5
Industry	267.0	288.5	302.7	308.6	323.4	440.5	438.5	453.2	466.7
Construction	104.0	97.0	108.0	117.0	118.0	132.7	153.7	176.5	183.5
Transportation	62.0	71.0	70.7	72.7	71.5	155.7	155.6	159.1	163.0
Communications	11.9	12.1	11.4	11.5	11.1	19.8	21.7	22.8	23.2
Trade	132.4	204.6	215.6	213.9	235.0	167.7	165.9	176.7	184.2
Other productive activities	0.1	2.2	3.8	6.1	6.7	--	--	--	--
Nonproductive	208.9	257.4	270.2	289.3	301.7	561.9	553.6	587.1	618.0
Community services & housing	14.3	20.1	26.2	27.7	28.5	--	--	--	--
Science & technology	--	3.6	9.2	9.7	10.0	--	--	--	--
Education	74.0	97.2	97.1	106.4	109.4	--	--	--	--
Culture & art	15.4	16.3	18.0	17.5	12.9	--	--	--	--
Public health	41.4	52.5	63.0	61.2	62.0	--	--	--	--
Finance & insurance	60.4	64.1	52.3	53.0	--	--	--	--	--
Administration									
Other nonproductive activities	3.4	3.6	4.4	13.5	25.9	--	--	--	--

Activity	1975	1976	1977	1978	1979	1980	1981	1982
Total	2393.8	2469.2	2626.1	2733.1	2768.2	2733.8	2824.4	2881.7
Productive	1732.4	1783.2	1973.4	2017.5	2013.6	1968.5	2007.6	2036.9
Agriculture*	685.1	684.9	635.6	660.2	637.5	644.3	639.4	636.3
Industry	472.2	477.4	567.3	552.9	553.7	546.1	576.4	599.9
Construction	208.0	243.2	300.3	318.9	319.3	273.4	266.3	260.7
Transportation	164.1	174.2	158.5	161.4	169.2	171.4	180.9	179.5
Communications	23.7	24.4	20.6	21.2	21.5	21.8	22.7	23.5
Trade	179.3	179.1	286.5	296.1	303.8	302.0	310.7	324.1
Other productive activities	–	–	4.6	6.8	8.6	9.5	11.2	12.9
Nonproductive	661.4	686.0	652.7	715.6	754.6	765.3	816.8	844.8
Community services& housing	–	–	.58.9	85.9	92.9	93.1	90.8	85.7
Science& technology	–	–	32.8	17.4	18.7	19.0	20.3	21.3
Education	–	–	273.4	303.6	314.6	329.5	347.8	357.0
Culture & art	–	–	25.9	23.2	28.5	30.3	32.5	35.0
Public health	–	–	109.6	117.5	120.8	126.7	138.2	153.7
Finance& insurance	–	–	8.2	8.6	9.6	10.8	11.9	13.3
Administration	–	–	137.9	140.4	150.5	141.3	151.9	151.5
Other nonproductive activities	–	–	6.0	19.0	19.0	14.6	23.4	27.3

Sources: **1962-66**: *Boletín estadístico, 1970*, p. 34; **1971**: *Anuario estadístico de Cuba, 1975*, p. 44; **1972-76**: *Anuario estadístico de Cuba, 1976*, p. 50; **1977**: *Anuario estadístico de Cuba, 1978*, p. 57; **1978**: *Anuario estadístico de Cuba, 1979*, p. 57; **1979**: *Anuario estadístico de Cuba, 1980*, p. 57; **1980-82**: *Anuario estadístico de Cuba, 1982*, p. 115.

Note: Columns may not add to totals because of unreported or overreported residuals. Dashes mean no information.
*Includes forestry.

Table 14. Economically Active Population in 1970, by Economic Activity

Activity	No. of Workers	%
All activities	2,633,309	100.00
Industry	533,258	20.25
Mining, except nickel	7,659	0.29
Nickel mining & processing	5,600	0.21
Manufacture of metal products, except machinery & equipment	20,853	0.79
Manufacture & assembly of nonelectrical machinery & equipment	43,422	1.65
Manufacture & assembly of electrical & electronic machinery & equipment	8,180	0.31
Manufacture of transportation equipment	64,109	2.43
Construction materials & processing of nonmetallic minerals	20,774	0.79
Petroleum refining	2,979	0.11
Chemicals	21,803	0.83
Textiles & leather	55,669	2.11
Sugar & by-products	96,780	3.68
Processed foods	70,649	2.68
Beverages & tobacco	46,731	1.77
Electricity	6,618	0.25
Woodworking & furniture	23,225	0.88
Publishing & printing	11,065	0.42
Other industrial activities n.e.c.	27,142	1.03
Agriculture	790,356	30.01
Sugar agriculture	183,510	6.97
Nonsugar agriculture	253,511	9.63
Livestock	108,229	4.11
Forestry	19,557	0.74
Fishing	17,381	0.66
Agricultural services	71,619	2.72
Other agricultural services n.e.c.	136,549	5.19
Construction	157,182	5.97
Housing	4,988	0.19
Buildings & structures for production & service activities	64,156	2.44
Road work	19,850	0.75
Utility lines, including underground lines	2,531	0.10

Table 14—Continued

Activity	No. of Workers	%
Construction of dams, ports, shoring	13,546	0.51
Construction services	1,996	0.08
Assembly	7,825	0.30
Project design	5,113	0.19
Maintenance of construction projects & other construction activities n.e.c.	37,177	1.41
Transportation	146,233	5.55
Air	2,078	0.08
Maritime	24,507	0.93
Road	103,542	3.93
Railroad	13,034	0.49
Animal-drawn	3,062	0.12
Communications	15,155	0.58
Postal & telegraphic	7,826	0.30
Telephone	5,620	0.21
International radio communication	895	0.03
Radio broadcasting (except technical personnel & programmers)	814	0.03
Trade	305,958	11.62
Domestic (wholesale)	61,672	2.34
Domestic (retail)	94,395	3.58
Foreign	2,315	0.09
Restaurants & food services	94,778	3.60
Personal & domestic services	52,798	2.01
Social services	621,957	23.62
Other activities	25,781	0.98
Political & mass organizations	23,064	0.88
Other activities n.e.c.	2,717	0.10
Activities not well specified	37,439	1.42

Source: Junta Central de Planificación, *Censo de población y viviendas 1970*, pp. 511-512.

Table 15. State and Private Civilian Employment
(thousands of employees)

Year	Total Employment	State Sector	%	Private Sector	%
1962	1,823	1,083	59.4	740	40.6
1964	1,885	1,369	72.6	516	27.4
1966	1,993	1,517	76.1	476	23.9
1971	2,402	2,082	86.7	320	13.3
1972	2,426	2,126	87.6	300	12.4
1973	2,526	2,246	88.9	280	11.1
1974	2,573	2,313	89.9	260	10.1
1975	2,626	2,394	91.2	232	8.8
1976	2,669	2,469	92.5	200	7.5
1977	2,790	2,608	93.5	182	6.5

Source: Banco Nacional de Cuba, Cuba: *Economic Development and Prospects*, p. 11.

for nonproductive sphere investments are not available in the *Anuario*. Regarding nonproductive sphere investments, information on the type of investment is only available for 1981 (table 25).

In view of the lack of appropriate capital stock and investment data and complete absence of data on returns to land, constructing value-added weights on the basis of returns to factors appears to be unfeasible. Since, as noted above, the returns-to-labor data appear to be reasonably complete, a question might be whether the wage bill data alone, if they could be adjusted to make them into a continuous series, could be used as proxies for total value added. This proxy relationship would be appropriate if the share of value added attributable to labor inputs were similar across all economic sectors. Partial information on the industrial sector for 1964 suggests that this is not the case. As is indicated in table 26, the labor share of total value added by branches within the industrial sector ranged from 98 percent for wood products and furniture to 16 percent for petroleum and by-products. Thus, using wage bill data alone as proxies for total value added would be distortive, tending to assign heavier weight to relatively labor-intensive sectors at the expense of those that are capital- or land-intensive.

Estimating Value-Added Weights from GVO Data and Value-Added/GVO Coefficients

The value-added weights that I propose to use in the construction of activity indexes for Cuba are essentially derived by applying value-added/GVO coefficients to GVO data for categories of productive and nonproductive output. In keeping with the "bottom-up" procedure, I have attempted to define index categories at the most disaggregated level possible subject to data availability and usefulness of the index for economic analysis. The GVO data refer to 1974, the only year for which value of non-material services data are available; the value-added/GVO coefficients originate from a variety of sources and typically refer to an earlier period. The implicit assumption in this procedure is that value-added/GVO ratios are relatively stable over time.

GVO Data

The Cuban government provides only minimal data on global indicators, and those that have been published are subject to frequent revisions and changes in methodology. At different points, the Cuban government has published data on GSP, GMP, and Net Material Product (NMP), but only GSP is available for the entire period 1962–80, albeit not calculated with a consistent methodology throughout. Data on the value of nonmaterial services were first published in early 1982 in a special publication of CEE.

In May 1982, CEE hosted an international seminar of specialists on the topic of the conversion of national product statistics from MPS to SNA. The seminar was the culmination of a cooperative project begun more than two years earlier by ECLA and CEE with the objective of developing a methodology that would yield Cuban macroeconomic data comparable to those for the rest of Latin America.[10]

Two documents were prepared for discussion at the seminar: a general summary of the United Nations MPS/SNA conversion methodology, prepared by ECLA,[11] and an exercise in applying the SNA methodology to Cuban data for 1974, carried out by CEE.[12] The CEE document is of crucial importance, since it contains the only official Cuban estimates on the value of nonmaterial services and on value added by the productive and nonproductive sectors (table 27). In the mentioned exercise, CEE estimated GVO in 1974 at 15,642.3 million pesos, with 13,482.5 million pesos (86.2 percent) contributed by the productive sphere and 2,159.8 million pesos (13.8 percent) by the nonproductive sphere; total value added amounted to 9,239.3 million pesos (59.1 percent of GVO), of which 4,286 million were payments to labor inputs and 4,953.3 million pesos were payments to nonlabor inputs.

For purposes of the index calculations, it is imperative to disaggregate the GVO data in table 27 to estimate the contribution by individual economic sectors and branches. For productive activities, this could be accomplished using data on components of GSP in 1974 available in the statistical yearbooks. However, this is not readily achievable, since different output valuation methodologies were used in calculating GVO in the conversion exercise and in the GSP data. GSP data for 1974 reported in the statistical

Table 16. Economically Active Population in 1970, by Occupational Category

Activity	Total	State	Private	Small Farmer	Occupational Category Owner	Self-Employed	Unpaid Helper	Unrecorded
All activities	2,633,309	2,288,406	35,192	230,525	108	29,990	34,395	14,693
Industry	533,258	530,727	645		4	1,755	24	103
Mining, except nickel	7,659	7,658						1
Nickel mining & processing	5,600	5,600						
Manufacture of metal products, except machinery & equipment	20,853	20,851						2
Manufacture & assembly of nonelectrical machinery & equipment	43,422	43,411						11
Manufacture & assembly of electrical & electronic machinery & equipment	8,180	8,174						6
Manufacture of transportation equipment	64,109	64,067						42

Construction materials & processing of nonmetallic minerals	20,774	20,713	27		2	28	1	3
Petroleum refining	2,979	2,978				26	1	6
Chemicals	21,803	21,741	29		1			7
Textiles & leather	55,669	54,916	160			580	5	2
Sugar & by-products	96,780	96,778						
Processed foods	70,649	70,469			1	88	6	7
Beverages & tobacco	46,731	46,730	78					1
Electricity	6,618	6,617				856	9	1
Woodworking & furniture	23,225	22,063	290					7
Publishing & printing	11,065	11,064				177	2	1
Other industrial activities n.e.c.	27,142	26,897	61			177	2	5
Agriculture	790,356	495,073	24,139	230,525	40	6,236	34,289	54
Sugar agriculture	183,510	139,358	8,058	32,128	7	516	3,438	5
Nonsugar agriculture	253,511	85,301	10,090	132,007	12	2,818	23,272	11
Livestock	108,229	102,057	663	4,868	3	228	405	5
Forestry	19,557	19,073	165			291	27	1
Fishing	17,381	15,923	221		4	1,212	13	8
Agricultural services	71,619	71,277	170		1	109	49	13

Table 16—Continued

Activity	Total	State	Private	Small Farmer	Owner	Self-Employed	Unpaid Helper	Unrecorded
						Occupational Category		
Other agricultural activities	136,549	62,084	4,772	61,522	13	1,062	7,085	11
Construction	157,182	156,003	209			948	6	16
Housing	4,988	4,987						1
Buildings & structures for production & service activities	64,156	64,152						1
Road work	19,850	19,848						2
Utility lines, including underground lines	2,531	2,528						3
Construction of dams, ports, shoring	13,546	13,545						1
Construction services	1,996	1,995						1
Assembly	7,825	7,824						1
Project design	5,113	5,112						1

Maintenance of construction projects & other construction activities n.e.c.	37,177	36,012	209		948	6	2
Transportation	146,223	122,966	6,648	40	16,509	23	37
Air	2,078	2,077					1
Maritime	24,507	24,502					5
Road	103,542	81,598	6,411				
Railroad	13,034	13,033					
Animal-drawn	3,062	1,756	237		1,065	4	1
Communications	15,155	15,092	55		3		5
Postal & telegraphic	7,826	7,825					1
Telephone	5,620	5,619					1
International radio	895	841	50		1		3
Radio broadcasting, except technical personnel & programmers	814	807	5		2		
Trade	305,958	300,537	1,570	16	3,773	29	33
Domestic (wholesale)	61,672	61,670					2
Domestic (retail)	94,395	93,903	155	4	319	7	7
Foreign	2,315	2,315					

Table 16—Continued

Activity	Total	State	Private	Small Farmer	Occupational Category Owner	Self-Employed	Unpaid Helper	Unrecorded
Restaurants & food services	94,778	94,591	124		1	46	10	6
Personal & domestic services	52,798	48,058	1,291		11	3,408	12	18
Social services	621,957	620,716	586		4	486	19	146
Other activities Political & mass organizations	25,781	24,150	1,340		4	280	5	2
Other activities	23,064	23,063						1
n.e.c.	2,717	1,087	1,340		4	280	5	1
Activities not well specified	37,439	23,142						14,297

Source: Junta Central de Planificación, *Censo de población y viviendas 1970*, pp. 679-680.

Table 17. Employment in 1979, by Occupational Category (thousands)

Activity	Total	State	Private	Small Farmer	Member of Co-op	Self-Employed	Unpaid Helper
All activities	3270.3	3053.0	13.4	160.1	5.7	27.6	10.4
Industry	651.9	649.8	0.8	0.5	0.1	0.5	*
Construction	256.5	255.8	0.2	0.1	0.0	0.4	*
Agriculture & forestry	716.0	546.0	9.0	138.2	5.0	9.6	8.3
Transportation & communications	202.7	195.8	1.4	0.1	0.0	5.4	0.0
Trade	265.5	264.5	*	0.4	*	0.4	*
Other productive activities	7.7	7.5	0.0	0.1	0.0	0.1	*
Community & personal services	94.7	91.5	0.3	*	0.0	2.8	0.0
Education, culture, art	373.8	373.2	*	0.1	*	0.2	0.1
Public health, social assistance, sports, tourism	148.7	148.4	*	*	0.0	0.2	0.0
Other nonproductive activities	316.8	314.9	0.3	0.9	*	0.6	*
Activities not well specified	236.0	205.5	1.2	19.6	0.4	7.4	1.8

Source: Comité Estatal de Estadísticas, Dirección de Demografía, Encuesta demográfica nacional 1979, p 35.
Notes: Columns may not add to totals because of rounding.
*Fewer than 100 persons.

yearbooks were calculated on the basis of "circulación completa" (complete circulation), presumably equivalent to the gross turnover valuation method; according to this method, GSP in 1974 amounted to 13,423.5 million pesos. The GVO data reported in the conversion exercise, however, were calculated on the basis of value "a salida de empresa" (at enterprise exit), an approach reportedly equivalent to the enterprise method and the valuation method used exclusively to calculate GSP since 1977. Using the enterprise exit valuation method, CEE estimated GSP in 1974 at 12,479 million pesos, 7.6 percent lower than under the gross turnover valuation methodology.

For 1975 and 1976, official data on GSP and its components calculated according to both valuation methodologies are available. Using these data I have attempted to determine whether a stable relationship exists between the main components of GSP across valuation methodologies. The results of the test suggest that such a relationship did hold for 1975 and 1976. (The test and its results are presented in Appendix D.) Thus, I assumed that the ratios relating output under the two valuation methods for 1975 and 1976 were also applicable to the main components of GSP in 1974 and estimated the value of output at enterprise exit for the principal components of GSP in 1974.

Table 28 presents estimates of the value of output at enterprise exit produced by sectors within the productive sphere in 1974, following the methodology described above. Also included in table 28 are estimates of GVO for sectors within the productive sphere in 1974. With the exception of the trade sector, the table presents identical results at the sector level. However, GVO in the trade sector is higher, by 1,003.5 million pesos, than the contribution of this sector to GSP, reflecting the different treatment of meals purchased away from home in the SNA and the MPS.[13]

To obtain GVO data for the productive sphere at the level of branches of

Table 18. Economically Active Population in 1970 and Employment in 1979, by Occupational Category

Activity	% of Total			
	State		Private[a]	
	1970[b]	1979	1970[b]	1979
All activities[c]	87.76	93.84	12.24	6.16
Productive activities	83.16	91.39	16.84	8.61
Industry	99.52	99.68	0.48	0.32
Construction	99.26	99.71	0.74	0.29
Agriculture & forestry	62.64	76.25	37.36	23.75
Transportation & communications	85.57	96.58	14.43	3.42
Trade	98.24	99.62	1.76	0.38
Other productive activities	--	99.57	–	0.43
Nonproductive activities	99.58	99.36	0.42	0.64
Community & personal services	--	99.65	–	3.35
Education, culture, art	--	99.84	–	0.16
Public health, social assistance, sports, tourism	--	99.83	–	0.17
Other nonproductive activities	--	99.38	–	0.62

Source: Tables 16 and 17.
Notes: Dashes mean information not available.
[a]Includes the following occupational categories: private, small farmers, member of a cooperative, owner, self-employed, and unpaid helper
[b]Excludes those who failed to record their occupational category in the census
[c]Excludes activities not well specified

industry, further manipulation of the estimates in table 28 is required. Conceptually, GVO data for certain economic sectors (industry, agriculture, transportation) could be disaggregated to estimate GVO for branches within these sectors, using a technique analogous to the one used above to estimate GVO valued at enterprise exit for sectors; that is, the hypothesis that the distribution of output at the branch level under one valuation methodology is a reasonable proxy for the distribution under the other could be tested. If such a hypothesis were validated, the ratios relating output under the two valuation methods could be used to estimate GVO valued at enterprise exit for branches of industry.

This procedure is not feasible, however, since the definitions of branches within the major economic sectors were changed at the same time as the valuation methodologies. Table 29 lists the branches for which value of output data are available under each of the two systems. Within the industrial sector, value of output data are available for fourteen branches under the complete circulation valuation methodology and for twenty-one under enterprise exit. Although in some cases the correspondence between the two sets of branches appears close (electricity, chemicals, beverages, and tobacco), there exist substantial differences in others. For example, the

Table 19. Capital Stock of State Industrial Sector circa 1963, Valued at Acquisition Prices, by Type (million pesos)

Industry	Total		Type			
	Value	%	Transportation Equipment	Buildings	Machinery & Equipment	Other
Total	1262.9	100.0	170.7	299.2	692.2	100.8
Food, bev., tobacco	202.2	16.0	15.6	70.6	83.9	32.1
Sugar	551.9	43.7	121.4	96.6	311.8	22.1
Textiles	40.7	3.2	0.5	13.1	25.3	1.8
Apparel & footwear	21.6	1.7	0.6	6.4	12.6	2.0
Wood products	16.3	1.3	1.2	7.8	4.9	2.4
Paper, paper prods.	56.8	4.5	0.7	12.5	40.1	3.5
Printing & publishing	15.5	1.2	0.7	3.3	10.8	0.7
Leather products	4.8	0.4	0.2	1.5	2.7	0.4
Rubber products	17.4	1.4	1.2	4.6	10.9	0.7
Chemicals	68.2	5.4	3.4	20.7	36.4	7.7
Petroleum	113.1	9.0	12.2	14.0	73.1	13.8
Nonmetallic mineral products	61.8	4.9	6.5	17.9	32.3	5.1
Basic metals	26.3	2.1	0.1	6.8	17.0	2.4
Metal products	57.0	4.5	6.4	20.7	24.8	5.1
Other manuf. prods.	9.3	0.7	0.0	2.7	5.6	1.0

Source: "El desarrollo industrial de Cuba," *Cuba Socialista*, pt. 2, no. 57 (May 1966): 113.

complete circulation methodology recognizes (1) nickel, (2) mining (excluding nickel), and (3) metallurgy and metalworking as separate branches of industry, whereas the enterprise exit valuation methodology purportedly considers the same activities under the headings of (1) ferrous mining and metallurgy, (2) nonferrous mining and metallurgy, (3) nonelectrical machinery, and (4) metal products. Bridging these differences in classification is not possible because there are no disaggregated data on the value of each of the outputs of these branches.

For the purpose of constructing economic activity indexes, it is desirable

**Table 20. Total Value of State Investment
(million pesos at current prices)**

Year	Total Value
1962	574
1963	696
1964	772
1965	842
1966	930
1967	1,032
1968	918
1969	897
1970	669
1971	964
1972	1,094
1973	1,475
1974	1,712
1975	2,304
1976	2,588
1977	2,766
1978	2,624
1979	2,609
1980	2,739
1981	3,206
1982	2,996

Sources: 1962-64: United Nations, *Statistical Bulletin.*
1965-68: *Boletín estadístico 1971.*
1969: *Anuario estadístico de Cuba 1972.*
1970: United Nations, *Yearbook of National Accounts 1977.*
1971-78: Comité Estatal de Estadísticas, *Cifras estadísticas 1980.*
1979-82: *Anuario estadístico de Cuba 1982.*

to use the most disaggregated classification scheme possible. Thus, I decided to make estimates of GVO at the branch level for 1974 following the classification used by the CEE in presenting data valued at enterprise exit. In table 30, the contribution by branches to output of the industrial, agricultural, and construction sectors for 1975 to 1977 is presented in terms of both value and share of the sector's output. As expected, there is considerable variation in the shares for specific branches across the three years, reflecting both secular and cyclical changes in the structure of the economy. The branch distribution of output for 1975 has been used as a proxy for the distribution in 1974, since it was the closest year for which data were available. (The objection could be raised that the selection of the branch distribution for 1975 as a proxy for 1974 understates the role of the sugar industry, since the world price of sugar plummeted in 1975 after recording historic highs in 1974. However, since the 1974 world price for sugar was abnormally high, the relative importance of the sugar industry in 1975 probably reflects more closely the *average* contribution by this branch to the economy over a longer time period.) Disaggregated estimates of GSP and GVO for the productive sphere in 1974 made using the method described above are reported in table 31.

Disaggregation of GVO in the nonproductive sphere presents special difficulties. As indicated in table 27, GVO of the nonproductive sphere in 1974 was estimated at 2,159.8 million pesos. According to the CEE conversion exercise,[14] such a total represents the value of services performed by "nonproductive enterprises," 183 million pesos; housing, 92.5 million pesos, including owner-occupied dwellings, 73.3 million pesos, and services provided by "budgeted" units, 19.2 million pesos; and services performed by "budgeted" units, 1,884.3 million pesos. Unfortunately, there is no

Table 21. State Investment, by Sector (percentages)

Sector	State Investment				
	1962	1963	1964	1965	1966
Agriculture	29.4	24.3	30.5	40.5	40.4
Industry	23.1	31.6	29.1	18.1	16.7
Construction	4.3	5.8	4.6	3.8	2.2
Transport & communications	9.5	9.6	9.1	11.7	14.3
Commerce	4.4	3.3	3.5	4.6	3.2
Housing & community services	13.5	11.5	11.4	9.4	9.6
Education, culture, research	8.1	7.0	5.3	5.0	4.4
Health	2.0	1.6	1.9	1.6	1.2
Other*	5.7	5.3	4.6	5.3	8.0

Source: *Boletín estadístico 1966*, p. 102, as cited by Carmelo Mesa-Lago, *The Economy of Socialist Cuba*, p. 45.
*Includes administration and finance, defense and internal security, and other minor activities in the material and nonmaterial sectors.

Table 22. Gross Investment, by Sector (million pesos at current prices)

Sector	Gross Investment								
	1970	1975	1976	1977	1978	1979	1980	1981	1982
Total	800.1	2304.2	2588.2	2765.9	2623.6	2605.8	2739.1	3205.7	2996.4
Productive sphere	686.1	1782.5	2038.7	2197.6	2054.5	2041.5	2212.5	2670.5	2500.3
Industry	163.3	630.1	807.9	966.5	897.1	1003.7	1007.1	1134.1	1058.5
Construction	84.0	141.3	164.5	162.1	112.3	89.8	114.5	132.6	131.3
Agriculture	253.6	559.6	553.9	540.1	446.0	435.5	584.5	786.9	737.1
Forestry	7.0	17.5	16.7	12.1	15.2	14.7	17.4	21.1	29.9
Transportation	142.2	357.4	408.7	417.9	469.3	383.7	375.6	449.7	385.2
Communications	10.9	30.6	35.7	39.0	47.2	42.8	30.0	41.9	63.0
Trade	25.1	41.9	46.4	54.1	61.6	59.5	74.5	88.8	84.1
Other productive activities	0.0	4.1	4.9	5.8	5.8	11.8	8.9	15.4	11.2
Nonproductive sphere	114.0	521.7	549.5	568.3	569.1	564.3	526.6	535.2	496.1
Community & personal services	61.1	170.3	155.3	167.6	207.5	227.6	250.9	277.9	217.5
Science & technology	5.1	17.7	21.1	23.7	13.9	13.7	19.2	17.1	23.1
Education	19.5	237.9	262.2	247.5	221.7	189.5	132.9	108.2	62.1
Culture & arts	3.6	6.8	7.6	0.2	13.1	15.0	11.7	12.7	11.1
Public health, welfare, sports, tourism	13.2	46.7	51.8	54.1	61.7	59.8	57.7	72.2	102.6
Finance & insurance	0.0	0.0	0.0	0.0	0.0	0.8	1.6	5.9	4.1
Administration	3.3	40.0	49.8	55.0	51.2	57.9	51.2	36.8	72.8
Other nonproductive activities	8.2	2.3	1.7	12.2	0.0	0.0	1.4	4.4	2.8

Sources: 1970, 1975: CEE, Cuba en cifras 1981, p. 56; 1976-82: Anuario estadístico de Cuba 1982, p. 135.

information on which activities are performed by either "nonproductive enterprises" or by "budgeted" units. Although the conversion exercise provides detailed data on GVO and value added by labor and nonlabor inputs for the banking and insurance sector (table 32), these detailed data are of limited use, since it is not known whether the enterprises that performed these services fall under "nonproductive enterprises" or "budgeted" units.

The possibility of disaggregating the GVO data for the nonproductive sphere using information on the wage bill or on employment has been investigated. Since either one of these two disaggregating schemes implicitly assumes uniformity with respect to either employment/GVO or returns to labor/GVO across nonproductive sectors, conditions that are violated in the productive sphere and that we may posit are similarly violated with respect to the nonproductive sphere, I have rejected them.

The disaggregating scheme that I have selected is based on state budget allocations for financing activities in the nonproductive sphere. It is not

Table 23. Total Value of State Investment, by Sector (million pesos)

| Sector | Total Value | | | | | | | |
	1960	1965	1970	1975	1976	1977	1978	1979
Total	388	858	800	1,777	2,593	2,553	2,473	2,564
Productive								
sphere	222	730	686	1,197	1,869	1,581	1,767	2.064
Industry	29	185	163	194	704	728	766	1,028
Construction	15	32	84	97	121	126	93	90
Agriculture &								
forestry	97	360	261	568	609	535	581	575
Transportation &								
communications	77	122	153	324	405	143	269	313
Commerce	5	31	25	24	30	49	58	58
Nonproductive								
sphere	166	128	114	580	724	972	706	500
Housing & community services	--	--	--	--	--	26	111	123
Education, culture, research	--	--	--	--	--	245	224	194
Health, sports, tourism	--	--	--	--	--	43	50	59

Source: Council for Mutual Economic Assistance, *Statisticheskii ezhegodnik,* 1979, 1980, tables 47, 51.
Notes: Dashes mean data not available.

possible to rely on the distribution of budgeted state expenditures in 1974, however, since data on the state budget for that year have not been published. Table 33 reproduces the available state budget data related to expenditures in nonproductive activities;[15] the state budget has not been made public for periods other than 1962–65 and 1978–85 and it has even been suggested by some officials that a national budget may not have been prepared for some of the interim years.[16] Thus, using the distribution of budgeted expenditures by activity in 1978 as a proxy for the distribution of GVO in 1974, I have estimated GVO for six activities of the nonproductive sphere: (1) housing and community services; (2) education and public health; (3) social security, welfare, cultural, and scientific activities; (4) public administration; (5) defense and internal order; and (6) other nonproductive activities. These estimates are presented in table 34.

Value-Added Data

In 1964–65 *Nuestra Industria. Revista Económica*, the economic journal of the Ministry of Industries, published two important articles introducing an input-output (I-O) table for enterprises under the jurisdiction of the ministry and pointing out several applications of the I-O table to planning and economic analysis.[17] According to these sources, the 45 x 45 I-O table was compiled using data for the first semester of 1963 provided by

Table 24.   Gross Investment, by Type (million pesos at current prices)

Year	Total Gross Investment	Construction & Assembly	Capital Goods	Other
1970	800.1	339.2	416.0	44.8
1975	2304.2	1210.1	685.8	408.3
1976	2588.2	1273.1	930.1	385.0
1977	2765.9	1314.0	1060.0	391.9
1978	2623.6	1383.3	888.4	351.9
1979	2605.8	1362.4	892.1	351.3
1980	2739.1	1329.5	1031.0	378.6
1981	3205.7	1474.7	1199.9	531.1
1982	2996.4	1044.8	1232.6	719.0

Source: **1970, 1975**: CEE, *Cuba en cifras 1981*, p. 56;
1976-82: *Anuario estadístico de Cuba 1982*, p. 135.

Table 25. Gross Investment in Nonproductive Sectors, by Sector and Use (million pesos at current prices)

Use

Sector	1981				1982			
	Total	Construction & Assembly	Equipment	Other	Total	Construction Assembly	Equipment	Other
Total	499.4	342.6	119.3	37.5	496.1	293.1	163.1	39.9
Community & personal services	252.2	218.2	21.9	12.1	217.5	175.9	27.3	14.3
Science & technology	17.3	3.9	10.5	2.9	23.1	2.2	14.2	6.7
Education	101.2	62.8	33.2	5.2	62.1	28.4	29.9	3.8
Culture & arts	12.1	7.0	3.9	1.2	11.1	3.5	6.3	1.3
Public health, welfare, sports, tourism	67.8	41.8	21.7	4.3	102.6	61.0	37.0	4.6
Finance & insurance	5.7	1.7	3.9	0.1	4.1	3.0	0.9	0.2
Administration	38.5	5.5	22.9	10.1	72.8	17.9	46.2	8.7
Other nonproductive activities	4.6	1.7	1.3	1.6	2.8	1.2	1.3	0.3

Source: CEE, Cuba en cifras 1981, p. 57; and 1982, p. 57.

all enterprises then under the jurisdiction of the Ministry of Industries (thus, neither sugar industrial activities, which were under the jurisdiction of the Ministry of the Sugar Industry, nor food-processing activities, under the Ministry of the Food Industry, were explicitly included in the I-O table). Following the practice of CPEs, the direct requirements matrix is available but not so the matrix of transactions flows.[18] The final (direct plus indirect) requirements matrix, the inverse of the direct requirements matrix, is also available.[19]

The direct requirements matrix, which provides information on the purchase of goods and services by each of forty-five industries, provides valuable information on value added. This comes about because the I-O table records not only an industry's purchase of goods and services from

Table 26.   Composition of Value Added in 1964 (percentages)

Industry	Value Added	
	Labor	Nonlabor
Food, beverages, tobacco*	47	53
Textiles	60	40
Apparel & footwear	55	45
Wood products & furniture	98	2
Paper	46	54
Printing & publishing	55	45
Leather	40	60
Rubber	29	71
Chemicals	21	79
Petroleum & by-products	16	84
Nonmetallic minerals	61	39
Basic metals	63	37
Metalworking	67	33
Other industrial activities	52	48

Source: "El desarrollo industrial de Cuba," Cuba socialista, pt. 2, 6, no. 57 (May 1966):110.
*Excluding sugar

other industries within the Ministry of Industries, from units outside the ministry, and from foreigners (imports), but also purchases of labor and non-labor inputs. The segment of the I-O table that provides information on purchase of labor and nonlabor inputs is reproduced in table 35; these direct requirements coefficients per 100 pesos' worth of an industry's output can be interpreted as the ratio to GVO of value added by labor, nonlabor and labor plus nonlabor factors.

Table 27. GVO and Value Added in 1974 (million pesos)

Activity	GVO	%	Value Added			Value Added/GVO (%)		
			Total	Labor	Nonlabor	Total	Labor	Nonlabor
All activities	15642.3	100.0	9239.3	4286.3	4953.3	59.1	27.4	31.7
Productive sphere	13482.5	86.2	7816.5	3083.2	4733.3	58.0	22.9	35.1
Nonproductive sphere	2159.8	13.8	1422.8	1202.8	220.0	65.9	55.7	10.2

Source: CEE, "Cuba: Conversión de los principales indicadores macroeconómicos del Sistema de Balances de la Economía Nacional (SBEN) al Sistema de Cuentas Nacionales (SCN 1974," tables 1 and 2, pp. 15-16.

Table 28. Estimated GSP and GVO for Productive Sectors, 1974 (million pesos)

Sector	GSP	GVO
All activities	12479.0	13482.5
Agriculture	1507.5	1507.5
Forestry	77.4	77.4
Fishing	93.6	93.6
Industry	6210.8	6210.8
Construction	1086.9	1086.9
Transportation	891.0	891.0
Communications	76.1	76.1
Trade	2535.7	3639.2

Source: GSP—See Appendix D, and text, p. 54; GVO—See text, p. 55.

Table 29.   Statistical Detail for Selected Economic Sectors

Complete Circulation Methodology	Enterprise Exit Methodology
Industry	
Electricity	Electricity
Mining, excluding nickel	Fuel
Metallurgy & metalworking	Ferrous mining & metallurgy
Mining & processing of nonmetallic minerals	Nonelectrical machinery
Petroleum & by-products	Electronics
Chemicals	Chemicals
Textiles & leather	Paper & cellulose
Sugar & by-products	Printing
Processed foods	Wood products
Beverages & tobacco	Construction materials
Wood & wood products	Glass & ceramics
Printing & publishing	Textiles
Other	Apparel
	Leather products
	Sugar
	Processed foods
	Fishing
	Beverages & tobacco
	Other
Agriculture	
Sugar	Sugar
Nonsugar	Nonsugar
Livestock	Livestock
	Agricultural services
Transportation	
Railroad	Railroad
Motor	Motor
Maritime	Maritime
Air	Air
	Cargo handling

Two observations related to table 35 are in order. First, the wide disparity across industries regarding the share of value added attributable to labor and to nonlabor inputs reinforces the concern raised earlier (in the context of discussing the data in table 26) regarding the risks in using coefficients of value added by labor or nonlabor inputs to estimate value added for large segments of the economy or in using only one of the two coefficients to estimate total value added. Second, a cursory comparison of the value-added coefficients in table 35 with some estimated coefficients for 1953 (table 36) suggests that, in general, the 1963 value added/GVO coefficients were considerably higher than in 1953 and, further, that the share of value added attributable to labor inputs in 1963 was typically higher than in 1953. Although these general trends are not surprising, given the economic policies implemented by the revolutionary government in the 1960s (for example, increase in wages, nationalization of enterprises, and reduction in private sector profits), the fact that they are reflected in the value-added information suggests the sensitivity of this body of data to the deep economic changes that began in Cuba in 1959.

Value-Added Weights

Table 37 presents the set of value-added weights that I have used in the calculation of activity indexes for revolutionary Cuba. (The weights reported are given in value terms; a set of value-added coefficients could be obtained by dividing value added by each sector or branch by total value added.) These weights have been constructed using my estimates of GVO in 1974 and estimated value-added/GVO coefficients. For the productive sphere the value-added/GVO coefficients used refer to the structure of production in 1963. This procedure assumes implicitly that the relationship between GVO and value added that existed in 1963 is applicable to 1974 as well. For the nonproductive sphere, no value-added data at the level of sectors have been found and therefore the value-added weights merely represent the estimated structure of GVO in 1974.

In making my estimates of value added by branches of industry I have attempted to take advantage of the very detailed value-added coefficients data available from the I-O table (table 35). Where possible, I have matched the productive branches to I-O cells and used the value-added/GVO coefficients to represent the branch. In some cases it is clear that a productive branch contains more than one of the industries in the I-O matrix. For example, the beverages and tobacco branch contains activities in I-O cells 17 (soft drinks), 18 (beer and malt), 19 (cigarettes), 31 (wine and liquors), and 37 (cigars), with the value-added/GVO coefficients ranging from 82 to 60 percent. However, GVO data are not available at this same level of disaggregation. (As noted earlier, the available I-O table does not contain actual value data;

Table 30. Branch Contribution to Output of Selected Economic Sectors (enterprise exit valuation methodology)

| | Contribution to Output | | | | | |
| | 1975 | | 1976 | | 1977 | |
Sector	Million Pesos	%	Million Pesos	%	Million Pesos	%
Industry	6724.2	100.00	7015.6	100.00	6995.8	100.00
Electricity	144.6	2.15	158.6	2.26	183.4	2.62
Fuel	428.1	6.37	411.4	5.86	403.3	5.76
Ferrous mining & metallurgy	61.8	0.92	61.5	0.88	74.0	1.06
Nonferrous mining & metallurgy	59.7	0.89	65.0	0.93	72.3	1.03
Nonelectrical machinery	307.1	4.57	360.2	5.13	376.4	5.38
Electronics	152.5	2.27	148.8	2.12	116.5	1.67
Metal products	106.6	1.59	110.7	1.58	112.9	1.61
Chemicals	652.6	9.71	648.4	9.24	551.7	7.89
Paper & cellulose	80.9	1.20	88.6	1.26	83.4	1.19
Printing	85.0	1.26	88.6	1.26	95.0	1.36
Wood products	131.8	1.96	127.6	1.82	138.8	1.98
Construction materials	274.9	4.09	287.7	4.10	307.4	4.39
Glass & ceramics	31.3	0.47	29.1	0.41	28.1	0.40
Textiles	142.0	2.11	143.1	2.04	127.5	1.82
Apparel	288.9	4.30	301.0	4.29	347.6	4.97
Leather products	183.2	2.72	194.3	2.77	185.1	2.65

Sugar	625.7	9.31	608.4	8.67	686.3	9.81
Processed foods	1295.0	19.26	1313.8	18.73	1359.9	19.44
Fishing	85.6	1.27	106.2	1.51	103.1	1.47
Beverages & tobacco	1363.5	20.28	1537.6	21.92	1438.9	20.57
Other	223.4	3.32	225.0	3.21	204.2	2.92
Agriculture	1537.7	100.00	1595.3	100.00	1664.9	100.00
Sugar	553.6	36.00	557.2	34.93	629.4	37.80
Nonsugar	365.2	23.75	384.4	24.10	362.4	21.77
Livestock	603.2	39.23	637.9	39.99	657.5	39.49
Agricultural services	15.7	1.02	15.8	0.99	15.6	0.90
Transportation	1006.3	100.00	1035.9	100.00	1095.7	100.00
Railroad	57.6	5.72	63.2	6.10	91.2	8.32
Motor	513.1	50.99	590.5	57.00	614.4	56.07
Maritime	249.2	24.76	213.6	20.62	203.8	18.60
Air	48.6	4.83	54.6	5.27	66.1	6.03
Cargo handling	137.8	13.69	114.0	11.00	120.2	10.97

Source: Anuario estadístico de Cuba 1980, p. 50.
Note: Percentages may not add to 100 because of rounding.

**Table 31.   Disaggregated Estimates of GSP and GVO for Productive
Sectors, 1974 (million pesos)**

Sector	GSP	GVO
Total	12479.0	13482.5
Agriculture	1507.5	1507.5
Sugar	542.7	542.7
Nonsugar	358.0	358.0
Livestock	591.4	591.4
Agricultural services	15.4	15.4
Forestry	77.4	77.4
Industry	6210.8	6210.8
Electricity	133.5	133.5
Fuel	395.6	395.6
Ferrous mining & metallurgy	57.1	57.1
Nonferrous mining & metallurgy	55.3	55.3
Nonelectrical machinery	283.8	283.8
Electronics	141.0	141.0
Metal products	98.8	98.8
Chemicals	603.1	603.1
Paper & cellulose	74.5	74.5
Printing	78.3	78.3
Wood products	121.7	121.7
Construction materials	254.0	254.0
Glass & ceramics	29.2	29.2
Textiles	131.0	131.0
Apparel	267.1	267.1
Leather products	169.6	169.6
Sugar	578.2	578.2
Processed foods	1195.0	1195.0
Fishing	78.9	78.9
Beverages & tobacco	1258.9	1258.9
Other	206.2	206.2
Construction	1086.9	1086.9

Table 31—Continued

Sector	GSP	GVO
Transportation	891.0	891.0
Railroad	51.0	51.0
Motor	454.4	454.4
Maritime	220.6	220.6
Air	43.0	43.0
Cargo handling	122.0	122.0
Communications	76.1	76.1
Trade	2535.7	3539.2

Sources: GSP—Tables 28 and 30, and text, pp. 57, 58; GVO—Text, pp. 57, 58.

Table 32. Output Measures for Banking and Insurance Services, 1974 (million pesos)

Output Measures	Banking	Insurance	Banking & Insurance
GVO	23.0	1.4	24.4
Intermediate consumption	8.0	0.0	8.0
Value added	15.0	1.4	16.4
Value added by labor	14.0	0.2	14.2
Value added by nonlabor factors	1.0	1.2	2.2
Value added/GVO (%)	65.2	100.0	67.2
Value added by labor/GVO (%)	60.9	14.3	58.2
Value added by nonlabor/ GVO (%)	4.3	85.7	9.0

Source: Comité Estatal de Estadísticas, "Cuba: Conversión de los principales indicadores macroenonómicos del Sistema de Balances de la Economía Nacional (SBEN) al Sistema de Cuentas Nacionales (SCN) 1974," Annex 1, p. 21.

Table 33. State Budget Allocations for Financing of Nonproductive Activities (million pesos)

Sector	Allocation							
	1962		1963		1964		1965	
	Pesos	%	Pesos	%	Pesos	%	Pesos	%
Total	1219.7	100.0	1192.8	100.0	1270.1	100.0	1344.0	100.0
Housing & community services	92.7	7.6	96.3	8.1	128.7	10.1	135.7	10.1
Education & public health ⎫ Social security, welfare, cultural & scientific activities ⎭	568.9	46.6	610.2	51.2	626.7	49.3	695.6	51.8
Public administration	195.0	16.0	145.5	12.2	143.8	11.3	136.8	10.2
Defense & internal order	247.0	20.3	213.7	17.9	221.2	17.4	213.2	15.9
Other nonproductive activities	116.1	9.5	127.2	10.7	149.7	11.8	162.7	12.1

Sector	1978		1979		Allocation 1980		1981	
	Pesos	%	Pesos	%	Pesos	%	Pesos	%
Total	4732.9	100.0	5134.7	100.0	5217.0	100.0	5980.8	100.0
Housing & community services	326.6	6.9	398.4	7.8	363.7	7.0	412.1	6.9
Education & public health	1532.8	32.4	1684.8	32.8	1800.2	34.5	1848.3	30.9
Social security, welfare, cultural & scientific activities	1150.0	24.3	1242.2	24.2	1315.1	25.2	1436.4	24.0
Public administration	540.1	11.4	517.3	10.1	483.7	9.3	675.1	11.3
Defense & internal order	784.0	16.6	840.9	16.4	810.9	15.5	842.1	14.1
Other nonproductive activities	399.4	8.4	451.1	8.8	443.4	8.5	766.8	12.8

Source: Based on official Cuban data as quoted by Carmelo Mesa-Lago, "The Economy: Caution, Frugality, and Resilient Ideology," p. 139, supplemented with official data.

rather, it consists of direct input coefficients obtained after dividing the value of an industry's purchases by its GVO.) I have considered the possibility of obtaining GVO at the level of the I-O cells by operating with available labor-requirements-per-one-peso's-worth-of-output coefficients (table 38); however, such manipulation requires information on employment at the same level of detail as the I-O cells, and such data are not available.

Table 34. GVO of Nonproductive Sphere in 1974 and Estimated GVO for Selected Nonproductive Activities (million pesos)

Activity	GVO	%
Nonproductive sphere	2159.8	100.0
Housing & community services	149.0	6.9
Education & public health	699.8	32.4
Social security, welfare, cultural & scientific activities	524.8	24.3
Public administration	246.2	11.4
Defense & internal order	358.5	16.6
Other activities	181.4	8.4

Source: Estimated based on data in tables 27 and 33.

Table 35.   Purchases of Labor and Capital Inputs per 100 Pesos of
Output

I-O	Industrial Activity	Direct Requirements Coefficient		
		Labor	Capital	Value Added
1.	Automotive	16.117	26.107	42.224
2.	Cement	24.761	34.908	59.669
3.	Ceramics	55.091	1.612	56.703
4.	Electricity	30.142	45.219	75.361
5.	Fertilizers	12.224	2.439	14.663
6.	Ferrous metallurgy	32.654	7.102	39.756
7.	Nonferrous metallurgy	23.006	27.146	50.152
8.	Mining	87.644	(35.605)	52.039
9.	Nickel & cobalt	26.408	41.892	68.300
10.	Petroleum	7.052	41.939	48.991
11.	Paper & artificial wood	25.448	17.148	42.636
12.	Basic chemicals	43.474	2.311	45.785
13.	Salt	34.422	35.291	69.713
14.	Agricultural machinery	40.321	10.317	50.638
15.	Naval construction	73.220	(5.751)	66.469
16.	Metalworking	46.994	8.480	55.474
17.	Soft drinks	19.475	46.029	65.504
18.	Beer & malt	19.930	61.988	81.918
19.	Cigarettes	19.442	40.423	59.865
20.	Paper & cardboard	22.523	21.759	44.282
21.	Apparel	27.761	18.101	45.862
22.	Leather products	45.885	15.720	61.605
23.	Metal containers	26.816	10.137	36.953
24.	Electrical equipment	26.022	31.008	57.030
25.	Matches	28.987	58.326	87.313
26.	Hard fibers	24.878	30.696	55.574
27.	Rubber	21.116	45.674	66.790
28.	Flour	23.656	28.944	52.600
29.	Textiles	31.589	25.496	57.085
30.	Soap & perfumes	9.931	52.983	62.914
31.	Wine & liquors	7.465	73.209	80.674
32.	Wood	56.694	4.578	61.272
33.	Paint	17.173	38.718	55.891
34.	Plastics	39.570	32.166	71.736
35.	Pharmaceuticals	11.063	63.528	74.591
36.	Recovery of raw materials	55.920	11.024	66.944
37.	Cigars	44.229	6.955	51.184

Table 35—Continued

| I-O | Industrial Activity | Direct Requirements Coefficient | | |
		Labor	Capital	Value Added
38.	Tanneries	17.689	25.748	43.437
39.	Knitted fabrics & apparel	34.404	28.917	63.321
40.	Glass	34.066	24.493	58.559
41.	Specialty textiles	21.261	31.350	52.611
42.	Printing	42.454	15.248	57.702
43.	Toys	46.764	6.687	53.451
44.	Local industries	35.591	13.463	49.054
45.	Other industries	98.066	(22.955)	75.111

Source: Adapted from direct requirements matrix in Zoila González Maicas, "La matriz de insumo-producto: un nuevo instrumento de planificación industrial," *Nuestra Industria. Revista Económica* 2, no. 8 (August 1964): 68-75.

Table 36.   GVO and Value Added in 1953 (million pesos)

Sector	GVO	Value Added Labor	Value Added Nonlabor	Value Added Total	Value Added as % of GVO
Total	5285.2	934.0	749.7	1683.7	31.9
Agriculture, forestry, hunting, fishing	472.4	236.2	138.1	374.3	79.2
Mining	46.5	12.3	21.9	34.2	73.5
Manufacturing	1433.7	233.4	224.5	457.9	31.9
Foodstuffs	785.7	126.2	94.6	220.8	28.1
Beverages	115.4	14.4	26.9	41.3	35.8
Tobacco	43.5	7.9	13.1	21.0	48.3
Textiles	44.7	11.7	5.2	16.9	37.8
Footwear & apparel	56.4	10.6	10.2	20.8	36.9
Wood & wood products	18.4	2.4	1.2	3.6	19.6
Furniture	11.8	2.4	1.4	3.8	32.2
Paper & paper products	24.7	4.6	3.5	8.1	32.8
Printing & publishing	14.9	4.5	1.7	6.2	41.6
Leather & leather products	14.7	2.4	0.7	3.1	21.1
Rubber products	15.2	2.3	3.6	5.9	38.8
Chemicals	114.7	19.1	21.4	40.5	35.3
Oil refining & by-products	67.8	3.5	27.6	31.1	45.9
Construction materials	36.6	8.3	10.6	18.9	51.6
Basic metallurgy	27.0	3.4	2.8	6.2	23.0
Metal products, excluding machinery & transportation equipment	10.5	2.2	1.7	3.9	37.1
Nonelectrical machinery	11.8	2.7	1.8	4.5	38.1
Electrical machinery	2.5	0.6	0.3	0.9	36.0
Transportation equipment	5.0	1.8	0.5	2.3	46.0
Other manufactures	12.4	2.4	1.1	3.5	28.2
Construction	90.0	19.2	4.8	24.0	26.7
Electricity, gas, water, sanitary services	59.1	19.5	27.3	46.8	79.2
Electricity, electrical service, gas production & distribution	56.6	18.7	26.6	45.3	80.0
Heat, steam, water, sanitary services	2.5	0.8	0.7	1.5	60.0
Transportation, warehousing, communications	199.2	84.3	33.3	117.6	59.0
Maritime, railroad & other transportation activities	142.4	58.7	19.4	78.1	54.8
Warehousing	38.0	18.6	6.2	24.8	65.3
Communication	18.8	7.0	7.7	14.7	78.2
Wholesale & retail trade	2467.6	221.0	241.5	462.5	18.7
Wholesale	1060.5	82.1	93.3	175.4	16.5

Table 36—Continued

Value Added

Sector	GVO	Labor	Nonlabor	Total	Value Added as % of GVO
Retail	1407.1	138.9	148.2	287.1	20.4
Banking, insurance & real estate	141.9	37.6	33.1	70.7	49.8
Banking & other financial institutions	46.4	15.9	15.4	31.3	67.5
Insurance	68.9	19.2	12.2	31.4	45.6
Real estate	26.6	2.5	5.5	8.0	30.1
Services	225.4	57.7	17.7	75.4	33.5
Other activities not well specified	149.5	12.7	8.8	21.5	14.4

Source: Adapted from Tribunal de Cuentas, Dirección de Fiscalización Preventiva y Control de Presupuestos del Estado, "Análisis de los sectores económicos en Cuba y su tributación," table A.

Table 37.   Estimated Value-Added Weights, 1974 (million pesos)

Sector	GVO	Value Added/ GVO (%)	Estimated Value Added	Adjusted Value Added
Total	15642.3	58.4	9199.8	9239.3
Productive				
sphere	13482.5	57.2	7776.6	7816.5
A Agriculture	1583.2	76.1	1205.5	1211.7
1 Sugar	542.7	82.5	447.7	450.0
2 Nonsugar	358.0	92.3	330.4	332.1
3 Livestock	591.4	59.6	352.5	354.3
4 Agricultural services	15.4	80.8	12.4	12.5
5 Forestry	77.4	80.8	62.5	62.8
B Industry	6210.8	46.5	2886.1	2900.9
6 Electricity	133.5	75.4	100.7	101.2
7 Fuel	395.6	49.0	193.8	194.8
8 Ferrous mining & metallurgy	57.1	39.8	22.7	22.8
9 Nonferrous mining & metallurgy	55.3	50.2	27.8	27.9
10 Nonelectrical machinery	283.8	50.6	143.6	144.3
11 Electronics	141.0	57.0	80.4	80.8
12 Metal products	98.8	37.0	36.6	36.8
13 Chemicals	603.1	50.9	307.0	308.6
14 Paper & cellulose	74.5	43.5	32.4	32.6
15 Printing	78.3	57.7	45.2	45.4
16 Wood products	121.7	61.3	74.6	75.0
17 Construction materials	254.0	59.7	151.6	152.4
18 Glass & ceramics	29.2	57.7	16.9	17.0
19 Textiles	131.0	57.1	74.8	75.2
20 Apparel	267.1	45.9	122.6	123.2
21 Leather products	169.6	61.6	104.5	105.0
22 Sugar	578.2	27.3	157.9	158.7
23 Processed foods	1195.0	25.1	300.0	301.5
24 Fishing	78.9	90.8	71.6	72
25 Beverages & tobacco	1258.9	59.6	750.3	754.1
26 Other	206.2	34.5	71.1	71.5
C Construction	1086.9	63.3	688.0	691.5
D Transportation	891.0	72.4	645.0	648.3
27 Railroad	51.2	72.4	36.9	37.1
28 Motor	454.4	72.4	329.0	330.7

Table 37—Continued

Sector	GVO	Value Added/ GVO (%)	Estimated Value Added	Adjusted Value Added
29 Maritime	220.6	72.4	159.7	160.5
30 Air	43.0	72.4	31.1	31.3
31 Cargo handling	122.0	72.4	88.3	88.8
E Communications	76.1	72.4	55.1	55.4
F Trade	3539.2	64.9	2296.9	2308.7
Nonproductive sphere	2159.8	65.9	1422.8	1422.8
G Housing & community services	149.0	65.9	98.2	98.2
H Education & public health	699.8	65.9	461.2	461.2
I Social security, welfare, cultural, scientific activities	524.8	65.9	345.8	345.8
J Public administration	246.2	65.9	162.2	162.2
K Defense & internal order	358.5	65.9	236.3	236.3
L Other nonproductive activities	181.4	65.9	119.5	119.5

Sources: Col. 1 (GVO): Tables 31 and 34.
Col. 2 (Value Added/GVO coefficients):
   A Agriculture--derived from sum of estimated value added and GVO for each branch.
   1 Sugar--estimate for 1963 from table 10.
   2 Nonsugar--estimate for 1963 from table 10.
   3 Livestock--estimate for 1963 from table 10.
   4 Agricultural services--assigned the average value added/GVO coefficient for agriculture in 1963 from table 10.
   5 Forestry--assigned the average value added/GVO coefficient for agriculture for 1963 from table 10.
   B Industry--derived from sum of estimated value added and GVO for each branch.
   6 Electricity--estimate for 1963 from table 35, I-O 4 (Electricity).
   7 Fuel--estimate for 1963 from table 35, I-O 10 (Petroleum).
   8 Ferrous mining & metallurgy--estimate for 1963 from table 35, I-O 6 (Ferrous metallurgy).
   9 Nonferrous mining & metallurgy--estimate for 1963 from table 35, I-O 7 (Nonferrous metallurgy).
   10 Nonelectrical machinery--estimate for 1963 from table 35, I-O 14 (Agricultural machinery).
   11 Electronics--estimate for 1963 from table 35, I-O 24 (Electricl equipment).
   12 Metal products--estimate for 1963 from table 35, I-O 23 (Metal containers).
13 Chemicals--estimate for 1963 from table 10.

Table 37—Continued

14 Paper & cellulose--estimate for 1963 from table 35, unweighted average of I-O 11 (Paper & artificial wood) and I-O 20 (Paper & cardboard).

15 Printing--estimate for 1963 from table 35, I-O 42 (Printing).

16 Wood products--estimate for 1963 from table 35, I-O 32 (Wood).

17 Construction materials--estimate for 1963 from table 35, I-O 2 (Cement).

18 Glass & ceramics--estimate for 1963 from table 35, unweighted average of I-O 3 (Ceramics) and I-O 40 (Glass).

19 Textiles--estimate for 1963 from table 35, I-O 29 (Textiles).

20 Apparel--estimate for 1963 from table 35, I-O 21 (Apparel).

21 Leather products--estimate for 1963 from table 35, I-O 22 (Lather products).

22 Sugar--estimate for 1963 from table 10.

23 Processed foods--estimate for 1963 from table 10.

24 Fishing--estimate for 1963 from table 10.

25 Beverages & tobacco--estimate for 1963 from table 10.

26 Other--estimate for 1963 from table 10.

C Construction--estimate for 1963 from table 10.

D Transportation--estimate for 1963 from table 10.

27 Railroad--estimate for 1963 from table 10.

28 Motor--estimate for 1963 from table 10.

29 Air--estimate for 1963 from table 10.

30 Maritime--estimate for 1963 from table 10.

31 Cargo handling--estimate for 1963 from table 10.

E Communications--estimate for 1963 from table 10.

F Trade--estimate for 1963 from table 10.

G Housing & community services--estimate for 1974 from table 27.

H Education & public health--estimate for 1974 from table 27.

I Social security, welfare, cultural, scientific activities--estimate for 1974 from table 27.

J Public administration--estimate for 1974 from table 27.

K Defense & internal order--estimate for 1974 from table 27.

L Other nonproductive activities--estimate for 1974 from table 27.

Col. 3 (Estimated Value Added): calculated as product of cols. 1 & 2.

Col. 4 (Adjusted Value Added): for all activities, productive sphere activities and nonproductive sphere activities from table 27. For sectors and branches of productive sphere, estimated using value added by activities in productive sphere distributed proportional to composition of estimated value added in col. 3.

Note: Figures may not be internally consistent because of rounding.

Table 38.   Labor Requirements per Peso of Output

I-O	Industrial Activity	Man-Years per Peso of Output
1.	Automotive	0.00010
2.	Cement	0.00010
3.	Ceramics	0.00035
4.	Electricity	0.00009
5.	Fertilizers	0.00006
6.	Ferrous metallurgy	0.00015
7.	Nonferrous metallurgy	0.00011
8.	Mining	0.00048
9.	Nickel & cobalt	0.00015
10.	Petroleum	0.00002
11.	Paper & artificial wood	0.00012
12.	Basic chemicals	0.00018
13.	Salt	0.00025
14.	Agricultural machinery	0.00024
15.	Naval construction	0.00040
16.	Metalworking	0.00027
17.	Soft drinks	0.00009
18.	Beer & malt	0.00006
19.	Cigarettes	0.00004
20.	Paper & cardboard	0.00013
21.	Apparel	0.00023
22.	Leather products	0.00022
23.	Metal containers	0.00011
24.	Electrical equipment	0.00018
25.	Matches	0.00018
26.	Hard fibers	0.00017
27.	Rubber	0.00009
28.	Flour	0.00013
29.	Textiles	0.00015
30.	Soap & perfumes	0.00004
31.	Wine & liquors	0.00005
32.	Wood	0.00039
33.	Paint	0.00007
34.	Plastics	0.00026
35.	Pharmaceuticals	0.00006
36.	Recovery of raw materials	0.00035
37.	Cigars	0.00027

Table 38—Continued

I-O	Industrial Activity	Man-Years per Peso of Output
38.	Tanneries	0.00008
39.	Knitted fabrics & apparel	0.00023
40.	Glass	0.00017
41.	Specialty textiles	0.00012
42.	Printing	0.00013
43.	Toys	0.00052
44.	Local industries	0.00020
45.	Other industries	0.00027

Source: Enrique González Romero and Zoila González Maicas, "Algunas contribuciones al análisis y utilización de la matriz de insumo-producto," *Nuestra Industria. Revista Económica* 3, no. 12 (April 1965): 16.

3. Product/Services Weights

An essential datum for the construction of activity indexes for branches or sectors of the economy is the relative importance, in the base period, of each product or service produced. In a market economy, the prices commanded by products and services can perform this function. In trying to construct activity indexes for revolutionary Cuba, two critical problems arise: (1) there is very little information on prices in Cuba for 1974, the base period for the indexes, or for any other period; and (2) prevailing Cuban prices differ significantly from market-determined scarcity prices.

The Cuban Price System

Policies implemented by the Cuban revolutionary government soon after it gained power had as their objective the achievement of popular support through demand satisfaction.[1] These policies included (1) the already-mentioned First Agrarian Reform Law, which provided land to peasants; (2) creation of public service jobs primarily in construction, administration, and the armed forces; (3) an increase in the minimum salary of government employees; (4) support for demands by private sector labor unions for higher wages in collective bargaining agreements renegotiated in 1959; and (5) reductions, or freezes, in the retail prices of certain services and commodities.

Government tampering with the price system began in February 1959, when the government ordered a reduction in the rates charged by small electric plants servicing rural areas to bring them in line with lower rates charged in Havana.[2] In March 1959, the government took over the Cuban Telephone Company and repealed telephone service rate increases that had been granted by the previous government; in the same month, Law 135, the Rent Reduction Act, which scaled down residential rents by 30 to 50 percent, and Law-Decree 709, which provided for an immediate reduction of 15 percent in the retail prices of domestically produced pharmaceutical products and of 20 percent for those imported, were enacted. In July the prices of textbooks for elementary and secondary schools were reduced. In August Law 502 reduced residential electricity and gas rates charged by the Cuban Electric Company, the supplier of roughly 90 percent of all electric power publicly sold, and Law-Decree 1939 reduced by one-half cent per gallon the wholesale price of gasoline.

In preparation for the implementation of the first national economic plan (for 1962), JUCEPLAN was given the authority to control prices. On 15 November 1961, it issued regulations freezing retail and wholesale prices at the levels that prevailed on that date. Law 1000, enacted in February 1962, reaffirmed the November 1961 price freeze and called for the preparation of price lists covering all transactions and all enterprises. To deal with serious shortages of consumer products, the government instituted a national rationing system beginning in March 1962. Though there has been a progressive reduction in the number of products covered by the rationing system, it still remains in effect;[3] in 1982 a Cuban official estimated that rationed goods still represented 20 percent of manufactured goods and 25 percent of foodstuffs sold.[4] The basic price structure of 15 November 1961, slightly revised to account for the introduction of new products and encourage certain behavioral changes, such as energy conservation, prevailed in Cuba throughout the 1960s and 1970s.

Official Prices

The attempt to increase economic efficiency in the second half of the 1970s by implementing the Sistema de Dirección y Planificación de la Economía (Economic Management and Planning System, SDPE), focused considerable attention on the price system and the extent to which it required overhauling. As a first step, the Comité Estatal de Precios (State Price Committee, CEP) compiled lists of prices that prevailed on 31 March 1976; in this exercise CEP identified more than one million individual product prices and rates for services.[5] Neither the very detailed price lists for 1976 (129 volumes) nor an abridged version (2 volumes) are available to me. Claes Brundenius has had access to the latter, however, and has reported official retail price data for selected products effective in 1977 in a recent book.[6] Based on this source, official prices in 1977 for forty-nine consumer products are reported in table 39.

In mid-December 1981, the government announced a general upward revision of prices for a wide range of consumer products.[7] The stated purpose of the revision was to attempt to reverse the rising trend in subsidies being incurred by the state in maintaining consumer prices at the 15 November 1961 levels. Using a table published in the Cuban press at the time the price increases were announced, it is possible to learn the price of thirty-four consumer products before the price increase (table 40). Table 41

Table 39. Official Cuban Consumer Prices, 1977

Product	Unit	Price (pesos)
Bananas	KG	0.15
Beans, black	KG	0.37
Beef	KG	1.78
Beer	L	1.71
Blouses	KG	4.74
Bread	KG	0.50
Butter	KG	6.60
Cabbage	KG	0.18
Cheese	KG	0.55
Cloth, cotton	SM	1.50
Cloth, rayon	SM	10.00
Coffee	KG	2.09
Cucumbers	KG	0.24
Dresses	KG	15.88
Eggs	EA	0.08
Fish, canned	KG	1.54
Fish, fresh & frozen	KG	0.88
Flour, wheat	KG	0.22
Ice cream	L	0.95
Lard	KG	0.53
Malanga	KG	0.22
Malt	L	2.29
Meat, canned	KG	0.90
Milk, condensed	KG	0.44
Milk, evaporated	KG	0.46
Milk, pasteurized	L	0.26
Oil, vegetable	KG	0.73
Onions	KG	0.31
Pants	KG	15.00
Pineapple	KG	0.15
Plantains	KG	0.15
Pork	IG	1.65
Potatoes	KG	0.15
Poultry	KG	1.10
Rice	KG	0.42
Shirts	KG	5.22
Shoes, leather	PAIR	12.77
Skirts	KG	5.12

Table 39—Continued

Product	Unit	Price (pesos)
Soft drinks	L	0.24
Spaghetti	KG	0.66
Squash	KG	0.13
Sugar	KG	0.15
Suits	KG	78.22
Sweet potatoes	KG	0.13
Tomatoes	KG	0.18
Underwear	KG	1.55
Yams	KG	0.18
Yogurt	L	0.44
Yucca	KG	0.13

Source: Comité Estatal de Precios, "Lista oficial de precios," in Claes Brundenius, *Revolutionary Cuba: The Challenge of Economic Growth with Equity*, pp. 166-167.
Note: KG=kilogram; L=-liter; SM=square meter

reports official Cuban prices for sixty-three commodities, obtained by combining the data in tables 39 and 40. Each of the commodities is classified according to the product code identifying the output series in Appendix A; the table also reports the price data after converting them to correspond to the unit of measurement for which physical output data are available.[8]

Other Cuban Prices

In addition to official prices, prices in three other segmented markets may also be relevant: (1) the black market; (2) the government-sponsored parallel market; and (3) the *"mercados libres campesinos"* (free peasant markets). Unfortunately, there are no systematic price data relating to these markets nor time series data on the proportion of domestic sales transacted in each. It is clear, however, that over time the parallel market has played an increasing role. A Cuban official estimated that in 1982 the parallel market accounted for about 10 percent of total retail sales.[9] More recently, the minister of domestic trade has estimated that parallel market sales accounted for over 10 percent of domestic sales in 1983 and would account for as much as 15 percent of total sales in 1984.[10]

Black Market
Since the early 1960s, an illegal black market has existed alongside the

Table 40.   Official Cuban Consumer Prices, December 1981

Product	Unit	Price (pesos)
Bananas	LB	0.05
Beans, black,	LB	0.17
Beans, red	LB	0.17
Beef (1st grade)	LB	0.55
Beef (2d grade)	LB	0.44
Cigarettes	PACK	0.20
Cigars	EACH	0.12
Coffee	LB	0.96
Detergent	LB	0.30
Fuel, diesel	L	0.06
Garlic	LB	0.32
Gasoline	L	0.16
Grapefruit	LB	0.04
Lard	LB	0.24
Lemons	LB	0.09
Malanga	LB	0.07
Milk, condensed	CAN	0.20
Milk, evaporated	CAN	0.21
Milk, pasteurized	L	0.20
Oil, vegetable	LB	0.33
Onions	LB	0.14
Oranges	LB	0.06
Peppers, green	LB	0.22
Plantains	LB	0.07
Potatoes	LB	0.07
Rice	LB	0.20
Soap, bath	BAR	0.15
Soap, laundry,	BAR	0.14
Soft drinks	BOTTLE	0.05
Squash	LB	0.06
Sugar, raw	LB	0.05
Sugar, refined	LB	0.07
Tomatoes	LB	0.18
Yucca	LB	0.06

Source: *Granma* (14 December 1981): 3.

Table 41. Official Cuban Consumer Prices, 1977–1981

Product	Code	Reported		Converted	
		Unit	Price (pesos)	Unit	Price (pesos)
Fuel, diesel	BD	L	0.06	000MT	71600.00
Gasoline	BF	L	0.16	MT	217.00
Detergent	HU	LB	0.30	MT	661.00
Soap, laundry	HV	BAR	0.14	MT	617.00
Soap, bath	HW	BAR	0.15	MT	1176.00
Cloth, cotton	NA	SM	1.50	000SM	1500.00
Cloth, rayon	NC	SM	10.00	000SM	10000.00
Underwear	OA	KG	1.55	000U	176.00
Blouses	OC	KG	4.74	000U	984.00
Shirts	OD	KG	5.22	000U	1354.00
Pants	OE	KG	15.00	000U	8380.00
Skirts	OF	KG	5.12	000U	1900.00
Suits	OH	KG	78.22	000U	81630.00
Dresses	OI	KG	15.88	000U	8045.00
Footwear, leather	PD	PAIR	12.77	000PAIR	12770.00
Sugar, raw	QA	LB	0.055	000MT	121000.00
Sugar, refined	QB	KG	0.15	000MT	150000.00
Beef	RA	KG	1.78	MT	1780.00
Pork	RB	KG	1.65	MT	1650.00
Meat, canned	RC	KG	0.90	MT	900.00
Poultry	RD	KG	1.10	MT	1100.00
Flour, wheat	RE	KG	0.22	MT	220.00
Lard	RF	KG	0.53	MT	530.00
Milk, pasteurized	RI	L	0.26	MT	252.40
Milk, condensed	RJ	KG	0.44	MT	440.00
Milk, evaporated	RK	KG	0.46	MT	460.00
Cheese	RM	KG	0.55	MT	550.00
Butter	RN	KG	6.60	MT	6600.00
Yogurt	RO	L	0.44	MT	4580.00
Ice cream	RP	L	0.95	000GAL	3595.75
Oil, vegetable	RQ	KG	0.73	MT	730.00
Bread	RR	KG	0.50	MT	500.00
Spaghetti	RV	KG	0.66	MT	660.00
Coffee	RY	KG	2.09	MT	2090.00
Fish, fresh & frozen	R1	KG	0.88	MT	880.00
Fish, canned	R3	KG	1.54	MT	1540.00
Beer	TE	L	1.71	000HL	171000.00
Malt	TF	L	2.29	000HL	229000.00
Soft drinks	TG	L	0.24	000HL	24000.00
Cigars	TI	U	0.12	000U	120.00
Cigarettes	TJ	PACK	0.20	000000U	10000.00
Potatoes	XA	KG	0.15	MT	150.00
Potatoes, sweet	XB	KG	0.13	MT	130.00

Table 41—Continued

Product	Code	Reported		Converted	
		Unit	Price (pesos)	Unit	Price (pesos)
Malanga	XC	KG	0.22	MT	220.00
Yucca	XD	KG	0.13	MT	130.00
Yams	XE	KG	0.18	MT	180.00
Rice	XF	KG	0.42	MT	420.00
Beans, black	XI	KG	0.37	MT	370.00
Beans, red	XJ	LB	0.17	MT	370.00
Tomatoes	XL	KG	0.18	MT	180.00
Peppers, green	XM	LB	0.22	MT	490.00
Onions	XN	KG	0.31	MT	310.00
Garlic	XO	LB	0.32	MT	710.00
Squash	XP	LB	0.06	MT	130.00
Cucumbers	XQ	KG	0.24	MT	240.00
Cabbage	XS	KG	0.18	MT	180.00
Oranges	XT	LB	0.06	MT	130.00
Grapefruit	XU	LB	0.04	MT	88.00
Lemons	XV	LB	0.09	MT	198.00
Plantains	XX	KG	0.15	MT	150.00
Bananas	XY	KG	0.15	MT	150.00
Pineapple	XZ	KG	0.15	MT	150.00
Eggs	YD	U	0.08	000U	80.00

Sources: Tables 39 and 40.
Notes: SM=square meter; MT=metric ton; U=unit, each; L=liter; HL=hectoliter

official market. Despite periodic crackdowns and heavy sentences imposed on black marketeers, it has remained an important source of consumer and industrial goods. Traditionally, private farmers have been the main source of the supply of agricultural products entering the black market,[11] though homemade manufactured products, rationed goods purchased but not consumed, goods illegally diverted from state enterprises, and goods brought from abroad by technicians, diplomats, and the like, are also important. As illustrated in table 42, in the late 1970s, black market prices were generally several times higher than rationed prices.

Parallel Market

In an effort to increase the variety of consumer products, reduce the substantial monetary surplus built up during the 1960s and 1970s, and compete with the thriving black market, the government created an official "parallel market" in 1973. Typically, the parallel market is used to distribute agricultural and industrial products not available in sufficient quantities to make them available to the general public through the rationing system or to dispose of excess quantities of rationed goods.[12] Prices in the

Table 42.   Prices of Selected Goods in Different Markets, 1977–1978 (pesos)

Goods	Official	Parallel	Black
		Market	
Food/lb.			
Beef	0.44-0.55		8.0
Ham	1.30-2.70	6.0	10.0
Rice	0.21		2.0
Beans	0.18-0.20	1.25	2.0-3.0
Coffee	2.0		10.0-20.0
Fats	0.22-0.30		3.0
Manufactures			
Rum (bottle)		7.50-12.00	25.0[a]
Cigarettes (pack)	0.20	1.60-2.00	1.0[a]
Cigars (each)	0.12	1.50	2.0[a]
Shoes (pair)	3.50-10.5		70.0
Fabric (meter)	0.40-2.5	1.50-10.5	30.0
Gasoline (gallon)	0.60	2.0	1.0
Consumer durables[b]			
TV (b&w, 17")		650.0-900.0	
Refrigerator (small-med.)		650.0-850.0	
Record player		350.0-1200.0	
Car (Soviet Fiat	4500.0		
Car (U.S., 1950s)			5000.0-15000.0

Source: Carmelo Mesa-Lago, *The Economy of Socialist Cuba*, p. 163.
Notes: Blanks indicate no information.
[a]Goods of higher quality than those available through rationing or through the parallel market.
[b]Most available only through quotas to state enterprises; a few through the parallel market.

parallel market are typically severalfold higher that rationed prices, but apparently lower than black market prices (see table 42).[13]

Free Peasant Markets

Early in 1980, the government legalized peasant markets.[14] As a temporary, but open-ended, measure, private farmers or cooperative members were permitted to sell to the public output beyond the limit committed to be sold to state agencies (*acopio*). Prices were totally unregulated, with farmers allowed to charge whatever the market would bear. Sale of certain products, such as beef, sugar, tobacco, coffee, and cocoa, was not permitted. Reportedly, the peasant markets were extremely popular in 1980–81, with a wide range of food products and handicrafts offered for sale at several times the official prices.

In early 1982, however, the government lashed out at irregularities in the peasant markets, the lack of social contribution of peasants selling directly to the public, the very high prices, and the appearance of middlemen who were subverting the concept of the peasant markets.[15] In April 1982, President Castro openly criticized the way in which the peasant markets were operating and proposed a series of measures to bridle the fledgling markets, including the effective taxation of profits. According to Castro, in 1981 the peasant markets generated two hundred million pesos in sales but paid only four hundred thousand pesos in taxes, a grossly inadequate amount.[16] Reportedly, supplies in the peasant markets dried up in the second half of 1982 as farmers chose to withhold their output or resorted to sales in the black market.[17]

In September 1982, a new decree regulating the operation of peasant markets was passed. Among its provisions, it excluded from participation in the peasant markets all intermediaries, farmers not formally associated with the National Association of Small Farmers, and garden plot producers; stiffened the rules under which the fulfillment of *acopio* sales would have to be demonstrated; and levied a 20 percent tax on gross sales.[18] Under the new regulations, the peasant markets have continued to operate, but with only a fraction of the vigor they demonstrated prior to regulation.

Proxy Prices

Economic theory suggests that GDP growth rates measure either an economy's production potential or the welfare of its population. To measure the growth of production potential, the theoretical requirement is that relative prices should equal their relative marginal costs and the rate of return to each factor of production should be equal in all of its uses. This is the so-called factor-cost standard. To measure welfare, prices should be market-determined, reflecting consumer preferences.

The primary objective is to develop a set of estimates of growth in Cuba's production potential (GDP) that would be comparable to those of other market economies. To what extent can Cuban prices be deemed to represent factor costs?

Students of centrally planned economies generally agree that in these economies "prices are not an autonomous force determining production, resource allocation and consumption. Instead, prices are manipulated by the central authorities as one of various instruments to accomplish their planned goals."[19] My research, and that of others,[20] concludes that Cuba is no exception and that the Cuban price system does not perform the economic allocation functions it would normally perform in a market economy and violates the theoretical requirements that would permit direct use of Cuban prices as product weights in constructing activity indexes.

Recognizing that prices in centrally planned economies are not suitable for valuing output to construct growth rate estimates, Bergson has proposed that certain adjustments be made to prevailing prices (for example, deletion of turnover taxes and of subsidies on final goods and services), which would bring the latter closer to the theoretical standard. These adjustments yield estimates of adjusted factor cost (AFC), which, under some restrictive assumptions, can be used to value output.[21] However, because the production cost data that would be necessary are not available, it is not feasible to adjust existing Cuban price data to obtain estimates of AFC, which could be used as product/services weights in our indexes.

In view of the theoretical inadequacy of Cuban prices and the practical impossibility of computing AFC measures for Cuba, I have relied on a different approach to develop product/services weights to calculate the indexes. In essence, I have used prices formed in another economy (Guatemala, and in a few cases, the United States) as proxies for Cuban factor-cost prices. The implicit assumption is that relative prices formed by these market economies are good approximations of relative prices that would obtain for the Cuban economy if the price system there served traditional allocation functions or that would result from the application of the AFC methodology to prevailing Cuban prices.

I have relied heavily on prices in Guatemala in 1973 as proxies for Cuban prices. The prices were collected in Guatemala in November 1973 according to detailed specifications developed by the Programa de Estudios Conjuntos sobre Integración Económica Latinoamericana (Program of Joint Studies on Latin American Integration, ECIEL) as part of the United Nations International Comparisons Project. Prices were reported in domestic currency (quetzales); at the time, the exchange rate was 1 quetzal = 1 U.S. dollar. Most of the prices were consumer prices and referred to an average of different urban and rural areas throughout Guatemala; for intermediate products, prices referred to producers' prices.[22]

To supplement the sample of Guatemalan prices, particularly with regard to intermediate and capital goods, prices in the United States (in U.S. dollars) in November and December 1974 have been used. For nonferrous minerals and metal products, average prices were obtained from publications of the Bureau of Mines and the Bureau of Labor Statistics, respectively.[23] For leather, average prices from the Boston Leather Market, as reported in the trade magazine *Leather and Shoes*, were used

Overall, proxy prices were obtained for 132 products across a range of industrial and agricultural activities (see table 43). I was unsuccessful in obtaining meaningful prices (weights) for services activities, however. Thus, for those services sectors for which several physical indicator series were available and the calculation of a weighted sectoral index was required, this was done by assigning equal base-period weights to each of the series within a branch or sector.

Three important points should be made with regard to the use of proxy prices as product weights in these indexes. First, the absolute value of the prices does not enter into the index calculations. The concern in the indexes is strictly with *relative* prices in the base period of specific products *within* a branch of the economy. Thus, the finding that prices of gasoline and of motor oil and lubricants in the base period were $162.80 and $2,183.00 per metric ton, respectively, is of less interest than the datum that the ratio of price of gasoline to motor oil and lubricants was roughly 1:13.4. It is the relative prices that enter into the calculations.

Second, I have been careful, *within each branch*, to rely on proxy prices for the same country. That is, at the cost of not fully utilizing some of the available price data, I have consciously avoided mixing Guatemalan and U.S. prices within the same branch. To have done so would have gone against a body of empirical research that has found that the "law of one price" (the proposition that in the absence of transportation costs and trade restrictions, perfect commodity arbitrage ensures that identical goods produced by several countries are uniformly priced around the world) is systematically violated.[24] Thus, the product weights used refer to the relative prices within each branch that prevailed in a given country in a given time period.

And third, because relative prices are calculated within branches, the currency in which prices are denominated is not an issue and exchange rate conversion problems are avoided.

Table 43.   Proxy Prices, 1973–1974 (dollars)

Product	Code	Reported Unit	Reported Price (pesos)	Converted Unit	Converted Price (pesos)
Fuel oil	BC	L	0.11	000MT	128526.00
Natural gas, liquefied	BE	10KG	2.51	MT	251.00
Gasoline	BF	L	0.12	MT	162.80
Kerosene	BG	L	0.12	MT	149.00
Motor oil & lubricants	BH	L	1.92	MT	2183.00
Gas, manufactured	BJ	CM	0.83	000CM	830.00
Chromium, refractory	CA	SHORT TON	68.00	MT	74.96
Carbon steel	CB	NET TON	265.42	MT	292.58
Bars, carbon steel	CC	100 LB	13.89	MT	306.22
Rods, carbon steel	CD	100LB	9.67	MT	213.8
Pipes, cast-iron (water supply)	CG	100 FT[a]	423.89	MT	417.94
Pipes, cast-iron	CH	100 FT[b]	38.11	MT	368.50
Barbed wire	CJ	SPOOL[c]	19.57	MT	491.67
Nickel-cobalt oxide	DA	LB	1.75	MT	3858.05
Nickel-cobalt sinter	DB	OB	1.75	MT	3858.05
Nickel-cobalt sulfide	DC	LB	1.10	MT	2425.06
Copper concentrate	DD	LB	0.93	MT	2050.28
Road levelers	EC	U	17700.00	U	17700.00
Road rollers	ED	U	37459.00	U	37459.00
Water pumps	EG	U	209.65	U	209.65
Stoves, gas	EH	U	183.00	U	183.00
Buses	EJ	U	7330.00	U	7330.00
Cables, electrical, & wires	FA	00M[d]	8.30	MT	732.00
Cables, insulated electrical, & wires	FB	00M	43.00	000M	430.00
Refrigerators, household	FE	U	524.80	U	524.80
Battery, automobile	FF	U	43.20	U	43.20
Radio receivers, household	FG	U	53.75	U	53.75
Television receivers	FH	U	250.68	U	250.68
Pressure cookers	GG	U	17.04	000U	17040.00
Nails	GH	MT	357.50	MT	357.50
Tire tubes	H1	U	20.15	U	20.15
Footwear, rubber	H2	PAIR	3.65	000PAIR	3650.00
Matches	H4	BOX	0.02	000000BOX	20000.00
Salt	HB	KG	0.09	MT	90.00
Paints, oil-based	HQ	GAL	3.56	HL	94.05
Varnishes	HS	GAL	4.32	HL	114.12
Detergent, household	HU	U[e]	0.47	MT	783.30
Soap, laundry	HV	U[f]	0.06	MT	423.30
Soap, bath	HW	U[g]	0.23	MT	2300.00
Toothpaste	HX	U[h]	0.59	MT	5900.00
Tires	HZ	U	24.77	U	24.77
Paper, writing	IB	100 SHEETS[i]	0.09	MT	396.80
Paper bags	IG	00U	0.63	000U	6.30
Boxes, corrugated	IH	U	0.24	000U	240.00
Containers, waxed	II	U	0.043	000U	43.00
Books	JA	U	0.42	000U	420.00

Table 43—Continued

Product	Code	Reported Unit	Reported Price (pesos)	Converted Unit	Converted Price (pesos)
Magazines	JB	U	0.15	000U	150.00
Booklets	JC	U	0.30	000U	300.00
Notebooks	JD	U	0.12	000U	120.00
Sand	LA	CM	3.67	000CM	3670.00
Stone, crushed	LB	CM	2.30	000CM	2300.00
Cement	LC	100 LB	1.38	000MT	30420.00
Tiles, terrazzo	LD	SM	3.03	000SM	3030.00
Bricks	LF	000U	29.50	000U	29.50
Concrete products, prefabricated	LG	CM	174.67	000CM	174670.00
Refractory materials	LG	100 LB	2.25	MT	49.60
Pipes, concrete (water supply)	LI	Uj	19.85	000M	6512.46
Glass, flat	MA	SF	3.50	000SM	37363.70
Bottles	MB	U	0.13	000000U	130000.00
Tiles, bathroom	MD	U	0.035	000U	35.00
Cloth, cotton	NB	SM	0.82	000SM	820.00
Cloth, wool	NC	SM	0.79	000SM	790.00
Cloth, rayon	ND	SM	0.89	000SM	890.00
Rope, sisal	NE	KG	1.65	MT	1650.00
Socks	NF	PAIR	0.89	000PAIR	890.00
Underwear	OA	U	1.25	000U	1250.00
Outerwear	OB	U	5.71	000U	5710.00
Blouses	OC	U	3.55	000U	3550.00
Shirts	OD	U	11.25	000U	11250.00
Pants	OE	U	9.72	000U	9720.00
Skirts	OF	U	10.64	000U	10640.00
Sweaters	OG	U	4.25	000U	4250.00
Suits	OH	U	36.33	000U	36330.00
Dresses	OI	U	16.31	000U	16310.00
Leather	PA	SF	0.28	000SM	3013.90
Leather, sole	PB	LB	1.03	MT	2270.74
Hides, cattle	PC	LBk	0.22	000U	7700.00
Footwear, leather	PD	PAIR	10.51	000PAIR	10510.00
Sugar, raw	QA	KG	0.18	000MT	180000.00
Sugar, refined	QB	KG	0.26	000MT	260000.00
Beef, deboned	RB	KG	3.10	MT	3100.00
Pork	RB	KG	1.78	MT	1780.00
Meat, canned	RC	KG	2.75	MT	2750.00
Poultry, fresh	RD	KG	1.35	MT	1350.00
Flour, wheat	RE	KG	0.39	MT	390.00
Lard	RF	KG	1.06	MT	1060.00
Grease, hydrogenated	RH	KG	0.18	MT	180.00
Milk, fresh & pasteurized	RI	L	0.20	MT	194.00
Milk, evaporated	RK	KG	0.38	MT	380.00
Milk, powdered	RL	KG	1.04	MT	1040.00
Cheese	RM	KG	0.60	MT	600.00
Butter	RN	KG	0.31	MT	310.00

Table 43—Continued

Product	Code	Reported Unit	Reported Price (pesos)	Converted Unit	Converted Price (pesos)
Ice cream	RP	L	0.53	000GAL	2006.28
Vegetable oil, refined	RQ	KG	1.06	MT	1060.00
Bread	RR	KG	0.48	MT	480.00
Pasta	RU	KG	0.35	MT	350.00
Fruits & vegetables, canned	RX	KG	0.88	MT	880.00
Coffee, roasted	RY	KG	1.39	MT	1390.00
Fish, fresh & frozen	R1	KG	1.80	MT	1800.00
Seafood, fresh & frozen	R2	KG	3.85	MT	3850.00
Fish & seafood, canned	R3	KG	0.69	MT	690.00
Alcohol, denatured	TA	L	3.02	000HL	302000.00
Beverages, alcoholic	TC	L	1.50	000HL	150000.00
Wine	TD	L	0.45	000HL	45000.00
Beer	TE	U	0.30	000HL	63410.00
Soft drinks	TG	U	0.09	000HL	19020.00
Mineral water	TH	U	0.09	000HL	19020.00
Cigarettes	TJ	PACK[l]	0.24	000000U	12000.00
Fodder	UA	MT	150.33	MT	150.33
Lamps (household)	UC	U	0.25	U	0.25
Wood, unsawn	VA	CM	17.70	CM	17.70
Firewood	VB	CM	17.17	000CM	17170.00
Coffee	X6	KG	1.31	MT	1310.00
Potatoes	XA	KG	0.24	MT	240.00
Sweet potatoes	XB	KG	0.17	MT	170.00
Yucca	XD	KG	0.11	MT	110.00
Rice	XF	KG	0.39	MT	390.00
Corn	XG	KG	0.54	MT	540.00
Corn, sweet	XH	KG	0.21	MT	210.00
Beans, black	XI	KG	0.53	MT	530.00
Tomatoes	XL	KG	0.31	MT	310.00
Peppers, green	XM	KG	0.39	MT	390.00
Onions	XN	KG	0.44	MT	440.00
Garlic	XO	KG	1.07	MT	1070.00
Cabbage	XS	KG	0.10	MT	100.00
Oranges	XT	KG	0.24	MT	240.00
Lemons	XV	KG	0.20	MT	200.00
Bananas	XY	KG	0.16	MT	160.00
Pineapples	XZ	KG	0.39	MT	390.00
Eggs	YD	U	0.06	000U	60.00
Milk	YE	L	0.18	MT	180.00
Poultry	YF	KG	1.35	MT	1350.00

Notes: [a]1 ft=22.36 lbs; [b]1 ft=2.28 lbs; [c]1 spool=87.75 lbs; [d]1 m=0.25 lbs; [e]600 gms/unit; [f]5 ozs/unit; [g]100 gms/unit; [h]100 gms/unit; [i]100 sheets=0.5 lbs; [j]10 ft/unit; [k]35 lbs/unit; [l]20 cigarettes/pack
CM=cubic meter; SF=square foot; SM=square meter; M=meter; MT=metric ton; U=unit, each; L=liter; HL=hectoliter

4. Results

Using the data on physical output series, value-added weights, and product/service weights described above, and the aggregation formulae reported in Appendix E, estimates of Cuban economic activity during the period 1965–82 have been made. This section describes the steps in making the estimates and the behavior of the activity indexes; in the next chapter the results are compared with official data and with estimates made by an independent researcher.

Goods-Producing Sectors

Table 44 reports activity indexes computed for each of the branches in industry and agriculture using equation (1) in Appendix E. The branches are identified by an alphabetic code consistent with the classification scheme used for individual activity series. (The coding scheme is given in Appendix A.) Thus, according to table 44, activity indexes were calculated for twenty branches within the industrial sector (sectors A–U) and four within agriculture (sectors V–Y); within industry, the wood products branch has been excluded because of the lack of price data, and within agriculture, no appropriate activity series were identified for the agricultural services branch.

Examination of the behavior of the individual branch series in the goods-producing sectors suggests that there was a great deal of variation in the rate of growth of output across branches. Within industry, the most impressive growth performance was turned in by the electricity branch (sector A), with output increasing steadily throughout the period. Other industrial branches for which output expanded significantly were ferrous mining and metallurgy (C), electronics (F), paper and cellulose (I), printing (J), and construction materials (L). Other industrial branches, such as metal products (G), chemicals (H), leather products (P), processed foods (R), and fishing (S), experienced more modest growth. Output of a few, such as textiles (N), sugar (Q), and beverages and tobacco (T), actually stagnated over the

Table 44.   Calculated Activity Indexes for Goods-producing Sectors

Sector	Weight	1965	Activity Index 1966	1967	1968
Industrial sectors					
Index for sector: A--electricity	04	48	52	57	60
Index for sector: B--fuel	07	65	67	71	69
Index for sector: C--ferrous mining & metallurgy	01	21	33	45	50
Index for sector: D--nonferrous mining & metallurgy	01	98	94	107	119
Index for sector: E--nonelectrical machinery	05	10	44	37	21
Index for sector: F--electronics	03	58	31	27	29
Index for sector: G--metal products	01	16	37	25	30
Index for sector: H--chemicals	11	57	58	69	61
Index for sector: I--paper & cellulose	01	73	70	76	68
Index for sector: J--printing	02	50	42	56	63
Index for sector: L--construction materials	05	22	22	27	28
Index for sector: M--glass & ceramics	00	35	36	58	41
Index for sector: N--textiles	03	112	95	90	91
Index for sector: O--apparel	04	70	66	74	75
Index for sector: P--leather products	04	88	103	114	109
Index for sector: Q--sugar	06	114	84	116	99
Index for sector: R--processed foods	11	87	92	88	95
Index for sector: S--fishing	03	22	24	41	42
Index for sector: T--beverages & tobacco	26	132	140	155	159
Index for sector: U--other	03	63	61	65	63
Agricultural sectors					
Index for sector: V--forestry	05	56	55	57	83
Index for sector: W--sugar	38	98	74	95	96
Index for sector: X--nonsugar	28	61	74	72	67
Index for sector: Y--livestock	30	60	65	68	68
Index for industry	70	80	83	91	90
Index for agriculture	30	74	70	79	79
Index for goods-producing sectors		79	79	88	87

Table 44—Continued

Sector	Activity Index				
	1969	1970	1971	1972	1973

Industrial sectors

Sector	1969	1970	1971	1972	1973
Index for sector: A--electricity	63	81	83	87	95
Index for sector: B--fuel	76	81	84	88	95
Index for sector: C--ferrous mining & metallurgy	45	47	46	74	90
Index for sector: D--nonferrous mining & metallurgy	109	106	104	108	104
Index for sector: E--nonelectrical machinery	9	21	64	59	87
Index for sector: F--electronics	26	34	57	74	97
Index for sector: G--metal products	73	77	101	104	105
Index for sector: H--chemicals	24	31	70	81	86
Index for sector: I--paper & cellulose	67	65	82	89	96
Index for sector: J--printing	63	61	61	71	91
Index for sector: L--construction materials	24	27	47	73	90
Index for sector: M--glass & ceramics	47	42	68	78	75
Index for sector: N--textiles	81	60	75	81	93
Index for sector: O--apparel	71	61	71	83	91
Index for sector: P--leather products	105	95	109	109	109
Index for sector: Q--sugar	86	149	106	83	94
Index for sector: R--processed foods	93	93	98	100	98
Index for sector: S--fishing	50	71	81	90	98
Index for sector: T--beverages & tobacco	164	107	79	89	99
Index for sector: U--other	63	67	76	81	84

Agricultural sectors

Sector	1969	1970	1971	1972	1973
Index for sector: V--forestry	105	85	94	99	107
Index for sector: W--sugar	106	142	107	93	97
Index for sector: X--nonsugar	65	73	77	74	78
Index for sector: Y--livestock	63	63	68	81	89
Index for industry	91	82	83	88	96
Index for agriculture	82	96	86	85	90
Index for goods-producing sectors	88	86	84	87	95

Table 44—Continued

Sector	Activity Index				
	1974	1975	1976	1977	1978

Industrial sectors

Index for sector: A--electricity	100	109	119	128	141
Index for sector: B--fuel	100	106	97	104	106
Index for sector: C--ferrous mining & metallurgy	100	118	105	134	130
Index for sector: D--nonferrous mining & metallurgy	100	112	112	111	106
Index for sector: E--nonelectrical machinery	100	127	117	110	113
Index for sector: F--electronics	100	119	107	102	112
Index for sector: G--metal products	100	94	29	27	44
Index for sector: H--chemicals	100	110	105	83	97
Index for sector: I--paper & cellulose	100	122	130	122	127
Index for sector: J--printing	100	110	106	158	180
Index for sector: L--construction materials	100	118	121	122	122
Index for sector: M--glass & ceramics	100	120	103	102	118
Index for sector: N--textiles	100	109	105	112	116
Index for sector: O--apparel	100	111	110	110	117
Index for sector: P--leather products	100	112	110	93	111
Index for sector: Q--sugar	100	107	103	116	130
Index for sector: R--processed foods	100	105	109	117	118
Index for sector: S--fishing	100	85	124	115	138
Index for sector: T--beverages & tobacco	100	104	102	106	112
Index for sector: U--other	100	112	123	126	141

Agricultural sectors

Index for sector: V--forestry	100	100	119	135	134
Index for sector: W--sugar	100	104	106	121	140
Index for sector: X--nonsugar	100	103	108	98	101
Index for sector: Y--livestock	100	110	118	135	122
Index for industry	100	108	107	108	115
Index for agriculture	100	105	111	119	124
Index for goods-producing sectors	100	108	108	111	118

Table 44—Continued

Sector	Activity Index 1979	1980	1981	1982
Industrial sectors				
Index for sector: A--electricity	156	164	175	184
Index for sector: B--fuel	109	107	107	112
Index for sector: C--ferrous mining & metallurgy	138	120	130	111
Index for sector: D--nonferrous mining & metallurgy	102	117	122	116
Index for sector: E--nonelectrical machinery	127	74	86	72
Index for sector: F--electronics	148	128	160	107
Index for sector: G--metal products	25	46	50	56
Index for sector: H--chemicals	84	92	104	91
Index for sector: I--paper & cellulose	124	146	160	164
Index for sector: J--printing	198	171	176	161
Index for sector: L--construction materials	120	111	120	118
Index for sector: M--glass & ceramics	100	87	70	115
Index for sector: N--textiles	112	116	123	95
Index for sector: O--apparel	119	103	113	117
Index for sector: P--leather products	105	99	114	100
Index for sector: Q--sugar	132	117	135	137
Index for sector: R--processed foods	117	124	139	141
Index for sector: S--fishing	89	121	108	130
Index for sector: T--beverages & tobacco	115	116	111	127
Index for sector: U--other	142	156	169	153
Agricultural sectors				
Index for sector: V--forestry	145	142	144	146
Index for sector: W--sugar	141	125	137	138
Index for sector: X--nonsugar	103	128	143	144
Index for sector: Y--livestock	128	134	148	140
Index for industry	116	113	120	120
Index for agriculture	127	129	142	141
Index for goods-producing sectors	119	118	127	127

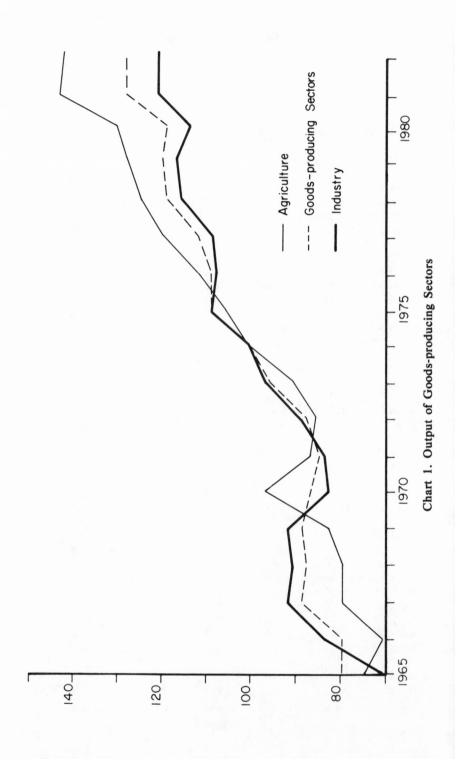

Chart 1. Output of Goods-producing Sectors

Agriculture
Goods-producing Sectors
Industry

140

120

100

80

1965   1970   1975   1980

period 1965–82. Within agriculture, output by the nonsugar agriculture (X), livestock (Y), and forestry (V) branches expanded steadily, whereas output of the sugar agriculture (W) branch tended to stagnate, except for the record harvest year 1970 and a growth spurt in 1977–78.

The individual branch indexes have been aggregated to calculate measures of activity for the industrial and agricultural sectors. This aggregation, which follows equation (2) in Appendix E, uses the branch indexes and the value-added weights reported in table 37. The weights, which are reported in table 44, have been normalized among the branches for those activity indexes that are available; this procedure implicitly imputes to branches that are not represented the average rate of growth of the represented branches.

The bottom of table 44 reports the output indexes for industry and agriculture, respectively. These indexes are also plotted on chart 1. Thus, according to the calculations, industrial output at constant prices rose from an index level of 80 in 1965 to 91 in 1967 and declined or stagnated subsequently; it began to recover in 1972 and rose sharply in 1975 (by 8 percent) and in 1978 (by 6.6 percent). Industrial output showed no significant improvement in 1979 and declined slightly in 1980; it recovered strongly in 1981 (6.2 percent increase) and showed no change in 1982. Meanwhile, agricultural output, as measured by these indexes, behaved erratically during 1965–71, expanded steadily during 1972–78, stagnated during 1978–80, grew by over 10 percent in 1981, and contracted slightly in 1982. Over the entire period 1965–82, industrial output grew at an average annual rate of 2.4 percent, compared with an annual average growth rate of 3.9 percent for agricultural output.

The last line in table 44 combines the output indexes for industry and agriculture using equation (3) in Appendix E to obtain a single output measure for the goods-producing sectors. According to this measure (see chart 1), production of goods expanded strongly in 1967, showed no growth during 1968–72, and began to recover in 1973. The record after 1974 is mixed, with significant output expansions recorded in 1975 (8 percent), 1977 (2.8 percent), 1978 (6.3 percent), and 1981 (7.6 percent), and very little growth, or no growth at all, in 1976, 1979, and 1980. Goods production showed no improvement in 1982 compared to 1981. Over the entire period 1965–82, output of goods-producing sectors grew at an average annual rate of 2.8 percent.

Services Sectors

Activity series for the services sectors are severely limited and no data are available on weights for each service within a sector (that is, prices). As noted earlier, satisfactory nonmonetary output series for several activities in services sectors were not available and series on employment have been used to represent changes in output. However, as discussed in chapter 2, consistent series on employment at the level of economic sectors are not available; instead, there are three unconnected employment subseries for the periods 1962–66, 1971–76, and 1977–82. It is clear that employment categories were redefined beginning with 1977, as the data on the distribution of employment by sectors *within* the productive and non-productive spheres shift significantly between 1976 and 1977. For example, there is a whopping gain from 179,100 to 281,600 employees in the trade sector at the expense of agriculture, transportation, and communications (table 13).[1] The immediate result is an artificial 57.2 percent increase in employment in the trade sector between 1976 and 1977 and a jump of the same magnitude in the activity index for the trade sector estimated based on these data.

To deal with this anomaly, I have assumed that employment in the trade sector expanded between 1976 and 1977 at the same rate as overall employment (that is, 6.16 percent). Based on this assumption, I estimated the *level* of employment in 1976 comparable with the data for the period 1977–82 at approximately 265,300 workers (281,600/1.0616) and adjusted the reported employment data for 1971–75 so that the two subseries for 1971–76 and 1977–82 could be linked. The procedure has the desired result of smoothing the employment series for the period 1971–82 and permitting the use of the employment series as a reasonable proxy for growth of output in the trade sector.

Notwithstanding these deficiencies, I have calculated activity indexes for each of the services branches or sectors by assigning equal base-period weights to each of the series within a branch or sector. Table 45 reports the indexes for services branches or sectors constructed under this assumption. Also reported in table 45 are indexes indicative of growth of productive and nonproductive services obtained by aggregating individual indexes corresponding to productive services (A-H) and nonproductive services (I-N) using value-added weights (from table 37). These indexes are plotted on chart 2.

A cursory examination of the activity indexes in table 45 suggests that over the entire period 1965–82, output of services sectors tended to grow quite rapidly, more so than the output of goods-producing sectors. Further, economic activity in nonproductive services sectors as a group expanded more rapidly than in productive services sectors. Within the group of productive services, the best growth performances were turned in by air transportation (E) and maritime transportation (D), and the worst by construction (A). All five sectors related to nonproductive services for which activity indexes have been calculated showed a tendency to expand over the period 1965–82. In particular the social security, welfare,

Chart 2. Output of Productive and Nonproductive Services Sectors

—— Non-productive Services

—— Productive Services

Table 45.   Calculated Activity Indexes for Services Sectors

Sector	Weight	Activity Index			
		1965	1966	1967	1968

Productive service sectors

Sector	Weight	1965	1966	1967	1968
Index for sector: A--construction	.19	58	72	118	74
Index for sector: B--railroad (transportation)	.01	110	117	143	153
Index for sector: C--motor (transportation)	.09	77	75	75	84
Index for sector: D--maritime (transportation)	.04	29	40	43	64
Index for sector: E--air (transportation)	.01	48	53	64	58
Index for sector: F--cargo handling (transportation)	.02	83	76	78	75
Index for sector: G--communications	.02	146	144	151	153
Index for sector: H--trade	.62	78	86	88	71

Nonproductive service sectors

Sector	Weight	1965	1966	1967	1968
Index for sector: I--housing & community services	.08	62	65	83	106
Index for sector: J--education & public health	.39	57	59	62	64
Index for sector: K--social security, welfare, cultural & scientific activities	.29	49	53	59	85
Index for sector: L--public administration	.14	47	47	61	79
Index for sector: N--other nonproductive activities	.10	66	70	82	106
Index for productive services	.72	73	81	91	74
Index for nonproductive services	.28	55	57	65	80
Index for all services		68	75	84	76
Index for domestic machinery & equipment for investment	--	27	39	33	24
Index for domestic consumer goods	--	107	112	121	124
Index for domestic investment, goods & services	--	50	64	97	62
Index for domestic consumer goods & services	--	81	85	93	102

Table 45—Continued

Sector	Activity Index				
	1969	1970	1971	1972	1973

Productive service sectors

Index for sector: A--construction	55	46	45	86	96
Index for sector: B--railroad (transportation)	158	138	126	120	97
Index for sector: C--motor (transportation)	94	91	82	81	90
Index for sector: D--maritime (transportation)	63	65	99	89	82
Index for sector: E--air (transportation)	76	87	90	99	107
Index for sector: F--cargo handling (transportation)	80	94	91	89	96
Index for sector: G--communications	155	150	144	123	105
Index for sector: H--trade	66	61	91	90	96

Nonproductive service sectors

Index for sector: I--housing & community services	111	104	105	95	93
Index for sector: J--education & public health	74	73	75	79	91
Index for sector: K--social security, welfare, cultural & scientific activities	85	77	77	88	99
Index for sector: L--public administration	82	78	69	70	84
Index for sector: N--other nonproductive activities	110	104	104	94	92
Index for productive services	69	65	83	89	95
Index for nonproductive services	85	81	80	83	93
Index for all services	74	69	82	88	94
Index for domestic machinery & equipment for investment	15	26	62	64	91
Index for domestic consumer goods	125	95	85	92	99
Index for domestic investment, goods & services	45	41	49	81	95
Index for domestic consumer goods & services	105	88	83	88	96

Table 45—Continued

Sector	Activity Index				
	1974	1975	1976	1977	1978

Productive service sectors

Index for sector: A--construction	100	100	97	107	75
Index for sector: B--railroad (transportation)	100	106	116	146	181
Index for sector: C--motor (transportation)	100	124	147	144	157
Index for sector: D--maritime (transportation)	100	132	132	138	131
Index for sector: E--air (transportation)	100	114	140	141	160
Index for sector: F--cargo handling (transportation)	100	105	104	113	121
Index for sector: G--communications	100	105	120	126	131
Index for sector: H--trade	100	94	97	103	109

Nonproductive service sectors

Index for sector: I--housing & community services	100	110	119	121	150
Index for sector: J--education & public health	100	111	121	123	128
Index for sector: K--social security, welfare, cultural & scientific activities	100	108	121	122	125
Index for sector: L--public administration	100	111	119	118	124
Index for sector: N--other nonproductive activities	100	110	118	120	380
Index for productive services	100	100	104	110	110
Index for nonproductive services	100	110	120	122	154
Index for all services	100	103	109	114	122
Index for domestic machinery & equipment for investment	100	124	113	107	113
Index for domestic consumer goods	100	105	106	109	115
Index for domestic investment, goods & services	100	106	101	107	85
Index for domestic consumer goods & services	100	108	113	116	135

Table 45—Continued

Sector	Activity Index			
	1979	1980	1981	1982

Productive service sectors

Index for sector: A--construction	96	72	70	72
Index for sector: B--railroad (transportation)	191	213	238	244
Index for sector: C--motor (transportation)	160	172	177	178
Index for sector: D--maritime (transportation)	130	129	123	128
Index for sector: E--air (transportation)	180	204	231	267
Index for sector: F--cargo handling (transportation)	135	141	143	138
Index for sector: G--communications	139	169	235	231
Index for sector: H--trade	111	111	114	119

Nonproductive service sectors

Index for sector: I--housing & community services	140	140	140	137
Index for sector: J--education & public health	129	127	132	135
Index for sector: K--social security, welfare, cultural & scientific activities	131	130	150	162
Index for sector: L--public administration	133	124	134	133
Index for sector: N--other nonproductive activities	380	292	468	546
Index for productive services	116	113	117	121
Index for nonproductive services	156	145	172	184

Index for all services | 127 | 122 | 132 | 138 |

Index for domestic machinery & equipment for investment	135	93	113	85
Index for domestic consumer goods	114	116	118	126
Index for domestic investment, goods & services	106	77	81	75
Index for domestic consumer goods & services	135	131	145	155

cultural, and scientific activities sector (K) and the education and public health sector (J) showed sustained growth over the entire period. It should be noted that since employment data, subject to the limitations already remarked, are used to represent output in several nonproductive sectors, the results are highly tentative. Over the entire period 1965–82, economic activity of productive services sectors grew at an average annual rate of growth of 3 percent, while for nonproductive services sectors the corresponding average annual growth rate was 7.4 percent. Activity in services sectors (productive and nonproductive services combined) expanded at an average annual rate of 4.3 percent over the period 1965–82, compared with a growth rate of 2.8 percent for goods-producing sectors.

Also in table 45 are reported aggregations of the individual activity indexes, which attempt to contrast the behavior of sectors producing goods and services for accumulation (that is, investment) and for consumption. Using the indexes for nonelectrical machinery and electronics to represent the production of investment goods and those for textiles, apparel, leather products, processed foods, fishing, and beverages and tobacco to represent the production of consumer goods, activity indexes have been calculated for those two groupings (these indexes are plotted on chart 3). Also calculated are indexes of activities in sectors producing goods and services for investment and consumption by assuming that the output of the construction sector contributes to investment activities, and all of the nonproductive services sectors contribute to consumption (chart 4).

It is clear from table 46 and chart 3 that output of goods for investment increased sharply over the entire period 1965–82, albeit from very low levels in the early part of the period. Production of investment goods stagnated from 1965 to 1968 and bottomed out in 1969; production rose sharply thereafter through 1975. In more recent years, production of investment goods has fluctuated severely, peaking in 1979 and declining subsequently. Output of consumption goods experienced no significant growth over the entire period 1965–82. After expanding rapidly from 1965 to 1969, output declined in the next two years, bottoming out in 1971. A slow recovery process began in 1972; by 1982, production of consumer goods was only slightly higher than it was during 1968–69.

When series representing activity in services associated with accumulation and consumption are also taken into account, the picture changes significantly. As can be seen from chart 4, inclusion of the construction sector in the broader index for investment goods and services tends to smooth out many of the annual fluctuations in the investment goods index and to reduce significantly the pattern of growth over the entire 1965–82 period. In contrast, inclusion of nonproductive services in the broader index for consumer goods and services tends to improve the growth performance substantially.

Interestingly, to some extent, changes in output of investment goods appear to be inversely correlated with changes in output of consumer goods (chart 3), illustrating policy shifts that have emphasized accumulation (that is, investment) versus consumption. The same relationship seems to hold when the broader indexes for investment goods and services and for consumer goods and services are analyzed (chart 4).

Macroeconomic Aggregates

Using the individual indexes for economic branches and sectors and value-added weights, measures have been calculated that closely approximate three widely used macroeconomic aggregates: the material product, GSP, and GDP. The following indexes have been aggregated to calculate

Table 46. Estimated Output Indicators for Cuba, 1965–1982 (1974=100)

Year	Industry	Agriculture	Material Product	GSP	GDP
1965	80	74	76	76	73
1966	83	70	78	80	77
1967	91	79	92	89	86
1968	90	79	85	81	81
1969	91	82	84	79	80
1970	82	96	80	76	77
1971	83	86	78	83	83
1972	88	85	87	88	87
1973	96	90	95	95	95
1974	100	100	100	100	100
1975	108	105	106	104	105
1976	107	111	105	106	108
1977	108	119	111	111	113
1978	115	124	112	114	120
1979	116	127	116	118	123
1980	113	129	111	116	120
1981	120	142	118	122	130
1982	120	141	119	124	133

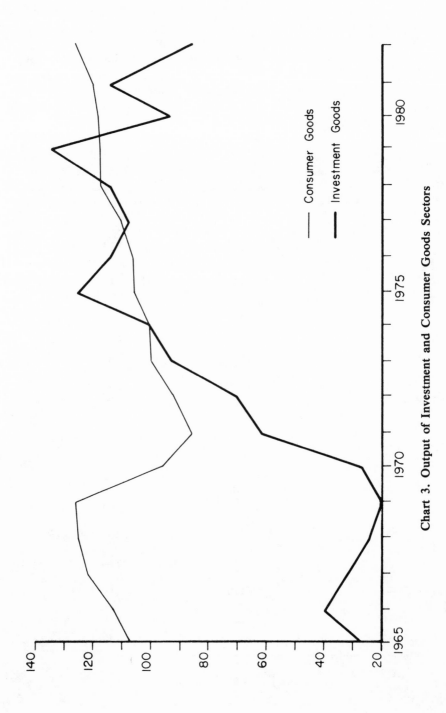

Chart 3. Output of Investment and Consumer Goods Sectors

—— Consumer Goods

—— Investment Goods

1965   1970   1975   1980

20 40 60 80 100 120 140

these special measures: (1) for the material product, the indexes for industry, agriculture, and construction; (2) for GSP, indexes for industry, agriculture, and productive services; and (3) for GDP, indexes for all productive and nonproductive activities. The measures are given in table 46 and plotted on chart 5.

According to the estimates, during the 1965–82 period, the material product expanded at an average annual rate of 2.6 percent, compared to an average annual growth rate of 2.9 percent for GSP and 3.4 percent for GDP. The higher growth rates in GSP and GDP compared with the material product are consistent with the finding, reported earlier, that output of the services sectors tended to grow more rapidly than that of the goods-producing sectors. As is apparent from chart 5, the growth pattern of these measures has been far from steady. All three measures suggest that the Cuban economy expanded strongly during 1965–67 and, beginning with 1968, entered into a period of decline that lasted through 1971. After 1970–71, all three measures point to substantial economic growth, although they do not coincide on how long the growth swing turned out to be. The severity of the 1967–71 recession is clearly illustrated by all three series. It is not until 1973 (1972 for GDP) that the activity levels achieved in 1967 are surpassed. Thus, during 1967–73, the material product expanded at a rate of 0.5 percent per annum, while GSP and GDP grew at an average annual rate of 1.1 percent and 1.7 percent, respectively.

The three estimated measures suggest somewhat different growth patterns for the period 1974–82. According to the estimated index of growth of the material product, significant expansion took place only in 1975, 1977, 1979, and 1981. Overall, the material product grew at an average annual rate of 2.2 percent during 1974–82. The measures for GSP and GDP, which include the output of services sectors, both showed more sustained and faster growth during 1974–82: an average annual growth rate of 2.7 percent for GSP, and 3.6 percent for GDP. All three estimated series suggest either no growth or a growth slowdown toward the end of the 1970s, followed by a growth spurt in 1981. According to the estimates, the material product was essentially stagnant during the period 1977–80; growth of GSP and GDP slowed down in 1978–79. All three series suggest that output actually contracted in 1980, compared with 1979, and recovered strongly in 1981, when the material product expanded by 6.3 percent, GSP by 5.2 percent, and GDP by 8.3 percent. All three series expanded marginally in 1982, with the material product rising by 0.8 percent, GSP by 1.6 percent, and GDP by 2.3 percent.

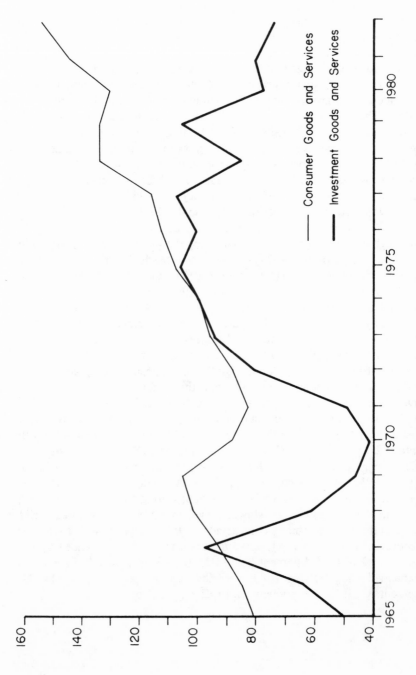

Chart 4. Output of Investment and Consumer Goods and Services Sectors

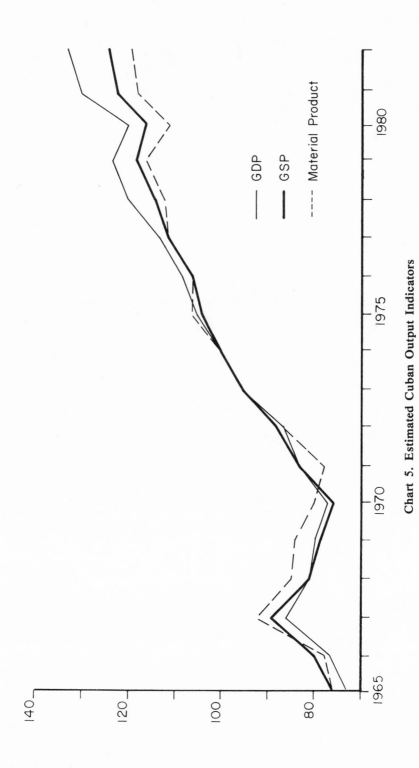

Chart 5. Estimated Cuban Output Indicators

GDP

GSP

Material Product

5. Comparisons with Other Measures

This chapter compares the estimated output indicators for industry, agriculture, the material product, GSP, and GDP with official data and with estimates developed by others. Table 47 contains indexes of growth of the value of industrial and agricultural production and GSP calculated from official Cuban data. The index for the material product has been constructed from official data on the value of output of the industrial, agricultural, and construction sectors. Also in table 47 is an index series on GDP for the period 1971–80 based on GDP estimates that appeared in a publication of the Banco Nacional de Cuba.[1] This publication does not indicate how, or by whom, the GDP series was calculated, although it presumably originates with the CEE, since the estimate of GDP for 1974 is very close to that in the CEE MPS/SNA conversion exercise (reported in table 27).[2]

Table 48 presents indexes of economic activity for industry, agriculture, the material product, and GDP based on the work of Claes Brundenius.[3] Brundenius developed indexes of material product for the principal goods-producing sectors and for the material product for the periods 1946–61, 1961–1968 and 1968–80. The Laspeyres-type indexes he developed ideally would reflect changes over time in material product at constant prices and be free of the methodological problems that affect Cuban official data on the value of gross output. However, in the construction of his indexes, Brundenius relied on Cuban official prices for consumer goods sectors; as has been discussed before, Cuban official prices are conceptually inappropriate for constructing indexes that reflect the growth in Cuban production potential. (More recently, Brundenius has indicated he also used Peruvian prices in his index calculations, but he has not indicated either the frequency with which he relied on these proxy prices or whether he used a combination of Cuban and Peruvian prices within the same economic branch.)[4] Moreover, for basic and intermediate product sectors, for which he could not obtain Cuban official prices, Brundenius relied on official data on the gross value of output as indicators of economic performance for the period 1968–80. Because these data suffer from the same lack-of-consistency problems that plague GSP and other macroeconomic indicators, Brundenius's growth rate estimates for industry and the material product for 1968–80 have to be interpreted with caution.

Brundenius has also made estimates of GDP using a version of the scaling-up method, that is, by adding to his estimates for the material product estimates of the value of nonmaterial services. As noted earlier, official time series data on the value of nonmaterial services are not available. Brundenius has estimated the value of nonmaterial services for each of the years 1958–81, using as proxy total government expenditures on social services in 1965 and moving the latter forward and backward by applying to it the growth rates of the education and public health components

Table 47.   Official Output Indicators for Cuba, 1965–1982 (1974=100)

Year	Industry	Agriculture	Material Product	GSP	GDP
1965	54	85	57	50	
1966	53	83	56	50	
1967	59	88	63	54	
1968	58	107	64	55	
1969	59	102	63	54	
1970	74	94	72	62	
1971	78	87	75	67	69
1972	83	92	82	77	79
1973	93	96	93	89	92
1974	100	100	100	100	100
1975	125	106	121	104	110
1976	130	110	126	105	112
1977	130	132	129	124	117
1978	140	140	139	121	132
1979	147	149	144	126	133
1980	151	153	147	131	154
1981*	177	173	171	151	NA
1982*	187	168	176	157	NA

Source: Industry, Agriculture, Material Product, GSP: *Anuario estadístico de Cuba 1982*, and earlier volumes; GDP: Banco Nacional de Cuba, *Economic Report* (August 1982), p. 30.
*Calculated using growth rates that reflect data at constant prices of 1981.

of his estimated indexes of basic needs performance in Cuba.[5]

Table 49 compares average annual growth rates over selected time periods for industry, agriculture, the material product, GSP and GDP obtained from official data, the estimates made by Brundenius (GSP excluded), and the estimated indexes. The raw indexes are plotted on charts 6-10.

Charts 6 and 7 compare the behavior of the estimated indexes of growth for the industrial and agricultural sectors with the official measures and with Brundenius's estimates. It is clear from chart 6 that the official measure of output for the industrial sector implies a growth rate that outstrips both those

Table 48. Cuban Output Indicators, 1965–1981, based on
Brundenius's Estimates (1974=100)

Year	Industry[a]	Agriculture[b]	Material Product	GDP
1965	56	91	62	73
1966	56	86	60	72
1967	62	92	66	74
1968	61	93	65	78
1969	60	90	62	76
1970	74	103	73	76
1971	78	89	75	75
1972	83	90	82	82
1973	93	94	93	92
1974	100	100	100	100
1975	112	104	112	110
1976	116	109	117	120
1977	117	114	122	130
1978	127	124	131	138
1979	130	126	133	141
1980	129	129	136	145
1981	NA	NA	159	158

Source: Claes Brundenius, Revolutionary Cuba: The Challenge of Growth with Equity, pp. 39, 149-152.
[a]Adjusted to include fishing.
[b]Adjusted to exclude fishing.

obtained from the estimates and those made by Brundenius. For all four
subperiods in table 49, the estimated indexes suggest slower growth
performance than do the other two measures. For example, according to the
estimates, industrial output expanded at an average annual rate of 5.7
percent in 1971–75 and 0.9 percent in 1976–80, whereas the official data
imply growth rates during these two periods of 11.1 percent and 3.9 percent
per annum, respectively, and Brundenius estimates 8.6 percent and 2.9
percent per annum, respectively.

For agriculture (chart 7), the differences in the behavior of the three series

**Table 49. Average Annual Growth Rates for Selected Indicators of
Cuban Economic Activity (percentages)**

Indicator	Average Annual Growth Rate			
	1966-70	1971-75	1976-80	1981-82
Industry				
Official	6.5	11.1	3.9	11.2
Brundenius	5.7	8.6	2.9	NA
Estimated	0.5	5.7	0.9	3.1
Agriculture				
Official	2.0	2.4	7.6	4.8
Brundenius	2.5	0.2	4.4	NA
Estimated	5.3	1.8	4.2	4.5
Material product				
Official	4.8	10.9	4.0	9.4
Brundenius	3.3	8.9	4.0	NA
Estimated	1.0	5.8	0.9	3.5
GSP				
Official	4.4	10.9	4.7	9.5
Estimated	0.0	6.5	2.2	3.4
GDP				
Official	NA	12.3*	7.0	NA
Brundenius	0.8	7.7	5.7	NA
Estimated	1.1	6.4	2.7	5.3

Source: Calculated from tables 46, 47, 48.
*1972-75

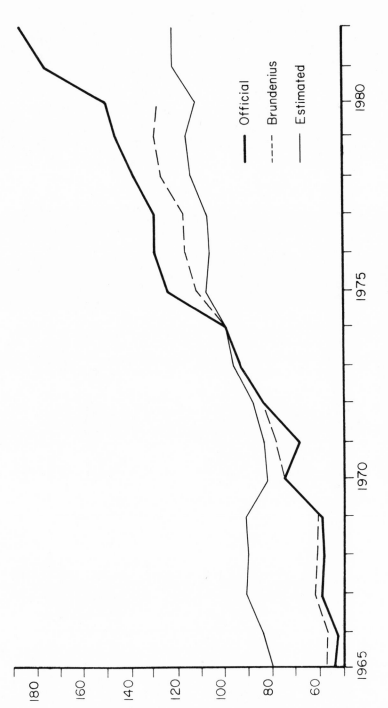

Chart 6. Measures of Cuban Industrial Output

Official
Brundenius
Estimated

1965   1970   1975   1980

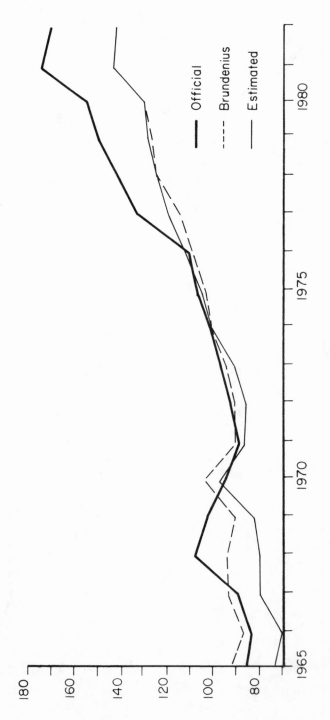

Chart 7. Measures of Cuban Agricultural Output

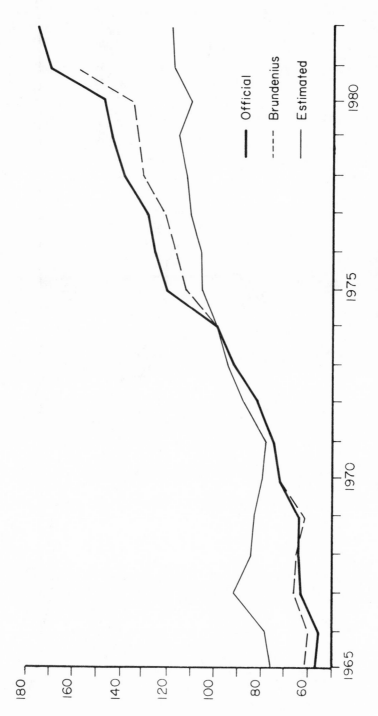

Chart 8. Measures of Cuban Material Product

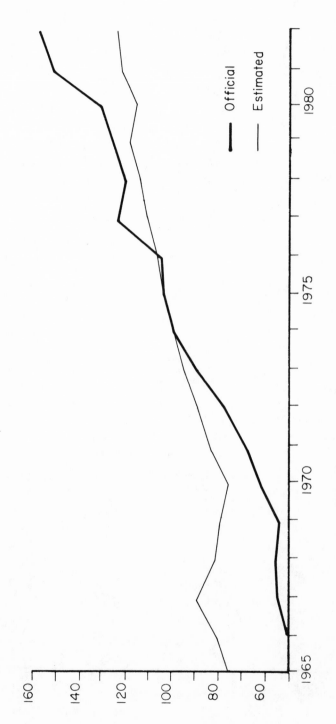

Chart 9. Measures of Cuban Global Social Product

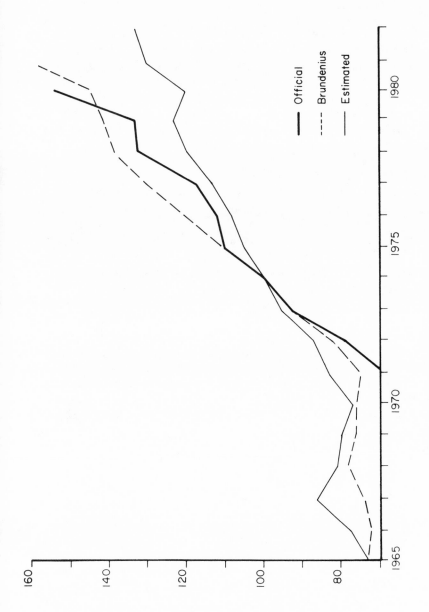

Chart 10. Measures of Cuban Gross Domestic Product

Official
Brundenius
Estimated

are less pronounced. My estimated index tracks Brundenius's estimates rather closely throughout; this is not surprising, since the methodology I have used and the one Brundenius used for the agricultural sector are probably quite close (the major difference being that Brundenius relied on Cuban official prices, whereas I used proxy prices). Neither my estimates nor Brundenius's pick up the large increase in output reported in the official data for 1968. Beginning in 1977, the official measure diverges abruptly from the two sets of estimates, implying a rapid pattern of agricultural growth during 1976–82 inconsistent with that obtained from the physical output data. My index for the material product (industry, agriculture, and construction) suggests considerably more sluggish growth throughout the period 1965–82 than that implied by the official data or the estimates made by Brundenius (chart 8).

For all subperiods in table 49, my estimated GSP measures consistently suggest slower growth rates than those implied by the official data. For 1966–70, my estimated measures indicate no growth, compared with 4.4 percent annual growth for the official series; for 1971–75 and 1976–80, the estimated index implies GSP growth at a rate roughly one-half of the official rate (6.5 percent versus 10.9 percent, and 2.2 percent versus 4.7 percent). For 1981–82, the official series yields a rate of growth of 9.5 percent, compared to 3.4 percent for the estimated index (chart 9).

Chart 10 compares the behavior of the Banco Nacional de Cuba's GDP series with my estimates and those Brundenius made. As was the case with the other indexes, the estimated GDP series suggests more sluggish growth than implied by the official series or Brundenius's estimates. My estimated series indicates that Cuban GDP expanded at an annual average rate of 6.4 percent in the first half of the 1970s, compared to 12.3 percent for the official series and 7.7 percent based on the estimates made by Brundenius. According to the Banco Nacional de Cuba series, GDP grew at a pace of 7.0 percent per annum in the second half of the 1970s, whereas Brundenius estimates the GDP growth rate at 5.7 percent and my indexes yield a rate of growth of 2.7 percent per annum.

6. Conclusions

Consistent with the contention that official macroeconomic data are not suitable for assessing Cuban real economic growth over time, or for comparing Cuba's economic performance with that of other market economies, I have prepared a set of alternative measures of real Cuban economic growth that, theoretically, come closer to meeting these objectives.

The measures I have prepared follow a long tradition of efforts by Western analysts to estimate real economic growth of centrally planned economies and uses a well-known and well-established methodology. However, in applying the methodology to revolutionary Cuba, I have faced a number of conceptual and data difficulties, such as inadequate product selection, lack of appropriate price information and data to estimate adjusted factor cost, scanty and dated information on value added, and unexplained changes in official statistical series. I have dealt with each of these problems in various ways—by assuming, for instance, that the sample of physical output series published in statistical yearbooks is representative of the universe of Cuban economic activities, or by assigning equal value weights to certain services activities for which prices could not be obtained. Reasonable analysts might disagree with some of these approaches, and I welcome constructive dialogue on alternative sources of data and methods to use to resolve some of these problems.

The indexes I have constructed suggest that the Cuban economy expanded moderately over the period 1965–82. They further suggest that growth was quite uneven over the entire period. Thus, no sustained economic growth occurred in the second half of the 1960s; levels of output for 1970 were roughly at the same level as five years earlier. Beginning in 1970 and stretching to about 1975 or 1976, my indexes suggest rapid real economic growth, followed by a period of sluggishness in the second half of the 1970s and an actual contraction in output in 1980. This unevenness in growth fits closely the patterns presented in a very detailed assessment of the Cuban economy over this period by Carmelo Mesa-Lago.[1] In 1981 the economy rebounded strongly but it is not clear that the same pace was maintained in 1982. Thus, according to my estimates, the material product was essentially stagnant in 1982 (0.8 percent growth) while the broader indicators of economic activity in which services sectors are more heavily represented, such as GSP and GDP, rose modestly (1.6 percent and 2.3 percent, respectively).

My measures of real economic growth and official macroeconomic indicators or estimates prepared by an independent researcher agree broadly in terms of growth trends but differ sharply in terms of magnitudes. According to my estimates, the Cuban economy expanded at a considerably slower pace than would be implied by official data or estimates by Brundenius. Generally, my calculated indexes yield real economic growth rates roughly one-half as large as those obtained from the official data or the estimates made by Brundenius.

Appendix A. Physical Output Data

Table A-2 contains time series of annual observations on physical or nonmonetary output for the period 1965–82. The data originate from the following official Cuban publications:

Junta Central de Planificación, Dirección Central de Estadística, *Boletín estadístico*. Issues for 1964, 1966, 1967, 1970, 1971.

_____, *Compendio estadístico de Cuba*. Issues for 1965, 1966, 1967, 1968, 1974.

Comité Estatal de Estadísticas, *Anuario estadístico de Cuba*. Issues for 1972, 1973, 1974, 1975, 1976, 1977, 1978, 1979, 1980, 1981, 1982.

_____, *Cifras estadísticas 1980*.

_____, *Compendio del anuario estadístico de Cuba*. Issues for 1975, 1976, 1977, 1978.

_____, *Cuba en cifras*. Issues for 1980, 1981, 1982.

_____, *Desarrollo económico y social de Cuba durante el período 1958–1980*.

_____, *Estadísticas quinquenales de Cuba 1965–1980*.

In addition to a description, each series in table A-2 has a four-character label. The first two characters in the field identify the commodity/service, with the first indicating the economic branch and sector and the second the commodity within that branch/sector. For the goods-producing sectors (industry, agriculture), the last two characters in the field are coded PY (for physical units), and for the services sectors they are coded PA. Thus, the series designated as CBPY is a series for physical production for product B (carbon steel) within economic branch C (nonferrous mining and metallurgy). The branch/sector codes are given in table A-1.

The unit of measure applicable to each of the series is identified using the following abbreviations:

BX	boxes
CM	cubic meters
GAL	gallons
GwH	gigawatt hours
GRS	gross (that is, 144 units)
HL	hectoliters (that is, 100 liters)
HA	hectares
HRS	hours
KM	kilometers
LIT	liters
M	meters
MT	metric tons
PAS	passengers
SM	square meters
U	unit, one

Table A-1.   Branch/Sector Codes

Sector		Branch/ Sector Code	Sector		Branch/ Sector Code
Goods-producing			**Services**		
Industry	Electricity	A	Construction		A
	Fuel	B			
	Ferrous mining &		Transportation	Railroad	B
	metallurgy	C		Motor	C
	Nonferrous mining			Maritime	D
	& metallurgy	D		Air	E
	Nonelectrical machinery	E		Cargo handling	F
	Electronics	F			
	Metal products	G	Communications		G
	Chemicals	H			
	Paper & cellulose	I	Trade		H
	Printing	J			
	Wood products	K	Housing & community services		I
	Construction materials	L			
	Glass & ceramics	M	Education & public health		J
	Textiles	N			
	Apparel	O	Social security, welfare, cultural,		
	Leather products	P	scientific activities		K
	Sugar	Q			
	Processed foods	R	Public administration		L
	Fishing	S			
	Beverages & tobacco	T	Defense & internal order		M
	Other	U			
Agriculture	Sugar	W	Other nonproductive activities		N
	Nonsugar	X			
	Livestock	Y			
	Forestry	V			
	Agricultural services	Z			

Table A-2.   Cuban Economic Indicators

Label	Product/Service	Unit	1965	1966	1967
AAPY	Electric power	GwH	2913.4	3119.3	3413.1
BAPY	Crude oil	MT	57000.0	69000.0	1161.6
BCPY	Fuel oil	000MT	1898.6	1973.3	1930.0
BDPY	Diesel oil	000MT	528.2	559.2	615.2
BEPY	Liquefied natural gas	MT	51578.0	48121.0	56959.0
BFPY	Gasoline	MT	809700.0	777600.0	854000.0
BGPY	Kerosene	MT	202004.0	250213.0	275556.0
BHPY	Motor oil & lubricants	MT	66669.0	67952.0	79719.0
BIPY	Natural gas	000CM	--	--	--
BJPY	Manufactured gas	000CM	66095.3	71871.2	73931.3
CAPY	Refractory chromium	MT	40994.0	37530.0	43005.6
CBPY	Carbon steel	MT	35973.9	66619.7	102371.0
CCPY	Carbon steel bars	MT	26200.0	74900.0	88900.0
CDPY	Carbon steel rods	MT	--	62614.4	98636.0
CEPY	Steel forgings	MT	--	--	1005.0
CFPY	Steel castings	MT	--	--	2514.6
CGPY	Cast-iron pipes (water supply)	MT	6231.0	9028.1	10241.9
CHPY	Cast-iron pipes	MT	1171.5	1569.1	1721.8
CIPY	Iron castings	MT	--	--	3243.6
CJPY	Barbed wire	MT	7285.6	3735.8	3177.2
DAPY	Nickel-cobalt oxide	MT	9561.6	9382.2	10174.2
DBPY	Nickel-cobalt sinter	MT	8738.6	7270.9	9550.7
DCPY	Nickel-cobalt sulfide	MT	9936.2	11201.4	12712.8
DDPY	Copper concentrate	MT	6001.9	5429.3	5209.6
DEPY	Aluminum shapes	MT	0.0	826.6	798.8
EBPY	Ind. air cond. & refrig. equip.	U	0.0	0.0	852.0
ECPY	Road levelers	U	--	--	--
EDPY	Road rollers	U	0.0	0.0	0.0
EEPY	Combines for sugarcane harvesting	U	--	--	--
EFPY	Sugarcane carts	U	2000.0	--	723.0
EGPY	Water pumps	U	--	--	6488.0
EHPY	Gas stoves	U	10288.0	46024.0	34878.0
EIPY	Kerosene stoves	U	--	--	0.0
EJPY	Buses	U	0.0	0.0	0.0
EKPY	Fishing boats	U	--	--	--
FAPY	Electrical cables & wire	MT	0.0	0.0	483.1
FBPY	Insul. elec. cables & wires	000M	23588.8	17197.2	15322.6
FCPY	Elec. wire (for elec. motors)	MT	0.0	0.0	0.1
FDPY	Telephone wire	000M	4943.5	4828.7	3703.3
FEPY	Household refrigerators	U	11871.0	1711.0	730.0
FFPY	Automobile batteries	U	102100.0	62400.0	88939.0
FGPY	Household radio receivers	U	81888.0	41417.0	9000.0
FHPY	Television receivers	U	0.0	0.0	0.0
GAPY	Steel structures	MT	--	--	329.2
GBPY	Stainless steel tanks	U	--	--	--
GCPY	Steel cans	000U	--	--	--
GDPY	Aluminum cans	000U	--	--	36030.3
GEPY	Electrodes (for welding)	MT	--	--	969.8
GFPY	Bottle caps	000GRS	10380.4	10194.3	11792.1
GGPY	Pressure cookers	000U	27.4	115.8	63.1
GHPY	Nails	MT	--	5953.0	4536.1
H1PY	Tire tubes	U	106600.0	110500.0	172749.0

Table A-2—Continued

Label	Product/Service	Unit	1965	1966	1967
H2PY	Rubber footwear	000PAIR	--	--	--
H3PY	Plastic tubing (for elec. conn.)	000M	2378.8	1826.6	1129.8
H4PY	Matches	000000BX	277.9	322.7	333.5
H5PY	Refined glycerine	MT	656.7	800.9	1967.2
HAPY	Iron pyrites	MT	--	--	--
HBPY	Salt	MT	74196.3	57431.4	68397.7
HCPY	Anhydrous ammonia	MT	--	--	--
HDPY	Sulfuric acid (98%)	MT	201500.0	230300.0	270341.3
HEPY	Caustic soda (50%)	MT	3138.0	3803.8	3538.0
HFPY	Oxygen	000CM	3655.4	3645.1	3515.0
HGPY	Acetylene gas	000CM	555.8	581.0	844.0
HHPY	Insecticides	MT	2461.0	2288.0	3651.0
HIPY	Superphosphates	MT	--	--	29615.0
HJPY	Ammonium nitrate	MT	--	--	2803.0
HKPY	Urea	MT	--	--	--
HLPY	Complex fertilizers	MT	16165.0	23048.0	18605.0
HMPY	Mixed fertilizers	MT	456544.0	490678.0	758948.0
HNPY	Granulated fertilizers	MT	--	--	10329.0
HOPY	Rayon cord	MT	--	1526.0	1857.0
HPPY	Rayon yarn	MT	714.0	671.0	711.0
HQPY	Oil-base paints	HL	30048.5	28434.4	26478.0
HRPY	Latex & acrylic paints	HL	12715.2	31320.0	24125.3
HSPY	Varnishes	HL	2827.7	4462.7	3586.0
HTPY	Enamels	HL	16973.6	26080.0	26080.0
HUPY	Household detergent	MT	12614.0	14997.3	13884.1
HVPY	Laundry soap	MT	36732.3	32906.0	39529.4
HWPY	Hand soap	MT	12721.7	11798.3	14475.4
HXPY	Toothpaste	MT	1115.4	1218.1	1779.7
HYPY	Torula yeast	MT	0.0	0.0	0.0
HZPY	Tires	U	197000.0	305700.0	413916.0
IAPY	Bagasse pulp	MT	--	--	--
IBPY	Writing paper	MT	18769.9	16354.7	18900.0
ICPY	Gray cardboard	MT	9717.7	11878.9	12796.0
IDPY	Cardboard for corrugating	MT	5405.3	6550.6	8562.0
IEPY	Kraft cardboard	MT	14472.4	20723.9	21575.0
IFPY	Bristol board	MT	10725.9	7474.0	10091.0
IGPY	Paper bags	000U	0.0	165600.0	179300.0
IHPY	Corrugated boxes	000U	29413.7	35697.5	34746.8
IIPY	Waxed containers	000U	110800.0	75500.0	97202.4
IJPY	Multilayered paper bags	000U	36361.3	37651.3	44129.9
JAPY	Books	000U	--	--	8519.9
JBPY	Magazines	000U	--	--	9829.1
JCPY	Booklets	000U	--	--	7454.6
JDPY	Notebooks	000U	52554.2	37512.7	55331.7
JEPY	Cigarette labels	000000U	1030.0	1093.0	1254.2
KAPY	Sawn wood	CM	73600.0	60100.0	58682.0
KBPY	Wooden boxes	000U	9283.1	9940.5	10578.5
KCPY	Telephone poles	000CM	4.9	0.2	4.5
KDPY	Railroad ties	CM	68400.0	62400.0	35700.0
LAPY	Sand	CM	780.5	834.1	1091.0
LBPY	Crushed stone	CM	2027.4	2165.1	2813.0
LCPY	Cement	000MT	801.1	750.4	835.1
LDPY	Terrazzo tiles	000SM	--	110.1	116.2
LEPY	Floor tiles	000SM	1028.7	1186.9	1352.2
LFPY	Bricks	000U	64322.1	52598.5	74146.0
LGPY	Prefab. concrete blocks	000CM	--	111.4	137.9
LHPY	Refractory materials	MT	13489.1	12719.2	13684.9
LIPY	Concrete pipes (water				

134   Appendix A

Table A-2—Continued

Label	Product/Service	Unit	1965	1966	1967
	supply)	000M	42.1	37.4	27.4
LJPY	Fiberglass roof panels	000SM	2461.8	2820.1	3810.7
LKPY	Fiberglass pipes (water supply)	000M	--	--	--
LLPY	Cinder blocks	000U	17638.1	18854.5	19604.2
MAPY	Flat glass	000SM	--	--	100.4
MBPY	Bottles	000000U	68.6	70.6	129.2
MCPY	Medicine vials	000000U	70.1	77.7	72.1
MDPY	Bathroom tiles	000U	28551.3	25574.7	33287.3
MEPY	Bathroom fixtures	000U	92.6	90.0	76.2
NBPY	Cotton textiles	000SM	96100.0	108400.0	112470.3
NCPY	Wool textiles	000SM	398.5	309.1	316.2
NDPY	Rayon textiles	000SM	21259.8	6426.7	3187.2
NEPY	Sisal rope	MT	10805.4	9509.6	7908.3
NFPY	Socks	000U	--	--	--
OAPY	Underwear (incl. infants')	000U	50065.7	47064.9	52645.3
OBPY	Outerwear (incl. infants)'	000U	25792.4	25766.6	28534.4
OCPY	Blouses & gowns (excl. infants')	000U	1836.2	1874.7	1906.1
ODPY	Shirts (excl. infants')	000U	11943.3	10258.4	10988.9
OEPY	Pants (excl. infants')	000U	6185.1	6049.4	8028.6
OFPY	Skirts	000U	1198.2	1127.9	1169.4
OGPY	Sweaters (excl. infants')	000U	535.1	478.2	417.1
OHPY	Suits (excl. infants')	000U	146.2	103.2	105.1
OIPY	Dresses (excl. infants')	000U	789.2	585.2	611.6
OJPY	Cotton & rayon bags	000U	16325.5	12727.4	13629.1
OKPY	Kenaf bags	000U	3843.8	3431.3	10316.3
PAPY	Leather	000SM	1857.6	2827.1	3240.8
PBPY	Sole leather	MT	4929.5	6089.6	7693.0
PCPY	Cattle hides	000U	--	--	--
PDPY	Leather footwear	000PAIR	11002.7	12642.6	13674.4
QAPY	Raw sugar	000MT	6156.2	4537.4	6236.1
QBPY	Refined sugar	000MT	1002.1	735.9	1127.9
QCPY	Final syrups	000MT	2144.0	1181.2	1880.2
QDPY	Bagasse for industrial uses	MT	--	--	--
RAPY	Deboned beef	MT	97655.2	108463.3	99705.9
RBPY	Pork	MT	9869.0	6123.7	5466.5
RCPY	Canned meats	MT	20217.5	17411.6	14171.1
RDPY	Fresh poultry	MT	30576.0	21826.5	19623.7
REPY	Wheat flour	MT	137300.0	131500.0	130798.3
RFPY	Lard	MT	--	--	215.9
RGPY	Tallow	MT	6317.8	7102.9	6171.5
RHPY	Hydrogenated fats	MT	10743.4	10263.1	11430.8
RIPY	Fresh & pasteurized milk	MT	228500.0	323000.0	354412.3
RJPY	Condensed milk	MT	43964.6	46826.2	51629.8
RKPY	Evaporated milk	MT	12612.7	14038.2	14073.5
RLPY	Powdered milk	MT	2552.5	2395.6	2808.0
RMPY	Cheeses	MT	1102.3	1414.6	1119.2
RNPY	Butter	MT	2326.9	2840.0	3001.4
ROPY	Yogurt	MT	2870.5	7341.0	9665.5
RPPY	Ice cream	000GAL	1878.6	2663.8	3866.9
RQPY	Refined vegetable oil	MT	98486.4	88790.1	63786.5
RRPY	Bread	MT	184596.1	263553.6	315758.1
RSPY	Crackers	MT	29643.4	31876.5	34955.0
RTPY	Cookies	MT	23185.9	22291.9	22092.1
RUPY	Pasta	MT	25768.0	33976.3	38149.8

Table A-2—Continued

Label	Product/Service	Unit	1965	1966	1967
RVPY	Nougats	MT	--	--	1742.8
RWPY	Candies	MT	10198.4	9598.4	10812.4
RXPY	Canned fruits & vegetables	MT	80397.1	83842.5	72335.3
RYPY	Roasted coffee	MT	26690.0	22373.0	23635.6
R1PY	Fresh & frozen fish	MT	4492.7	3977.2	5344.2
R2PY	Fresh & frozen seafood	MT	2227.0	2408.2	2614.6
R3PY	Canned fish & seafood	MT	1828.9	1910.3	2395.6
SAPY	Fish catch	MT	25911.0	28433.0	48117.0
TAPY	Denatured alcohol	000HL	1427.1	1492.7	1700.3
TBPY	Anhydrous alcohol	HL	759532.0	381642.0	545744.0
TCPY	Alcoholic bev. (excl. wines)	000HL	169.9	169.3	153.0
TDPY	Wines	000HL	122.2	126.2	122.8
TEPY	Beer	000HL	993.0	1088.9	1359.6
TFPY	Malts	000HL	168.2	190.5	245.2
TGPY	Soft drinks	000HL	2405.9	2207.8	2126.4
THPY	Mineral water	000HL	1275.8	1305.8	1459.8
TIPY	Cigars	000U	656800.0	622800.0	726805.4
TJPY	Cigarettes	000000U	16462.3	18454.7	19627.8
TKPY	Pipe tobacco	MT	3.8	18.9	20.5
UAPY	Fodder	MT	559400.0	546900.0	579601.1
UBPY	Lamps (industrial use)	U	92961.0	64882.0	50430.0
UCPY	Lamps (household use)	U	45300.0	62100.0	58946.0
VABY	Unsawn wood (logs)	CM	--	--	--
VBPY	Firewood	000CM	961.7	946.2	980.0
WAPY	Sugarcane	000MT	52541.3	39572.3	51131.5
X1PY	Mangoes	MT	53554.0	8666.2	24764.7
X2PY	Guavas	MT	11240.4	12333.0	13558.3
X3PY	Avocados	MT	31817.5	12997.2	27540.7
X4PY	Papayas	MT	35190.6	66285.3	53284.4
X5PY	Coconuts	MT	12616.2	11428.0	10275.0
X6PY	Coffee	MT	--	33406.5	34245.9
X7PY	Cocoa	MT	2153.6	2018.5	1459.4
X8PY	Tobacco	MT	--	51786.8	45296.2
XAPY	Potatoes	MT	106167.4	140887.5	104172.1
XBPY	Sweet potatoes	MT	80720.7	153042.3	88392.3
XCPY	Malanga	MT	46628.5	71274.6	42413.3
XDPY	Yucca	MT	62120.5	96064.3	49170.4
XEPY	Yams	MT	8386.7	11684.3	5732.9
XFPY	Rice	MT	49893.1	68416.2	93731.4
XGPY	Corn	MT	--	17188.8	8462.4
XHPY	Sweet corn	MT	--	--	16037.0
XIPY	Black beans	MT	8204.1	9283.6	12878.6
XJPY	Red beans	MT	159.4	174.9	787.6
XKPY	Black-eyed peas	MT	2147.1	1093.5	397.8
XLPY	Tomatoes	MT	120032.4	133134.6	164135.3
XMPY	Green peppers	MT	6773.8	9303.9	17066.8
XNPY	Onions	MT	5802.4	10863.1	15477.1
XOPY	Garlic	MT	111.0	26.0	42.1
XPPY	Squash	MT	53155.5	40001.4	44958.9
XQPY	Cucumbers	MT	14851.5	11822.0	12696.9
XRPY	Melons	MT	32197.9	13331.5	23232.0
XSPY	Cabbage	MT	12316.7	13843.5	16462.7
XTPY	Oranges	MT	85880.6	117615.3	109790.9
XUPY	Grapefruit	MT	10541.7	12504.8	13197.9
XVPY	Lemons	MT	9377.5	7257.8	8127.6
XWPY	Tangerines	MT	4306.7	12718.0	4316.2
XXPY	Plantains	MT	67741.9	71855.0	58632.7
XYPY	Bananas	MT	36326.1	28967.3	26778.3

Table A-2—Continued

Label	Product/Service	Unit	1965	1966	1967
XZPY	Pineapple	MT	15765.0	9681.1	6677.7
YAPY	Cattle	MT	--	--	316516.2
YBPY	Pigs	MT	18439.0	13225.0	10558.1
YCPY	Honey	MT	3900.7	3710.6	3680.9
YDPY	Eggs	000U	920267.4	1019868.3	1177607.0
YEPY	Milk	MT	231268.0	329711.5	324120.6
YFPY	Poultry	MT	34194.5	25262.1	24509.0
AAPA	Housing units	U	5040.0	6271.0	10257.0
ABPA	Cattle barns	U	--	--	--
ACPA	Fac. for scholars, students	U	--	--	--
ADPA	Water & sewer lines laid	000000CM	--	--	--
AEPA	Farm acreage brought under irrigation	HA	--	--	--
AFPA	Acreage protected against flood	HA	--	--	--
AGPA	Unpaved roads	KM	--	--	--
AHPA	Paved roads	KM	--	--	--
BAPA	Passengers transported (rail)	M.PAS-KM	895.4	922.1	1168.1
BBPA	Freight transported (rail)	M.MT-KM	1322.5	1487.2	1703.4
CAPA	Passengers transported (road)	000PAS	1163248.2	1240932.3	1319907.6
CBPA	Freight transported (road)	M.MT-KM	637.1	590.9	557.1
DAPA	Passengers transported (maritime)	M.PAS-KM	22.6	28.3	29.0
DBPA	Freight transported (maritime)	M.MT-KM	6026.7	11153.9	14175.3
EAPA	Pass. transp. by natl. airline	M.PAS-KM	287.3	295.2	334.4
EBPA	Freight transp. by natl. airline	M.MT-KM	5.8	7.0	9.1
FAPA	Cargo loaded & unloaded	000000MT	20894.0	19129.7	19498.1
GAPA	Domestic mail sent	000U	75118.9	71747.4	67978.9
GBPA	International mail sent	000U	--	--	--
GCPA	International mail received	000U	--	--	--
GDPA	Telegrams sent	000U	13058.8	13504.3	15732.3
GEPA	Domestic telephone calls	000U	15663.7	16204.2	18113.8
HAPA	Workers in trade sector	000	213.9	235.0	--
IAPA	Workers in comm. svces. & housing	000	27.7	28.5	--
IBPA	Tourists lodged (dom. & intl.)	000	--	--	--
JAPA	Students	U	2152030.0	2097084.0	2216029.0
JBPA	Scholarship students	U	116555.0	147096.0	191298.0
JCPA	Students graduating	U	174578.0	169357.0	123755.0
JDPA	Medical consultations	000	12748.3	13659.1	16675.8
JEPA	Patients admitted	U	815998.0	844065.0	923608.0
JFPA	Emerg. rm. & polyclinic consult.	U	5009244.0	5964829.0	6785419.0
JGPA	Immunizations	U	4689907.0	4438715.0	3712946.0
KAPA	Patrons using library services	U	1126.1	1718.0	1623.4
KBPA	Books published	U	15408.2	9274.8	8570.2
KCPA	Newspapers run	000000	--	--	--

Table A-2—Continued

Label	Product/Service	Unit	1965	1966	1967
KDPA	Domestic radio broadcasting	HRS	--	--	--
KEPA	Artistic performances	U	9649.0	9247.0	12813.0
KFPA	Particip. in organized sports	U	586940.0	778226.0	1281224.0
KGPA	Workers in var. soc. activ.	000	--	--	--
LAPA	Workers in public administration	000	53.3	53.0	--
NAPA	Workers in nonprod. activities	000	--	--	--

Label	Product/Service	Unit	1968	1969	1970
AAPY	Electric power	GwH	3584.5	3782.3	4887.6
BAPY	Crude oil	MT	197752.3	206169.4	159141.3
BBPY	Fuel oil	000MT	2017.0	2269.9	2367.3
BCPY	Diesel oil	000MT	715.8	626.0	583.0
BDPY	Liquefied natural gas	MT	60791.0	58590.0	56512.0
BEPY	Gasoline	MT	713300.0	746935.0	745858.0
BFPY	Kerosene	MT	293994.0	325319.0	401220.0
BGPY	Motor oil & lubricants	MT	73662.0	87776.0	95401.0
BHPY	Natural gas	000CM	--	--	--
BIPY	Manufactured gas	000CM	75910.0	74903.0	76974.0
CAPY	Refractory chromium	MT	48513.4	45291.2	22835.5
CBPY	Carbon steel	MT	119794.0	119195.0	140042.9
CCPY	Carbon steel bars	MT	103900.0	87091.0	84965.7
CDPY	Carbon steel rods	MT	109502.0	100199.0	105739.8
CEPY	Steel forgings	MT	791.8	536.9	645.8
CFPY	Steel castings	MT	3811.6	5533.5	3595.5
CGPY	Cast-iron pipes (water supply)	MT	7982.8	3548.5	3594.5
CHPY	Cast-iron pipes	MT	1560.3	920.3	246.1
CIPY	Iron castings	MT	3522.0	3201.8	6157.5
CJPY	Barbed wire	MT	1511.2	1507.3	522.7
DAPY	Nickel-cobalt oxide	MT	11513.9	8721.7	10653.8
DBPY	Nickel-cobalt sinter	MT	8500.4	8949.9	7828.2
DCPY	Nickel-cobalt sulfide	MT	17306.7	17705.1	18292.8
DDPY	Copper concentrate	MT	5148.0	3845.3	400.1
DEPY	Aluminum shapes	MT	684.0	589.2	560.6
EBPY	Ind. air cond. & refrig. equip.	U	1382.0	343.0	604.0
ECPY	Road levelers	U	--	6.0	52.0
EDPY	Road rollers	U	0.0	0.0	0.0
EEPY	Combines for sugarcane harvesting	U	--	--	--
EFPY	Sugarcane carts	U	--	2479.0	24.0
EGPY	Water pumps	U	1858.0	1605.0	1497.0
EHPY	Gas stoves	U	21929.0	8068.0	6009.0
EIPY	Kerosene stoves	U	0.0	500.0	2155.0
EJPY	Buses	U	0.0	0.0	300.0
EKPY	Fishing boats	U	--	52.0	36.0
FAPY	Electrical cables & wire	MT	1166.8	1175.4	824.5
FBPY	Insul. elec. cables & wires	000M	14700.5	12653.8	13122.2
FCPY	Elec. wire (for elec. motors)	MT	123.3	65.2	148.0
FDPY	Telephone wire	000M	3385.3	4136.9	4631.3

Table A-2—Continued

Label	Product/Service	Unit	1968	1969	1970
FEPY	Household refrigerators	U	19.0	2080.0	5841.0
FFPY	Automobile batteries	U	96942.0	90522.0	95209.0
FGPY	Household radio receivers	U	20853.0	0.0	19135.0
FHPY	Television receivers	U	0.0	0.0	0.0
GAPY	Steel structures	MT	3790.6	1419.2	488.9
GBPY	Stainless steel tanks	U	--	--	--
GCPY	Steel cans	000U	--	--	--
GDPY	Aluminum cans	000U	34029.5	38522.7	31556.5
GEPY	Electrodes (for welding)	MT	1583.2	1068.3	984.6
GFPY	Bottle caps	000GRS	9216.1	8357.4	5743.8
GGPY	Pressure cookers	000U	64.3	52.4	117.9
GHPY	Nails	MT	6141.5	4938.5	3930.9
H1PY	Tire tubes	U	67036.0	124952.0	181063.0
H2PY	Rubber footwear	000PAIR	--	1042.9	6130.3
H3PY	Plastic tubing (for elec. conn.)	000M	1688.1	679.5	1063.6
H4PY	Matches	000000BX	382.8	395.6	370.7
H5PY	Refined glycerine	MT	2405.0	1554.1	2106.4
HAPY	Iron pyrites	MT	23153.6	19685.0	23699.0
HBPY	Salt	MT	65238.5	87640.3	88882.2
HCPY	Anhydrous ammonia	MT	2142.0	8998.0	20386.0
HDPY	Sulfuric acid (98%)	MT	322479.0	325736.0	321858.0
HEPY	Caustic soda (50%)	MT	3755.0	3483.0	3608.0
HFPY	Oxygen	000CM	4496.0	5280.0	5355.0
HGPY	Acetylene gas	000CM	1010.0	1142.0	1040.0
HHPY	Insecticides	MT	2486.0	4164.0	1413.0
HIPY	Superphosphates	MT	10592.0	15264.0	0.0
HJPY	Ammonium nitrate	MT	2397.0	2858.0	13542.0
HJPY	Urea	MT	--	--	--
HKPY	Complex fertilizers	MT	12783.0	15526.0	33769.0
HLPY	Mixed fertilizers	MT	818697.0	655408.0	504022.0
HMPY	Granulated fertilizers	MT	28302.0	23919.0	39668.0
HNPY	Rayon cord	MT	540.0	1402.0	1131.0
HOPY	Rayon yarn	MT	90.0	34.0	--
HQPY	Oil-base paints	HL	12499.0	9215.0	24088.0
HRPY	Latex & acrylic paints	HL	22020.6	5930.8	29930.4
HSPY	Varnishes	HL	2569.0	2208.0	4573.0
HTPY	Enamels	HL	9766.0	7744.0	30776.0
HUPY	Household detergent	MT	3834.2	12349.0	9999.9
HVPY	Laundry soap	MT	43277.5	41818.7	32493.8
HWPY	Hand soap	MT	16552.6	17354.4	15852.6
HXPY	Toothpaste	MT	1743.2	2104.4	1818.5
HYPY	Torula yeast	MT	0.0	0.0	0.0
HZPY	Tires	U	147698.0	356379.0	201918.0
IAPY	Bagasse pulp	MT	--	32569.0	33703.0
IBPY	Writing paper	MT	20942.0	19889.0	18904.0
ICPY	Gray cardboard	MT	12255.0	11467.0	11675.0
IDPY	Cardboard for corrugating	MT	8730.0	7545.0	8500.0
IEPY	Kraft cardboard	MT	19866.0	20168.0	16547.0
IFPY	Bristol board	MT	6452.0	8399.0	6737.0
IGPY	Paper bags	000U	124800.0	148400.0	113042.0
IHPY	Corrugated boxes	000U	34202.6	33715.3	32859.4
IIPY	Waxed containers	000U	38545.9	38322.0	44395.5
IJPY	Multilayered paper bags	000U	38146.2	16152.0	42369.8
JAPY	Books	000U	13199.5	15776.9	16336.9
JBPY	Magazines	000U	5780.6	5332.4	5627.8
JCBY	Booklets	000U	9892.4	10990.5	6919.3
JDPY	Notebooks	000U	53036.5	42292.9	45675.5

Table A-2—Continued

Label	Product/Service	Unit	1968	1969	1970
JEPY	Cigarette labels	000000U	1162.5	1248.6	1098.6
KAPY	Sawn wood	CM	46299.0	39120.0	28409.0
KBPY	Wooden boxes	000U	9034.2	7977.9	7928.8
KCPY	Telephone poles	000CM	3.7	4.9	2.9
KDPY	Railroad ties	CM	22500.0	38600.0	10100.0
LAPY	Sand	CM	1383.7	1230.0	1206.2
LBPY	Crushed stone	CM	291.0	2679.3	2913.0
LCPY	Cement	000MT	779.7	679.6	742.0
LDPY	Terrazzo tiles	000SM	89.3	133.0	134.4
LEPY	Floor tiles	000SM	1119.2	672.3	517.9
LFPY	Bricks	000U	48148.0	27203.3	31289.2
LGPY	Prefab. concrete blocks	000CM	161.8	140.8	162.6
LHPY	Refractory materials	MT	12948.1	9753.1	6585.6
LIPY	Concrete pipes (water supply)	000M	52.3	69.6	43.4
LJPY	Fiberglass roof panels	000SM	4633.4	3861.1	3689.8
LKPY	Fiberglass pipes (water supply)	000M	--	--	--
LLPY	Cinder blocks	000U	18463.2	13388.1	12873.6
MAPY	Flat glass	000SM	100.4	107.8	0.0
MBPY	Bottles	000000U	82.5	97.0	92.5
MCPY	Medicine vials	000000U	79.8	109.6	133.7
MDPY	Bathroom tiles	000U	17132.6	18225.5	17559.1
MEPY	Bathroom fixtures	000U	81.0	73.5	55.5
NBPY	Cotton textiles	000SM	105222.9	91312.2	75684.8
NCPY	Wool textiles	000SM	247.9	274.2	116.5
NDPY	Rayon textiles	000SM	5295.9	4438.1	2184.3
NEPY	Sisal rope	MT	10007.7	9789.7	6057.5
NFPY	Socks	000U	--	--	--
OAPY	Underwear (incl. infants')	000U	46908.4	39671.5	39264.9
OBPY	Outerwear (incl. infants')	000U	30757.1	30145.6	26198.3
OCPY	Blouses & gowns (excl. infants')	000U	1604.0	1512.9	1144.7
ODPY	Shirts (excl. infants')	000U	9805.8	9731.9	8239.7
OEPY	Pants (excl. infants')	000U	9909.2	9271.4	7484.9
OFPY	Skirts	000U	1118.4	1477.5	1215.9
OGPY	Sweaters (excl. infants')	000U	222.5	61.6	89.2
OHPY	Suits (excl. infants')	000U	93.7	51.0	9.9
OIPY	Dresses (excl. infants')	000U	541.4	351.4	141.6
OJPY	Cotton & rayon bags	000U	14100.1	15674.7	15568.5
OKPY	Kenaf bags	000U	6130.7	4950.9	3514.2
PAPY	Leather	000SM	2758.1	2957.7	2495.5
PBPY	Sole leather	MT	570.5	4876.2	3834.7
PCPY	Cattle hides	000U	--	1067.9	1057.3
PDPY	Leather footwear	000PAIR	13637.0	13260.9	12051.6
QAPY	Raw sugar	000MT	5164.5	4459.4	8537.6
QBPY	Refined sugar	000MT	1012.2	892.9	1002.7
QCPY	Final syrups	000MT	1587.2	1526.7	2989.8
QDPY	Bagasse for industrial uses	MT	--	--	--
RAPY	Deboned beef	MT	110759.0	104482.0	104926.0
RBPY	Pork	MT	5048.4	2550.6	7561.4
RCPY	Canned meats	MT	17242.4	15525.2	14624.4
RDPY	Fresh poultry	MT	20173.9	15598.7	15573.0
REPY	Wheat flour	MT	137566.0	147874.5	159694.2
RFPY	Lard	MT	6.5	0.0	34.9
RGPY	Tallow	MT	6633.9	6451.3	6247.4
RHPY	Hydrogenated fats	MT	10369.6	9618.1	10472.5

Table A-2—Continued

Label	Product/Service	Unit	1968	1969	1970
RIPY	Fresh & pasteurized milk	MT	361767.4	436848.6	474505.3
RJPY	Condensed milk	MT	53555.6	56131.9	55240.4
RKPY	Evaporated milk	MT	14787.2	13137.8	12895.6
RLPY	Powdered milk	MT	2919.9	3554.8	3852.5
RMPY	Cheeses	MT	456.6	377.1	1173.8
RNPY	Butter	MT	1329.9	51.4	243.8
ROPY	Yogurt	MT	11881.2	13816.8	15850.4
RPPY	Ice cream	000GAL	5890.5	6872.4	8255.0
RQPY	Refined vegetable oil	MT	61456.7	57830.4	40445.0
RRPY	Bread	MT	360430.6	376493.8	387417.2
RSPY	Crackers	MT	30254.6	33104.7	29419.8
RTPY	Cookies	MT	5450.1	4707.9	12787.7
RUPY	Pasta	MT	42224.4	45992.5	44519.0
RVPY	Nougats	MT	1031.7	48.6	1067.3
RWPY	Candies	MT	12596.7	11368.2	10986.1
RXPY	Canned fruits & vegetables	MT	73074.1	51660.6	39343.7
RYPY	Roasted coffee	MT	24260.3	25793.4	25763.4
R1PY	Fresh & frozen fish	MT	2659.7	861.3	428.3
R2PY	Fresh & frozen seafood	MT	3173.0	5169.8	5387.4
R3PY	Canned fish & seafood	MT	2985.3	1859.6	2036.9
SAPY	Fish catch	MT	49120.0	58532.0	83840.0
TAPY	Denatured alcohol	000HL	1798.2	1850.7	910.1
TBPY	Anhydrous alcohol	HL	485623.0	267676.0	405286.0
TCPY	Alcoholic bev. (excl. wines)	000HL	168.8	126.8	107.3
TDPY	Wines	000HL	122.5	104.5	107.6
TEPY	Beer	000HL	784.1	658.8	1001.5
TFPY	Malts	000HL	496.3	656.8	524.2
TGPY	Soft drinks	000HL	2091.2	1582.3	871.2
THPY	Mineral water	000HL	1512.1	1445.4	1523.0
TIPY	Cigars	000U	723985.1	422355.5	363529.4
TJPY	Cigarettes	000000U	21756.4	25146.0	19806.4
TKPY	Pipe tobacco	MT	27.6	6.2	12.0
UAPY	Fodder	MT	557936.1	558559.8	594543.8
UBPY	Lamps (industrial use)	U	23243.0	20018.0	10349.0
UCPY	Lamps (household use)	U	59204.0	41577.0	39869.0
VAPY	Unsawn wood (logs)	CM	--	--	--
VBPY	Firewood	000CM	1427.8	1798.0	1456.6
WAPY	Sugarcane	000MT	51403.1	56680.8	75918.0
X1PY	Mangoes	MT	44834.5	9978.1	9056.9
X2PY	Guavas	MT	23992.7	20782.3	14098.3
X3PY	Avocados	MT	16149.9	16491.9	16080.2
X4PY	Papayas	MT	70497.7	35203.6	8584.4
X5PY	Coconuts	MT	23031.9	10884.3	10229.7
X6PY	Coffee	MT	29245.9	31649.7	19742.3
X7PY	Cocoa	MT	1938.5	1233.6	1329.6
X8PY	Tobacco	MT	46414.0	36271.0	31726.2
XAPY	Potatoes	MT	119533.8	95282.7	77334.7
XBPY	Sweet potatoes	MT	91176.5	45936.8	22016.6
XCPY	Malanga	MT	43553.7	35021.8	11988.9
XDPY	Yucca	MT	53354.6	37176.5	21959.9
XEPY	Yams	MT	2207.5	5101.8	2277.7
XFPY	Rice	MT	94938.9	177418.8	290888.3
XGPY	Corn	MT	6823.8	5840.4	3416.6
XHPY	Sweet corn	MT	26330.3	13876.0	13637.7
XIPY	Black beans	MT	6924.5	3748.2	4252.5
XJPY	Red beans	MT	637.3	160.8	125.6
XKPY	Black-eyed peas	MT	1765.5	2071.3	579.9

Table A-2—Continued

Label	Product/Service	Unit	1968	1969	1970
XLPY	Tomatoes	MT	98349.9	44614.4	62412.1
XMPY	Green peppers	MT	1954.9	11781.5	10933.7
XNPY	Onions	MT	18526.7	18568.2	11906.0
XOPY	Garlic	MT	51.7	139.7	276.9
XPPY	Squash	MT	27156.3	14051.4	20654.5
XQPY	Cucumbers	MT	11404.6	8444.7	10581.0
XRPY	Melons	MT	21462.7	7820.8	7219.9
XSPY	Cabbage	MT	15194.2	15136.4	10031.0
XTPY	Oranges	MT	120365.4	108142.8	122278.5
XUPY	Grapefruit	MT	14690.5	12579.8	16859.1
XVPY	Lemons	MT	11715.7	12348.2	8046.3
XWPY	Tangerines	MT	11662.8	11360.6	9184.6
XXPY	Plantains	MT	74561.6	93587.8	40578.0
XYPY	Bananas	MT	25046.1	28504.4	47239.4
XZPY	Pineapple	MT	7214.1	10476.1	14187.4
YAPY	Cattle	MT	360728.7	343189.7	340837.3
YBPY	Pigs	MT	9908.0	4192.3	11924.1
YCPY	Honey	MT	4473.3	4604.2	4480.7
YDPY	Eggs	000U	1205347.0	1288847.0	1402732.2
YEPY	Milk	MT	302102.3	250709.3	214368.9
YFPY	Poultry	MT	25641.4	20488.8	20448.7
AAPA	Housing units	U	6458.0	4817.0	4004.0
ABPA	Cattle barns	U	--	--	20.0
ACPA	Fac. for scholars, students	U	--	--	2.0
ADPA	Water & sewer lines laid	000000CM	--	--	--
AEPA	Farm acreage brough under irrigation	HA	--	--	--
AFPA	Acreage protected against flood	HA	--	--	--
AGPA	Unpaved roads	KM	--	--	1953.7
AHPA	Paved roads	KM	--	--	383.2
BAPA	Passengers transported (rail)	M.PAS-KM	1301.9	1433.8	1130.0
BBPA	Freight transported (rail)	M.MT-KM	1671.7	1485.0	1624.7
CAPA	Passengers transported (road)	000PAS	1508847.2	1556017.7	1547962.7
CBPA	Freight transported (road)	M.MT-KM	612.0	734.4	695.8
DAPA	Passengers transported (maritime)	M.PAS-KM	48.9	48.4	45.5
DBPA	Freight transported (maritime)	M.MT-KM	15309.6	14400.3	19461.6
EAPA	Pass. transp. by natl. airline	M.PAS-KM	330.3	448.2	507.4
EBPA	Freight transp. by natl. airline	M.MT-KM	7.5	9.5	10.9
FAPA	Cargo loaded & unloaded	000000MT	18756.3	19969.7	23442.0
GAPA	Domestic mail sent	000U	58281.2	43792.7	39971.5
GBPA	International mail sent	000U	94.1	88.6	82.4
GCPA	International mail received	000U	77.4	98.6	99.1
GDPA	Telegrams sent	000U	19558.3	22859.1	23087.7
GEPA	Domestic telephone calls	000U	19470.2	21523.0	21213.0
HAPA	Workers in trade sector	000	--	--	--
IAPA	Workers in comm. svces. & housing	000	--	--	--

Table A-2—Continued

Label	Product/Service	Unit	1968	1969	1970
IBPA	Tourists lodged (dom. & intl.)	000	--	--	--
JAPA	Students	U	2197558.0	2214281.0	2311837.0
JBPA	Scholarship students	U	206960.0	234152.0	201795.0
JCPA	Students graduating	U	128042.0	139278.0	131006.0
JDPA	Medical consultations	000	19121.1	21829.8	21504.6
JEPA	Patients admitted	U	963507.0	1033631.0	1073439.0
JFPA	Emerg. rm. & polyclinic consult.	U	7600015.0	7979934.0	7795441.0
JGPA	Immunizations	U	3161754.0	5094622.0	5427771.0
KAPA	Patrons using library services	U	1726.3	1998.8	2161.2
KBPA	Books published	U	13199.5	15776.9	16336.9
KCPA	Newspapers run	000000	--	--	--
KDPA	Domestic radio broadcasting	HRS	--	--	--
KEPA	Artistic performances	U	45190.0	43251.0	25800.0
KFPA	Particip. in organized sports	U	1371606.0	1177375.0	1094317.0
KGPA	Workers in var. soc. activ.	000	--	--	--
LAPA	Workers in public administration	000	--	92.8	88.4
NAPA	Workers in nonprod. activities	000	--	--	--

Label	Product/Service	Unit	1971	1972	1973
AAPY	Electric power	GwH	5021.0	5265.0	5703.4
BAPY	Crude oil	MT	120066.1	112152.7	137768.6
BCPY	Fuel oil	000MT	2375.8	2525.9	2672.9
BDPY	Diesel oil	000MT	657.0	712.9	865.1
BEPY	Liquefied natural gas	MT	57746.0	66929.0	66533.0
BFPY	Gasoline	MT	712081.0	802724.0	911030.0
BGPY	Kerosene	MT	439190.0	441290.0	451583.0
BHPY	Motor oil & lubricants	MT	110700.0	110239.0	118425.0
BIPY	Natural gas	000CM	5811.0	6914.1	14501.8
BJPY	Manufactured gas	000CM	78780.0	81977.0	88099.0
CAPY	Refractory chromium	MT	13885.0	37104.0	37164.0
CBPY	Carbon steel	MT	110802.7	186551.5	220655.0
CCPY	Carbon steel Bars	MT	95331.1	145116.1	189049.8
CDPY	Carbon steel rods	MT	111107.0	162669.6	194395.8
CEPY	Steel forgings	MT	1171.5	749.4	905.6
CFPY	Steel castings	MT	4159.9	4771.4	5460.3
CGPY	Cast-iron pipes (water supply)	MT	7832.7	10031.4	12203.0
CHPY	Cast-iron pipes	MT	1073.8	1637.3	1850.2
CIPY	Iron castings	MT	3052.4	4017.9	4906.6
CJPY	Barbed wire	MT	2018.9	8013.1	9479.8
DAPY	Nickel-cobalt oxide	MT	8893.8	8542.5	6607.0
DBPY	Nickel-cobalt sinter	MT	9106.9	9024.5	10441.0
DCPY	Nickel-cobalt sulfide	MT	18454.6	19222.3	18150.7
DDPY	Copper concentrate	MT	0.0	1827.3	2106.9
DEPY	Aluminum shapes	MT	715.9	1216.7	1936.8
EBPY	Ind. air cond. & refrig. equip.	U	2592.0	2893.0	747.0

Table A-2—Continued

Label	Product/Service	Unit	1971	1972	1973
ECPY	Road levelers	U	105.0	51.0	50.0
EDPY	Road rollers	U	0.0	30.0	20.0
EEPY	Combines for sugarcane harvesting	U	0.0	0.0	0.0
EFPY	Sugarcane carts	U	1606.0	1650.0	3906.0
EGPY	Water pumps	U	4256.0	5742.0	8818.0
EHPY	Gas stoves	U	30010.0	30000.0	40112.0
EIPY	Kerosene stoves	U	25381.0	50800.0	72250.0
EJPY	Buses	U	800.0	575.0	1137.0
EKPY	Fishing boats	U	53.0	87.0	105.0
FAPY	Electrical cables & wire	MT	1144.0	1329.9	1021.9
FBPY	Insul. elec. cables & wires	000M	19893.9	19174.0	32369.0
FCPY	Elec. wire (elec.motors)	MT	53.2	168.4	238.2
FDPY	Telephone wire	000M	7923.6	5192.0	4059.5
FEPY	Household refrigerators	U	20168.0	30097.0	40220.0
FFPY	Automobile batteries	U	90422.0	108340.0	111550.0
FGPY	Household radio receivers	U	12706.0	31283.0	23928.0
FHPY	Television receivers	U	0.0	0.0	0.0
GAPY	Steel structures	MT	1622.9	1447.9	1395.0
GBPY	Stainless steel tanks	U	213.0	351.0	218.0
GCPY	Steel cans	000U	370.6	495.8	500.9
GDPY	Aluminum cans	000U	43800.4	51942.5	52023.9
GEPY	Electrodes (for welding)	MT	1472.8	2041.5	648.2
GFPY	Bottle caps	000GRS	5958.0	8917.9	9970.7
GGPY	Pressure cookers	000U	300.8	350.0	414.4
GHPY	Nails	MT	7125.3	8196.2	6602.6
H1PY	Tire tubes	U	191798.0	206503.0	215428.0
H2PY	Rubber footwear	000PAIR	11209.6	11820.7	8985.1
H3PY	Plastic tubing (for elec. conn.)	000M	5021.5	5242.2	5894.6
H4PY	Matches	000000BX	428.2	457.2	439.6
H5PY	Refined glycerine	MT	1852.7	2138.7	2265.1
HAPY	Iron pyrites	MT	34559.0	71091.1	71850.6
HBPY	Salt	MT	103316.1	102059.8	123781.3
HCPY	Anhydrous ammonia	MT	14057.0	5556.0	24784.0
HDPY	Sulfuric acid (98%)	MT	368261.0	399656.0	384589.0
HEPY	Caustic soda (50%)	MT	3858.0	4318.0	3619.0
HFPY	Oxygen	000CM	5311.0	6400.0	7258.0
HGPY	Acetylene gas	000CM	1289.0	1376.0	1448.0
HHPY	Insecticides	MT	2988.0	3416.0	4424.0
HIPY	Superphosphates	MT	9266.0	38292.0	45008.0
HJPY	Ammonium nitrate	MT	5181.0	1606.0	18570.0
HKPY	Urea	MT	--	--	--
HLPY	Complex fertilizers	MT	24654.0	30.0	323.0
HMPY	Mixed fertilizers	MT	506104.0	582751.0	588395.0
HNPY	Granulated fertilizers	MT	34533.0	37645.0	42527.0
HOPY	Rayon cord	MT	1425.0	1521.0	1268.0
HPPY	Rayon yarn	MT	--	400.0	229.0
HQPY	Oil-base paints	HL	18991.0	28174.0	49583.0
HRPY	Latex & acrylic paints	HL	39178.0	42131.0	82697.0
HSPY	Varnishes	HL	0.0	4610.0	11635.0
HTPY	Enamels	HL	29125.0	24015.0	38722.0
HUPY	Household detergent	MT	15067.5	16664.8	17867.0
HVPY	Laundry soap	MT	40052.7	35324.5	39719.0
HWPY	Hand soap	MT	17181.3	15198.7	15750.5
HXPY	Toothpaste	MT	2404.7	3053.4	3414.6
HYPY	Torula yeast	MT	7323.0	6285.0	6797.0

Table A-2—Continued

Label	Product/Service	Unit	1971	1972	1973
HZPY	Tires	U	251224.0	381086.0	371468.0
IAPY	Bagasse pulp	MT	36047.0	35010.0	43011.0
IBPY	Writing paper	MT	21985.0	24687.0	26880.0
ICPY	Gray cardboard	MT	13473.0	12422.0	14264.0
IDPY	Cardboard for corrugating	MT	10499.0	9987.0	13601.0
IEPY	Kraft cardboard	MT	27722.0	19181.0	24204.0
IFPY	Bristol board	MT	9986.0	9342.0	12287.0
IGPY	Paper bags	000U	177178.0	160453.4	151725.1
IHPY	Corrugated boxes	000U	43300.6	45624.2	49540.1
IIPY	Waxed containers	000U	56913.4	67839.2	71357.3
IJPY	Multilayered paper bags	000U	50493.3	54782.8	69122.8
JAPY	Books	000U	13282.3	21035.4	28817.1
JBPY	Magazines	000U	6401.6	5269.1	4984.6
JCPY	Booklets	000U	6610.6	5774.1	2803.3
JDPY	Notebooks	000U	56112.0	52814.8	76081.6
JEPY	Cigarette labels	000000U	587.3	661.9	916.6
KAPY	Sawn wood	CM	37084.4	38207.4	52677.4
KBPY	Wooden boxes	000U	8541.8	8246.5	9019.0
KCPY	Telephone poles	000CM	1.8	4.0	--
KDPY	Railroad ties	CM	8108.0	17178.0	20610.0
LAPY	Sand	CM	1810.6	2596.	2875.2
LBPY	Crushed stone	CM	4183.6	6107.1	7434.9
LCPY	Cement	000MT	1088.1	1473.7	1757.4
LDPY	Terrazzo tiles	000SM	176.0	369.3	1028.9
LEPY	Floor tiles	000SM	1083.3	1737.1	2118.1
LFPY	Bricks	000U	46060.5	70727.4	64854.5
LGPY	Prefab. concrete blocks	000CM	339.3	581.7	733.5
LHPY	Refractory materials	MT	11625.8	13297.9	14607.9
LIPY	Concrete pipes (water supply)	000M	33.9	58.4	68.3
LJPY	Fiberglass roof panels	000SM	4467.6	5313.1	5202.4
LKPY	Fiberglass pipes (water supply)	000M	116.4	64.0	130.8
LLPY	Cinder blocks	000U	18604.1	27338.7	26513.1
MAPY	Flat glass	000SM	0.0	0.0	111.3
MBPY	Bottles	000000U	155.5	182.1	174.2
MCPY	Medicine vials	000000U	150.1	112.9	92.5
MDPY	Bathroom tiles	000U	25302.7	27862.9	31532.8
MEPY	Bathroom fixtures	000U	100.1	133.2	135.6
NBPY	Cotton textiles	000SM	87112.2	97794.6	117108.7
NCPY	Wool textiles	000SM	19.3	28.7	54.6
NDPY	Rayon textiles	000SM	8139.0	7358.2	6759.9
NEPY	Sisal rope	MT	6317.7	4918.5	6176.7
NFPY	Socks	000U	18566.6	20488.1	20749.4
OAPY	Underwear (incl. infants')	000U	47771.2	51789.2	55095.4
OBPY	Outerwear (incl. infants')	000U	30761.5	35868.3	39418.3
OCPY	Blouses & gowns (excl. infants')	000U	1527.1	1677.5	1767.9
ODPY	Shirts (excl. infants')	000U	9450.6	11099.6	11806.1
OEPY	Pants (excl. infants')	000U	8402.2	9775.8	11767.2
OFPY	Skirts	000U	1423.3	1768.6	1474.5
OGPY	Sweaters (excl. infants')	000U	301.1	343.1	388.2
OHPY	Suits (excl. infants')	000U	44.4	51.8	66.9
OIPY	Dresses (excl. infants')	000U	224.1	285.0	348.1
OJPY	Cotton & rayon bags	000U	14372.1	12760.6	11582.2
OKPY	Kenaf bags	000U	3585.7	3688.5	2441.6
PAPY	Leather	000SM	2924.0	2834.3	2810.5

Table A-2—Continued

Label	Product/Service	Unit	1971	1972	1973
PBPY	Sole leather	MT	3543.4	2900.9	1695.8
PCPY	Cattle hides	000U	977.9	928.0	804.0
PDPY	Leather footwear	000PAIR	14217.4	14390.0	14760.0
QAPY	Raw sugar	000MT	5762.5	4540.5	5188.1
QBPY	Refined sugar	000MT	904.7	705.8	759.7
QCPY	Final syrups	000MT	2207.3	1801.4	1757.1
QDPY	Bagasse for industrial uses	MT	--	217233.0	280769.0
RAPY	Deboned beef	MT	100783.1	99030.4	84567.4
RBPY	Pork	MT	10022.9	11397.8	12935.9
RCPY	Canned meats	MT	11696.6	13461.6	14604.4
RDPY	Fresh poultry	MT	17879.1	--	11706.2
REPY	Wheat flour	MT	175305.4	177565.9	178446.1
RFPY	Lard	MT	411.4	179.5	14.8
RGPY	Tallow	MT	5981.4	6811.6	5715.7
RHPY	Hydrogenated fats	MT	11555.9	12639.7	13214.6
RIPY	Fresh & pasteurized milk	MT	504733.2	528895.0	568639.9
RJPY	Condensed milk	MT	63374.7	35709.7	42856.1
RKPY	Evaporated milk	MT	14531.9	13709.5	15681.9
RLPY	Powdered milk	MT	3822.0	3779.8	4077.4
RMPY	Cheeses	MT	1515.7	1344.6	4329.1
RNPY	Butter	MT	109.8	2781.3	6278.0
ROPY	Yogurt	MT	18352.1	21404.6	23403.4
RPPY	Ice cream	000GAL	12039.2	13137.0	14181.1
RQPY	Refined vegetable oil	MT	56370.7	60185.3	51500.2
RRPY	Bread	MT	388481.4	392975.2	400678.1
RSPY	Crackers	MT	33765.7	36852.2	37770.0
RTPY	Cookies	MT	17268.7	21396.9	22020.0
RUPY	Pasta	MT	48746.5	50913.2	52771.6
RVPY	Nougats	MT	4.8	0.0	0.0
RWPY	Candies	MT	14892.2	16547.0	17247.5
RXPY	Canned fruits & vegetables	MT	57119.2	60511.8	75490.9
RYPY	Roasted coffee	MT	27200.3	26749.7	27191.2
R1PY	Fresh & frozen fish	MT	337.8	403.7	372.5
R2PY	Fresh & frozen seafood	MT	7028.6	8695.2	9345.8
R3PY	Canned fish & seafood	MT	2039.6	1820.4	3155.7
SAPY	Fish catch	MT	94928.0	105319.0	115052.0
TAPY	Denatured alcohol	000HL	663.2	701.8	701.6
TBPY	Anhydrous alcohol	HL	305173.0	353717.0	86560.0
TCPY	Alcoholic bev. (excl. wines)	000HL	263.5	378.4	382.5
TDPY	Wines	000HL	114.3	150.7	135.8
TEPY	Beer	000HL	1308.6	1665.5	1851.3
TFPY	Malts	000HL	558.4	584.1	495.3
TGPY	Soft drinks	000HL	936.7	1572.8	1795.6
THPY	Mineral water	000HL	1578.9	1389.3	1242.0
TIPY	Cigars	000U	277167.7	327033.0	352957.0
TJPY	Cigarettes	000000U	10246.8	11218.4	14971.2
TKPY	Pipe tobacco	MT	0.0	3.0	7.9
UAPY	Fodder	MT	673154.8	718740.3	745147.0
UBPY	Lamps (industrial use)	U	14240.0	16802.0	53982.0
UCPY	Lamps (household use)	U	63861.0	74200.0	173622.0
VAPY	Unsawn wood (logs)	CM	77038.0	79118.0	90916.0
VBPY	Firewood	000CM	1611.2	1697.4	1830.3
WAPY	Sugarcane	000MT	57315.7	50108.0	52005.0
X1PY	Mangoes	MT	33947.3	11494.3	48370.4
X2PY	Guavas	MT	18645.2	21778.9	21863.9
X3PY	Avocados	MT	11838.5	18368.4	18427.8

Table A-2—Continued

Label	Product/Service	Unit	1971	1972	1973
X4PY	Papayas	MT	14640.7	32430.4	37267.5
X5PY	Coconuts	MT	10578.4	12102.9	16784.2
X6PY	Coffee	MT	25986.3	24390.8	21027.7
X7PY	Cocoa	MT	1352.5	1899.9	1743.4
X8PY	Tobacco	MT	24757.2	39551.0	43547.6
XAPY	Potatoes	MT	75239.7	75745.1	55487.0
XBPY	Sweet potatoes	MT	39408.4	65803.9	87346.1
XCPY	Malanga	MT	13516.0	25770.3	19609.4
XDPY	Yucca	MT	26970.7	65449.8	72806.5
XEPY	Yams	MT	1319.8	2560.0	3125.7
XFPY	Rice	MT	285494.9	239063.3	236500.8
XGPY	Corn	MT	6469.9	5682.0	4581.2
XHPY	Sweet corn	MT	22016.9	17270.3	16828.5
XIPY	Black beans	MT	4408.1	5368.2	2221.5
XJPY	Red beans	MT	231.6	142.4	181.1
XKPY	Black-eyed peas	MT	553.9	573.5	395.3
XLPY	Tomatoes	MT	85045.9	57015.7	100579.9
XMPY	Green peppers	MT	7214.0	4812.4	16033.2
XNPY	Onions	MT	10153.5	6127.3	9636.7
XOPY	Garlic	MT	153.1	74.8	90.1
XPPY	Squash	MT	37444.8	30850.6	47993.5
XQPY	Cucumbers	MT	18763.3	22186.1	31060.1
XRPY	Melons	MT	11109.4	15178.7	21354.1
XSPY	Cabbage	MT	19148.4	16743.9	20715.9
XTPY	Oranges	MT	84842.6	110449.6	117047.7
XUPY	Grapefruit	MT	14266.6	19459.1	25475.2
XVPY	Lemons	MT	11348.4	11914.7	15504.6
XWPY	Tangerines	MT	8115.0	10875.9	9891.7
XXPY	Plantains	MT	45386.8	117354.2	111170.4
XYPY	Bananas	MT	56434.8	75164.2	76371.5
XZPY	Pineapple	MT	20817.4	32321.6	30924.3
YAPY	Cattle	MT	324636.0	31035.2	2699.0
YBPY	Pigs	MT	15628.8	17378.7	20872.3
YCPY	Honey	MT	4363.8	5421.8	4366.8
YDPY	Eggs	000U	1472508.1	1509302.4	1585971.7
YEPY	Milk	MT	227722.0	344254.1	379298.0
YFPY	Poultry	MT	23700.1	29759.2	35811.8
AAPA	Housing units	U	5014.0	16807.0	20710.0
ABPA	Cattle barns	U	58.0	218.0	334.0
ACPA	Fac. for scholars, students	U	5.0	43.0	43.0
ADPA	Water & sewer lines laid	000000CM	--	--	--
AEPA	Farm acreage brought under irrigation	HA	--	--	--
AFPA	Acreage protected against flood	HA	--	--	--
AGPA	Unpaved roads	KM	1314.5	1434.3	1511.5
AHPA	Paved roads	KM	481.6	622.6	531.9
BAPA	Passengers transported (rail)	M.PAS-KM	990.1	946.0	609.5
BBPA	Freight transported (rail)	M.MT-KM	1598.3	1503.7	1617.2
CAPA	Passengers transported (road)	000PAS	1685134.8	1771092.1	1872771.1
CBPA	Freight transported (road)	M.MT-KM	522.3	477.0	567.4
DAPA	Passengers transported (maritime)	M.PAS-KM	47.7	47.9	40.3
DBPA	Freight transported (maritime)	M.MT-KM	49614.5	40439.6	40717.8

Table A-2—Continued

Label	Product/Service	Unit	1971	1972	1973
EAPA	Pass. transp. by natl. airline	M.PAS-KM	546.6	563.9	564.5
EBPA	Freight transp. by natl. airline	M.MT-KM	10.8	12.8	15.0
FAPA	Cargo loaded & unloaded	000000MT	22817.3	22429.7	24084.9
GAPA	Domestic mail sent	000U	41599.0	39863.9	38282.8
GBPA	International mail sent	000U	79.2	54.8	40.8
GCPA	International mail received	000U	87.6	78.2	58.3
GDPA	Telegrams sent	000U	22933.0	19664.2	17689.7
GEPA	Domestic telephone calls	000U	21135.2	23744.8	24705.2
HAPA	Workers in trade sector	000	248.3	245.7	261.9
IAPA	Workers in comm. svces. & housing	000	--	--	--
IBPA	Tourists lodged (dom. & intl.)	000	--	--	--
JAPA	Students	U	2440421.0	2665335.0	2838564.0
JBPA	Scholarship students	U	177929.0	200240.0	257768.0
JCPA	Students graduating	U	166627.0	239057.0	312493.0
JDPA	Medical consultations	000	21740.9	23412.9	24127.5
JEPA	Patients admitted	U	1123119.0	1160420.0	1192775.0
JFPA	Emerg. rm. & polyclinic consult.	U	8802859.0	9330569.0	10514281.0
JGPA	Immunizations	U	5009418.0	3675479.0	5447381.0
KAPA	Patrons using library services	U	2505.7	2550.1	2809.8
KBPA	Books published	U	13282.3	21035.3	28817.1
KCPA	Newspapers run	000000	275.5	308.6	312.8
KDPA	Domestic radio broadcasting	HRS	--	--	35511.0
KEPA	Artistic performances	U	25277.0	63710.0	63826.0
KFPA	Particip. in organized sports	U	1214278.0	821017.0	1063813.0
KGPA	Workers in var. soc. activ.	000	--	86.3	98.0
LAPA	Workers in public administration	000	77.8	79.9	95.7
NAPA	Workers in nonprod. activities	000	--	--	--

Label	Product/Service	Unit	1974	1975	1976
AAPY	Electric power	GwH	6019.0	6592.9	7191.4
BAPY	Crude oil	MT	167978.0	226423.9	234849.6
BCPY	Fuel oil	000MT	2769.0	2822.1	2935.6
BDPY	Diesel oil	000MT	974.9	1083.3	961.9
BEPY	Liquefied natural gas	MT	69780.0	83225.0	90312.0
BFPY	Gasoline	MT	868055.0	947114.0	909442.0
BGPY	Kerosene	MT	423859.0	447017.0	453917.0
BHPY	Motor oil & lubricants	MT	136699.0	150957.0	103579.0
BIPY	Natural gas	000CM	19493.9	17247.8	21288.5
BJPY	Manufactured gas	000CM	96785.6	98741.8	109254.3
CBPY	Carbon steel	MT	250291.6	298488.8	250309.6
CCPY	Carbon steel bars	MT	205392.0	242634.7	229601.4
CDPY	Carbon steel rods	MT	215152.2	260590.2	235272.6
CEPY	Steel forgings	MT	1034.1	1197.0	1208.7
CFPY	Steel castings	MT	5949.4	8452.1	7173.0

Table A-2—Continued

Label	Product/Service	Unit	1974	1975	1976
CGPY	Cast-iron pipes (water supply)	MT	14424.0	13426.0	16350.9
CHPY	Cast-iron pipes	MT	1202.0	1760.0	1576.9
CIPY	Iron castings	MT	5290.1	5265.1	9476.5
CHPY	Barbed wire	MT	10990.6	12012.4	10015.5
DAPY	Nickel-cobalt oxide	MT	7464.6	9632.5	8286.0
DBPY	Nickel-cobalt sinter	MT	7466.0	8876.0	10143.5
DCPY	Nickel-cobalt sulfide	MT	18948.1	18818.8	18581.0
DDPY	Copper concentrate	MT	2877.2	2776.5	2897.6
DEPY	Aluminum shapes	MT	1702.6	2017.8	1803.0
EBPY	Ind. air cond. & refrig. equip.	U	4978.0	5675.0	5761.0
ECPY	Road levelers	U	50.0	90.0	283.0
EDPY	Road rollers	U	20.0	25.0	46.0
EEPY	Combines for sugarcane harvesting	U	0.0	0.0	0.0
EFPY	Sugarcane carts	U	3000.0	3600.0	2600.0
EGPY	Water pumps	U	14130.0	14851.0	3672.0
EHPY	Gas stoves	U	45079.0	53627.0	49327.0
EIPY	Kerosene stoves	U	100000.0	104000.0	79000.0
EJPY	Buses	U	1255.0	1718.0	1266.0
EKPY	Fishing boats	U	131.0	137.0	156.0
FAPY	Electrical cables & wire	MT	1164.2	1332.1	975.2
FBPY	Insul. elec. cables & wires	000M	28950.9	27285.8	30272.7
FCPY	Elec. wire (for elec. motors)	MT	223.1	302.6	351.8
FDPY	Telephone wire	000M	4767.0	4635.2	2780.4
FEPY	Household refrigerators	U	42001.0	50012.0	43687.0
FFPY	Automobile batteries	U	126416.0	139856.0	98837.0
FGPY	Household radio receivers	U	42223.0	112635.0	92352.0
FHPY	Television receivers	U	0.0	25600.0	28000.0
GAPY	Steel structures	MT	4129.2	1836.0	2128.9
GBPY	Stainless steel tanks	U	95.0	187.0	314.0
GCPY	Steel cans	000U	647.8	895.2	662.5
GDPY	Aluminum cans	000U	54916.8	52151.0	53028.1
GEPY	Electrodes (for welding)	MT	2291.5	2316.7	1456.1
GFPY	Bottle caps	000GRS	9686.0	9139.0	8954.9
GGPY	Pressure cookers	000U	450.0	415.9	70.2
GHPY	Nails	MT	9197.4	8902.6	5540.9
H1PY	Tire tubes	U	246443.0	255552.0	189874.0
H2PY	Rubber footwear	000PAIR	6267.1	7081.8	6571.0
H3PY	Plastic tubing (for elec. conn.)	000M	6673.8	7478.9	6873.4
H4PY	Matches	000000BX	414.3	424.4	425.1
H5PY	Refined glycerine	MT	2153.0	1941.1	2284.5
HAPY	Iron pyrites	MT	65161.0	72605.0	64241.0
HBPY	Salt	MT	138337.3	156826.1	151185.1
HCPY	Anhydrous ammonia	MT	69297.0	118124.0	96838.0
HDPY	Sulfuric acid (98%)	MT	383772.0	417974.0	391776.0
HEPY	Caustic soda (50%)	MT	4034.0	4027.0	4010.0
HFPY	Oxygen	000CM	7333.8	7877.7	8339.0
HGPY	Acetylene gas	000CM	1605.3	1661.0	1660.7
HHPY	Insecticides	MT	5200.0	5436.0	3591.0
HIPY	Superphosphates	MT	155633.0	43322.0	5070.0
HJPY	Ammonium nitrate	MT	98839.0	207860.0	140220.0
HKPY	Urea	MT	2774.0	3260.0	22661.0
HLPY	Complex fertilizers	MT	71215.0	10420.0	70720.0
HMPY	Mixed fertilizers	MT	585020.0	548300.0	638440.0

Table A-2—Continued

Label	Product/Service	Unit	1974	1975	1976
HNPY	Granulated fertilizers	MT	71820.0	98428.0	88648.0
HOPY	Rayon cord	MT	1674.0	2154.0	1637.0
HPPY	Rayon yarn	MT	336.0	145.0	0.0
HQPY	Oil-base paints	HL	48758.0	74706.0	43726.0
HRPY	Latex & acrylic paints	HL	90025.0	112753.0	70721.0
HSPY	Varnishes	HL	6986.0	7042.0	5914.0
HTPY	Enamels	HL	43091.0	46649.0	39064.0
HUPY	Household detergent	MT	15753.7	22010.1	21868.0
HVPY	Laundry soap	MT	39706.7	40615.6	42818.2
HWPY	Hand soap	MT	17209.7	17794.7	17773.0
HXPY	Toothpaste	MT	3420.6	3651.4	3758.8
HYPY	Torula yeast	MT	8509.0	7955.0	8231.0
HZPY	Tires	U	390810.0	367831.0	266360.0
IAPY	Bagasse pulp	MT	42607.0	36320.0	40947.0
IBPY	Writing paper	MT	28525.0	31967.0	32255.0
ICPY	Gray cardboard	MT	14632.0	15951.0	14794.0
IDPY	Cardboard for corrugating	MT	13829.0	11798.0	14611.0
IEPY	Kraft cardboard	MT	19287.0	10567.0	2716.0
IFPY	Bristol board	MT	11426.0	14104.0	12319.0
IGPY	Paper bags	000U	176298.0	169008.1	195297.6
IHPY	Corrugated boxes	000U	51131.8	69317.3	71007.1
IIPY	Waxed containers	000U	72243.7	80276.6	116565.5
IJPY	Multilayered paper bags	000U	70509.5	70522.6	66401.8
JAPY	Books	000U	30053.8	35208.0	34528.3
JBPY	Magazines	000U	5211.7	5735.1	5532.1
JCPY	Booklets	000U	4798.0	2501.6	3073.8
JDPY	Notebooks	000U	84876.1	91900.0	86698.5
JEPY	Cigarette labels	000000U	812.7	898.2	668.2
KAPY	Sawn wood	CM	50678.0	55482.0	41377.0
KBPY	Wooden boxes	000U	10218.1	12521.7	17415.0
KCPY	Telephone poles	000CM	--	5.3	3.7
KDPY	Railroad ties	CM	20716.0	20441.0	20084.0
LAPY	Sand	CM	3341.2	4204.1	4322.7
LBPY	Crushed stone	CM	7599.2	8919.0	9512.3
LCPY	Cement	000MT	1813.5	2083.1	2501.1
LDPY	Terrazzo tiles	000SM	1787.9	2007.4	2818.9
LEPY	Floor tiles	000SM	2045.2	2223.8	2055.2
LFPY	Bricks	000U	66691.3	76860.8	99942.8
LGPY	Prefab. concrete blocks	000CM	828.0	981.2	919.4
LHPY	Refractory materials	MT	13581.6	11414.4	12552.7
LIPY	Concrete pipes (water supply)	000M	105.6	135.9	118.9
LJPY	Fiberglass roof panels	000SM	5815.5	6619.9	6932.1
LKPY	Fiberglass pipes (water supply)	000M	116.8	147.8	140.2
LLPY	Cinder blocks	000U	30091.1	35853.9	37799.7
MAPY	Flat glass	000SM	402.8	455.7	351.2
MBPY	Bottles	000000U	160.5	201.1	182.6
MCPY	Medicine vials	000000U	103.4	94.1	86.7
MDPY	Bathroom tiles	000U	33336.8	33284.4	35570.6
MEPY	Bathroom fixtures	000U	156.8	160.1	171.1
NBPY	Cotton textiles	000SM	127979.6	137550.1	134062.3
NCPY	Wool textiles	000SM	244.8	360.1	265.5
NDPY	Rayon textiles	000SM	3757.3	6277.8	5117.4
NEPY	Sisal rope	MT	7147.0	7933.2	7036.6
NFPY	Socks	000U	22718.5	24161.4	23812.6
OAPY	Underwear (incl. infants')	000U	62680.6	66881.8	61018.2
OBPY	Outerwear (incl. infants')	000U	43124.1	47438.6	47576.1

Table A-2—Continued

Label	Product/Service	Unit	1974	1975	1976
OCPY	Blouses & gowns (excl. infants')	000U	2034.3	2035.6	2303.4
ODPY	Shirts (excl. infants')	000U	13071.5	15082.1	16036.3
OEPY	Pants (excl. infants')	000U	12466.3	13204.3	13397.4
OFPY	Skirts	000U	2037.7	2582.0	1719.8
OGPY	Sweaters (excl. infants')	000U	466.2	697.3	476.9
OHPY	Suits (excl. infants')	000U	70.0	72.5	76.4
OIPY	Dresses (excl. infants')	000U	317.8	409.8	349.9
OJPY	Cotton & rayon bags	000U	11048.0	12389.7	10026.8
OKPY	Kenaf bags	000U	3035.4	6923.0	7144.5
PAPY	Leather	000SM	2557.7	2087.7	2703.8
PBPY	Sole leather	MT	1879.8	2002.6	2137.6
PCPY	Cattle hides	000U	716.3	659.2	731.7
PDPY	Leather footwear	000PAIR	13512.4	15513.3	14979.0
QAPY	Raw sugar	000MT	5700.6	6193.1	5917.6
QBPY	Refined sugar	000MT	688.3	655.1	700.1
QCPY	Final syrups	000MT	2144.0	1181.2	1880.2
QDPY	Bagasse for industrial uses	MT	321861.0	327557.0	293772.0
RAPY	Deboned beef	MT	69789.0	67697.5	80523.6
RBPY	Pork	MT	18957.9	24211.6	29105.5
RCPY	Canned meats	MT	19162.9	26278.6	29014.7
RDPY	Fresh poultry	MT	11854.9	13471.8	18406.6
REPY	Wheat flour	MT	184331.1	176065.4	165351.2
RFPY	Lard	MT	244.7	240.2	1124.4
RGPY	Tallow	MT	5008.0	4458.1	5198.6
RHPY	Hydrogenated fats	MT	13471.3	14489.6	13619.1
RIPY	Fresh & pasteurized milk	MT	593797.6	611478.3	621369.8
RJPY	Condensed milk	MT	42688.3	46206.3	46520.7
RKPY	Evaporated milk	MT	14627.2	15911.4	15551.6
RLPY	Powdered milk	MT	2875.6	3459.4	2495.3
RMPY	Cheeses	MT	3937.4	6748.3	6978.0
RNPY	Butter	MT	6738.3	7800.9	5275.7
ROPY	Yogurt	MT	27108.6	40068.8	40636.5
RPPY	Ice cream	000GAL	14097.1	16266.7	17455.5
RQPY	Refined vegetable oil	MT	56672.3	59059.6	46332.5
RRPY	Bread	MT	409403.9	417185.5	421503.2
RSPY	Crackers	MT	39231.6	41820.8	43513.3
RTPY	Cookies	MT	21565.0	22178.2	21690.5
RUPY	Pasta	MT	52324.1	53246.6	52058.9
RVPY	Nougats	MT	0.0	0.0	0.0
RWPY	Candies	MT	17398.4	20271.9	21915.2
RXPY	Canned fruits & vegetables	MT	86727.6	98341.0	103327.6
RYPY	Roasted coffee	MT	27732.5	28411.6	23695.3
R1PY	Fresh & frozen fish	MT	554.2	702.1	1799.9
R2PY	Fresh & frozen seafood	MT	12356.1	10970.4	10163.3
R3PY	Canned fish & seafood	MT	2765.0	2547.4	2536.6
SAPY	Fish catch	MT	117460.0	100258.0	145122.0
TAPY	Denatured alcohol	000HL	708.0	670.5	686.1
TBPY	Anhydrous alcohol	HL	210831.0	96166.0	204656.1
TCPY	Alcoholic bev. (excl. wines)	000HL	327.8	419.6	320.3
TDPY	Wines	000HL	141.1	78.2	125.1
TEPY	Beer	000HL	1808.3	2110.7	2169.2
TFPY	Malts	000HL	477.5	420.3	371.8
TGPY	Soft drinks	000HL	1710.2	1569.6	1500.6
THPY	Mineral water	000HL	550.6	391.5	398.8
TIPY	Cigars	000U	374237.6	383264.0	360954.3

Table A-2—Continued

Label	Product/Service	Unit	1974	1975	1976
TJPY	Cigarettes	000000U	14531.9	15366.4	14759.6
TKPY	Pipe tobacco	MT	4.8	8.7	21.7
UAPY	Fodder	MT	890895.1	1001027.2	1095580.8
UBPY	Lamps (industrial use)	U	85400.0	121200.0	86000.0
UCPY	Lamps (household use)	U	96700.0	69120.0	74200.0
VAPY	Unsawn wood (logs)	CM	100154.0	108022.0	90519.0
VBPY	Firewood	000CM	1699.020	1688.6	2048.7
WAPY	Sugarcane	000MT	53635.4	55663.5	56828.2
X1PY	Mangoes	MT	60133.0	48874.5	46184.8
X2PY	Guavas	MT	23329.7	24422.5	30408.6
X3PY	Avocados	MT	20558.1	23359.2	21181.2
X4PY	Papayas	MT	45072.8	51071.4	75006.3
X5PY	Coconuts	MT	14180.9	14495.3	7884.9
X6PY	Coffee	MT	28794.6	17473.7	19045.3
X7PY	Cocoa	MT	1355.6	1246.0	1487.5
X8PY	Tobacco	MT	44685.1	41430.2	50714.2
XAPY	Potatoes	MT	87831.4	116738.2	145084.6
XBPY	Sweet potatoes	MT	83662.6	89846.8	78564.6
XCPY	Malanga	MT	25519.2	32517.1	45169.5
XDPY	Yucca	MT	67948.2	82478.6	84336.3
XEPY	Yams	MT	4041.3	7008.4	9592.3
XFPY	Rice	MT	309247.6	338030.5	335080.7
XGPY	Corn	MT	4727.7	3227.9	4079.0
XHPY	Sweet corn	MT	20177.7	17224.8	11656.8
XIPY	Black beans	MT	2384.6	3009.7	2455.1
XJPY	Red beans	MT	93.1	140.4	119.7
XKPY	Black-eyed peas	MT	384.7	652.4	307.1
XLPY	Tomatoes	MT	183475.0	184068.7	193923.6
XMPY	Green peppers	MT	22246.0	24357.5	29424.6
XNPY	Onions	MT	9991.3	9491.4	15057.5
XOPY	Garlic	MT	130.7	73.7	91.7
XPPY	Squash	MT	51009.7	73489.9	36572.1
XQPY	Cucumbers	MT	29420.8	39653.4	29261.8
XRPY	Melons	MT	31445.4	51925.8	34545.1
XSPY	Cabbage	MT	21543.1	23208.1	32678.5
XTPY	Oranges	MT	109381.1	126519.4	123987.7
XUPY	Grapefruit	MT	30685.6	25128.1	33797.3
XVPY	Lemons	MT	16630.5	14028.6	14633.6
XWPY	Tangerines	MT	11651.6	10154.7	17792.1
XXPY	Plantains	MT	102187.7	95208.4	106953.2
XYPY	Bananas	MT	84964.8	109921.4	131300.1
XZPY	Pineapple	MT	30154.6	22157.0	21416.4
YAPY	Cattle	MT	227765.5	218817.9	262073.9
YBPY	Pigs	MT	30504.6	38362.6	46315.4
YCPY	Honey	MT	6766.0	6497.4	6522.1
YDPY	Eggs	000U	1684299.2	1748893.5	1698465.6
YEPY	Milk	MT	420919.2	454292.0	527629.6
YFPY	Poultry	MT	45423.7	55914.5	62018.2
AAPA	Housing units	U	18552.0	18602.0	15342.0
ABPA	Cattle barns	U	305.0	270.0	152.0
ACPA	Fac. for scholars, students	U	63.0	68.0	110.0
ADPA	Water & sewer lines laid	000000CM	--	--	--
AEPA	Farm acreage brought under irrigation	HA	--	--	--
AFPA	Acreage protected against flood	HA	--	--	--
AGPA	Unpaved roads	KM	1404.3	1078.1	1032.0
AHPA	Paved roads	KM	639.4	804.2	673.2

Table A-2—Continued

Label	Product/Service	Unit	1974	1975	1976
BAPA	Passengers transported (rail)	M.PAS-KM	635.8	667.8	766.7
BBPA	Freight transported (rail)	M.MT-KM	1654.4	1765.8	1848.5
CAPA	Passengers transported (road)	000PAS	1940189.7	2172596.6	2327067.3
CBPA	Freight transported (road)	M.MT-KM	680.7	919.6	1188.4
DAPA	Passengers transported (maritime)	M.PAS-KM	50.7	75.5	90.6
DBPA	Freight transported (maritime)	M.MT-KM	48101.3	55799.3	41023.6
EAPA	Pass. transp. by natl. airline	M.PAS-KM	556.7	579.5	775.3
EBPA	Freight transp. by natl. airline	M.MT-KM	13.3	16.4	18.8
FAPA	Cargo loaded & unloaded	000000MT	25067.8	26445.2	25945.9
GAPA	Domestic mail sent	000U	40291.8	47714.7	55452.9
GBPA	International mail sent	000U	32.8	30.2	35.8
GCPA	International mail received	000U	55.9	52.9	63.9
GDPA	Telegrams sent	000U	16412.6	15943.3	15453.9
GEPA	Domestic telephone calls	000U	26212.6	31642.0	38375.3
HAPA	Workers in trade sector	000	272.7	256.6	265.3
IAPA	Workers in comm. svces. & housing	000	--	--	--
IBPA	Tourists lodged (dom. & intl.)	000	--	--	--
JAPA	Students	U	2964118.0	3267473.0	3547995.0
JBPA	Scholarship students	U	314543.0	382153.0	501915.0
JCPA	Students graduating	U	404344.0	507834.0	703611.0
JDPA	Medical consultations	000	24603.1	25505.3	25650.7
JEPA	Patients admitted	U	1213467.0	1249798.0	1214424.0
JFPA	Emerg. rm. & polyclinic consult.	U	11446051.0	12356513.0	12254287.0
JGPA	Immunizations	U	5698715.0	5987693.0	4636908.0
KAPA	Patrons using library services	U	2995.6	4127.9	4950.9
KBPA	Books published	U	29053.6	35208.0	35128.2
KCPA	Newspapers run	000000	310.9	330.6	353.3
KDPA	Domestic radio broadcasting	HRS	35927.0	37348.0	35914.0
KEPA	Artistic performances	U	49674.0	30029.0	41830.0
KFPA	Particip. in organized sports	U	1303734.0	1673049.0	2121754.0
KGPA	Workers in var. soc. activ.	000	105.6	101.4	103.2
LAPA	Workers in public administration	000	113.5	125.7	135.6
NAPA	Workers in nonprod. activities	000	--	--	--

Label	Product/Service	Unit	1977	1978	1979
AAPY	Electric power	GwH	7706.9	8481.3	9403.1

Table A-2—Continued

Label	Product/Service	Unit	1977	1978	1979
BAPY	Crude oil	MT	256385.9	288390.4	288200.0
BCPY	Fuel oil	000MT	3209.6	3100.6	3213.2
BDPY	Diesel oil	000MT	995.7	1083.1	1094.3
BEPY	Liquefied natural gas	MT	96862.0	101664.0	92172.0
BFPY	Gasoline	MT	833316.0	886749.0	872038.9
BGPY	Kerosen	MT	415592.0	426878.0	414636.0
BHPY	Motor oil & lubricants	MT	120138.0	126452.0	132902.0
BIPY	Natural gas	000CM	16972.7	10584.2	17531.3
BJPY	Manufactured gas	000CM	116331.6	124425.8	132586.6
CAPY	Refractory chromium	MT	20354.0	28776.0	28200.0
CBPY	Carbon steel	MT	330478.5	323561.7	327792.1
CCPY	Carbon steel bars	MT	292441.3	292755.3	313505.2
CDPY	Carbon steel rods	MT	289161.4	263138.4	303286.5
CEPY	Steel forgings	MT	1365.4	1971.9	2608.0
CFPY	Steel castings	MT	8252.4	6900.6	6986.5
CGPY	Cast-iron pipes (water supply)	MT	18957.2	18350.6	18108.0
CHPY	Cast-iron pipes	MT	1671.4	1985.7	1704.6
CIPY	Iron castings	MT	11426.6	11852.4	17768.3
CJPY	Barbed wire	MT	9785.1	7884.3	7876.6
DAPY	Nickel-cobalt oxide	MT	8996.8	8735.3	8189.9
DBPY	Nickel-cobalt sinter	MT	9629.1	9572.2	10861.9
DCPY	Nickel-cobalt sulfide	MT	18124.1	16479.3	13272.20
DDPY	Copper concentrate	MT	2582.9	2820.9	2839.9
DEPY	Aluminum shapes	MT	1157.8	1266.0	1455.8
EBPY	Ind. air cond. & refrig. equip.	U	3306.0	3568.0	3733.0
ECPY	Road levelers	U	0.0	100.0	140.0
EDPY	Road rollers	U	5.0	13.0	27.0
EEPY	Combines for sugarcane harvesting	U	30.0	165.0	360.0
EFPY	Sugarcane carts	U	3000.0	3000.0	3900.0
EGPY	Water pumps	U	1201.0	511.0	585.0
EHPY	Gas stoves	U	51717.0	51233.0	35652.0
EIPY	Kerosene stoves	U	102465.0	73272.0	107127.0
EJPY	Buses	U	1970.0	1805.0	2440.0
EKPY	Fishing boats	U	152.0	139.0	93.0
FAPY	Electrical cables & wire	MT	656.5	1387.5	2362.1
FBPY	Insul. elec. cables & wires	000M	21356.2	26313.2	42046.3
FCPY	Elec. wire (for elec. motors)	MT	153.8	193.7	373.1
FDPY	Telephone wire	000M	3657.8	3107.6	3753.2
FEPY	Household refrigerators	U	45000.0	45050.0	55000.0
FFPY	Automobile batteries	U	97397.0	136576.0	172000.0
FGPY	Household radio receivers	U	120005.0	120628.0	143273.0
FHPY	Television receivers	U	33000.0	51166.0	52414.0
GAPY	Steel structures	MT	8930.7	19210.1	24919.6
GBPY	Stainless steel tanks	U	193.0	295.0	68.0
GCPY	Steel cans	000U	787.5	663.0	749.2
GDPY	Aluminum cans	000U	53099.3	59300.3	39187.2
GEPY	Electrodes (for welding)	MT	2188.0	2404.4	2399.6
GFPY	Bottle caps	000GRS	8374.7	8145.9	9085.0
GGPY	Pressure cookers	000U	33.7	123.8	6.3
GFPY	Nails	MT	6803.7	7645.3	7411.6
H1PY	Tire tubes	U	150783.0	221043.0	193089.0
H2PY	Rubber footwear	000PAIR	2450.9	3038.0	2538.0
H3PY	Plastic tubing (for elec. conn.)	000M	7591.5	7090.3	6143.8
H4PY	Matches	000000BX	430.8	414.0	370.5

Table A-2—Continued

Label	Product/Service	Unit	1977	1978	1979
H5PY	Refined glycerine	MT	2027.0	1768.2	1822.8
HAPY	Iron pyrites	MT	81674.1	53715.208	28932.8
HBPY	Salt	MT	129454.4	130606.9	122487.3
HCPY	Anhydrous ammonia	MT	70001.0	47321.4	188745.4
HDPY	Sulfuric acid (98%)	MT	374834.0	346544.4	296538.8
HEPY	Caustic soda (50%)	MT	4706.0	4896.6	4463.5
HFPY	Oxygen	000CM	8633.4	10218.9	10690.4
HGPY	Acetylene gas	000CM	1642.6	1922.2	2274.4
HHPY	Insecticides	MT	2660.0	3013.0	4414.0
HIPY	Superphosphates	MT	9810.0	32399.0	14184.0
HJPY	Ammonium nitrate	MT	97225.0	69717.0	362851.0
HKPY	Urea	MT	16112.0	6946.0	21599.0
HLPY	Complex fertilizers	MT	59689.0	48715.4	72563.6
HMPY	Mixed fertilizers	MT	711896.0	796481.4	712899.6
HNPY	Granulated fertilizers	MT	91536.0	100269.5	87319.0
HOPY	Rayon cord	MT	440.0	1415.0	1586.1
HPPY	Rayon yarn	MT	257.0	297.0	0.0
HQPY	Oil-base paints	HL	31389.0	31600.0	47273.0
HRPY	Latex & acrylic paints	HL	73500.0	71100.0	71572.0
HSPY	Varnishes	HL	5523.0	5420.0	6834.0
HTPY	Enamels	HL	28930.0	25250.0	34797.0
HUPY	Household detergent	MT	16840.4	21308.4	15549.2
HVPY	Laundry soap	MT	34782.2	38166.8	34503.1
HWPY	Hand soap	MT	16207.0	17774.5	17154.2
HXPY	Toothpaste	MT	3637.1	4678.1	2932.8
HYPY	Torula yeast	MT	11165.0	21164.0	37661.0
HZPY	Tires	U	171949.0	294514.0	301954.0
IAPY	Bagasse pulp	MT	37537.0	33924.0	29500.0
IBPY	Writing paper	MT	31276.0	35643.0	34854.0
ICPY	Gray cardboard	MT	13545.0	15704.0	12322.0
IDPY	Cardboard for corrugating	MT	15303.0	14480.0	13151.0
IEPY	Kraft cardboard	MT	--	853.0	--
IFPY	Bristol board	MT	10283.0	10579.0	12872.0
IGPY	Paper bags	000U	184793.3	175248.3	155649.7
IHPY	Corrugated boxes	000U	67990.9	71352.4	74477.3
IIPY	Waxed containers	000U	94722.2	67979.6	43218.5
IJPY	Multilayered paper bags	000U	67400.0	76414.0	69749.8
JAPY	Books	000U	29766.5	46655.5	43712.4
JBPY	Magazines	000U	61337.1	62139.2	102321.5
JCPY	Booklets	000U	20410.2	15593.2	16974.4
JDPY	Notebooks	000U	98367.9	96159.5	90178.8
JEPY	Cigarette labels	000000U	768.1	811.4	904.7
KAPY	Sawn wood	CM	67965.0	73182.0	75286.0
KBPY	Wooden boxes	000U	9334.8	6968.2	6346.0
KCPY	Telephone poles	000CM	--	--	--
KDPY	Railroad ties	CM	19627.0	19909.0	25456.0
LAPY	Sand	CM	4233.4	4678.4	4496.8
LBPY	Crushed stone	CM	9682.5	9984.9	10500.8
LCPY	Cement	000MT	2656.3	2711.7	2612.8
LDPY	Terrazzo tiles	000SM	2256.4	2255.9	2274.6
LEPY	Floor tiles	000SM	2383.1	2519.2	2449.0
LFPY	Bricks	000U	113361.3	115426.4	115133.3
LGPY	Prefab. concrete blocks	000CM	915.1	893.6	883.2
LHPY	Refractory materials	MT	17412.6	17073.9	16316.9
LIPY	Concrete pipes (water supply)	000M	139.0	140.1	170.8
LJPY	Fiberglass roof panels	000SM	6238.7	5814.6	6040.3
LKPY	Fiberglass pipes (water supply)	000M	130.3	491.3	983.6

Table A-2—Continued

Label	Product/Service	Unit	1977	1978	1979
LLPY	Cinder blocks	000U	45119.2	48189.6	46079.7
MAPY	Flat glass	000SM	407.6	334.7	293.3
MBPY	Bottles	000000U	165.7	228.9	183.9
MCPY	Medicine vials	000000U	58.1	90.0	109.2
MDPY	Bathroom tiles	000U	29978.2	45373.4	59075.2
MEPY	Bathroom fixtures	000U	214.2	245.2	231.2
NBPY	Cotton textiles	000SM	148860.7	154404.3	148649.4
NCPY	Wool textiles	000SM	331.1	322.0	290.4
NDPY	Rayon textiles	000SM	2656.1	1529.0	1526.9
NEPY	Sisal rope	MT	6105.5	6144.0	5518.3
NFPY	Socks	000U	24892.9	26911.4	27073.4
OAPY	Underwear (incl. infants')	000U	58378.6	66754.5	66422.4
OBPY	Outerwear (incl. infants')	000U	45966.2	50444.4	51264.0
OCPY	Blouses & gowns (excl. infants')	000U	2328.5	2635.5	2183.3
ODPY	Shirts (excl. infants')	000U	16026.1	16600.0	16900.0
OEPY	Pants (excl. infants')	000U	13531.7	13971.0	14616.7
OFPY	Skirts	000U	2505.5	2396.7	2250.7
OGPY	Sweaters (excl. infants')	000U	428.2	114.0	325.5
OHPY	Suits (excl. infants')	000U	76.8	47.6	42.8
OIPY	Dresses (excl. infants')	000U	468.6	521.3	399.7
OJPY	Cotton & rayon bags	000U	9955.5	13758.4	10997.4
OKPY	Kenaf bags	000U	7561.5	9803.1	8680.8
PAPY	Leather	000SM	2637.1	3217.3	2925.2
PBPY	Sole leather	MT	1482.3	1908.4	1927.2
PCPY	Cattle hides	000U	845.7	1228.3	1238.6
PDPY	Leather footwear	000PAIR	12448.5	14685.4	13758.5
QAPY	Raw sugar	000MT	6705.1	7427.1	7515.1
QBPY	Refined sugar	000MT	742.5	860.6	898.7
QCPY	Final syrups	000MT	2171.0	2336.0	2474.5
QDPY	Bagasse for industrial uses	MT	330841.0	362773.0	358542.0
RAPY	Deboned beef	MT	87504.1	83386.5	78752.5
RBPY	Pork	MT	33707.0	34980.1	34027.8
RCPY	Canned meats	MT	31740.5	31124.1	30483.8
RDPY	Fresh poultry	MT	20385.5	19775.2	29184.1
REPY	Wheat flour	MT	176361.8	174928.9	169524.4
RFPY	Lard	MT	1394.3	1314.1	884.5
RGPY	Tallow	MT	5533.8	5276.2	4940.1
RHPY	Hydrogenated fats	MT	16119.7	16189.0	16423.7
RIPY	Fresh & pasteurized milk	MT	642465.4	651896.3	653742.3
RJPY	Condensed milk	MT	48185.4	43080.1	37102.4
RKPY	Evaporated milk	MT	14991.1	19854.7	28128.4
RLPY	Powdered milk	MT	2549.2	2278.3	2376.6
RMPY	Cheeses	MT	10123.0	8557.5	10054.5
RNPY	Butter	MT	6155.1	11465.9	10937.8
ROPY	Yogurt	MT	44461.8	43147.1	48449.7
RPPY	Ice cream	000GAL	17843.1	18851.0	18837.6
RQPY	Refined vegetable oil	MT	59735.4	52664.5	62683.1
RRPY	Bread	MT	429247.0	444063.5	441200.0
RSPY	Crackers	MT	42667.8	42014.1	40627.7
RTPY	Cookies	MT	20540.9	23631.1	22933.5
RUPY	Pasta	MT	51822.4	51672.0	52774.6
RVPY	Nougats	MT	1.3	--	--
RWPY	Candies	MT	22288.7	25142.6	21608.9
RXPY	Canned fruits & vegetables	MT	103372.6	99672.7	101846.0

Table A-2—Continued

Label	Product/Service	Unit	1977	1978	1979
RYPY	Roasted coffee	MT	15503.3	15984.6	14198.9
R1PY	Fresh & frozen fish	MT	13485.7	21726.8	11397.9
R2PY	Fresh & frozen seafood	MT	10043.0	11743.8	10571.2
R3PY	Canned fish & seafood	MT	2311.0	2293.9	1802.3
SAPY	Fish catch	MT	135420.0	162469.0	104788.0
TAPY	Denatured alcohol	000HL	770.7	772.9	802.1
TBPY	Anhydrous alcohol	HL	203740.0	564337.0	458249.2
TCPY	Alcoholic bev. (excl. wines)	000HL	284.3	319.4	358.8
TDPY	Wines	000HL	134.6	136.9	137.4
TEPY	Beer	000HL	2199.2	2338.3	2306.8
TFPY	Malts	000HL	279.8	179.9	221.0
TGPY	Soft drinks	000HL	1062.3	1249.6	1339.2
THPY	Mineral water	000HL	394.2	510.4	468.6
TIPY	Cigars	000U	352577.0	354214.4	295156.2
TJPY	Cigarettes	000000U	15880.5	16908.2	17376.5
TKPY	Pipe tobacco	MT	10.2	3.4	4.9
UAPY	Fodder	MT	1123643.0	1256317.9	1264259.7
UBPY	Lamps (industrial use)	U	60800.0	77900.0	36900.0
UCPY	Lamps (household use)	U	91600.0	81600.0	44300.0
VAPY	Unsawn wood (logs)	CM	97572.0	114421.0	120208.0
VBPY	Firewood	000CM	2338.9	2300.4	2486.7
WAPY	Sugarcane	000MT	65058.7	74942.0	75521.0
X1PY	Mangoes	MT	52181.0	19331.7	68773.4
X2PY	Guavas	MT	28795.1	31648.5	43491.0
X3PY	Avocados	MT	15953.0	24389.3	14100.6
X4PY	Papayas	MT	61845.9	49525.4	24222.6
X5PY	Coconuts	MT	11676.0	12204.4	13645.7
X6PY	Coffee	MT	15730.9	13368.9	22306.0
X7PY	Cocoa	MT	1285.5	1620.6	1408.3
X8PY	Tobacco	MT	42166.8	40364.4	33052.9
XAPY	Potatoes	MT	136985.4	173696.6	172152.7
XBPY	Sweet potatoes	MT	61606.9	54302.6	79202.2
XCPY	Malanga	MT	59304.2	117435.2	102170.3
XDPY	Yucca	MT	82850.6	85542.0	72155.5
XEPY	Yams	MT	8164.7	6415.2	8562.6
XFPY	Rice	MT	334176.6	344124.2	311835.0
XGPY	Corn	MT	1814.4	2402.0	2261.9
XHPY	Sweet corn	MT	11198.6	11118.6	9801.6
XIPY	Black beans	MT	1730.9	1777.6	1848.7
XJPY	Red beans	MT	54.2	76.1	161.0
XKPY	Black-eyed peas	MT	392.0	455.4	426.9
XLPY	Tomatoes	MT	145766.3	131778.1	157305.4
XMPY	Green peppers	MT	20606.3	31098.7	29812.5
XNPY	Onions	MT	8638.4	7831.5	9351.5
XOPY	Garlic	MT	7.5	36.5	50.8
XPPY	Squash	MT	25250.1	30981.8	24804.6
XQPY	Cucumbers	MT	24173.0	26847.8	24371.0
XRPY	Melons	MT	29177.7	26022.3	33121.7
XSPY	Cabbage	MT	14911.7	19143.4	10935.9
XTPY	Oranges	MT	131748.9	141418.3	136093.9
XUPY	Grapefruit	MT	11389.7	14251.8	12990.6
XVPY	Lemons	MT	13899.7	12068.9	15014.9
XWPY	Tangerines	MT	12817.6	22661.7	20665.7
XXPY	Plantains	MT	81135.8	91380.1	76570.3
XYPY	Bananas	MT	133662.3	149139.8	137777.2
XZPY	Pineapple	MT	17225.4	18097.1	14378.7
YAPY	Cattle	MT	269108.3	279858.9	266517.6
YBPY	Pigs	MT	52307.7	56034.3	55985.2
YCPY	Honey	MT	1345.1	640.6	538.4

Table A-2—Continued

Label	Product/Service	Unit	1977	1978	1979
YDPY	Eggs	000U	2241159.6	1721284.8	1831880.8
YEPY	Milk	MT	562278.4	609495.2	610669.3
YFPY	Poultry	MT	62780.3	57440.5	63785.3
AAPA	Housing units	U	20024.0	17072.0	14523.0
ABPA	Cattle barns	U	115.0	69.0	131.0
ACPA	Fac. for scholars, students	U	90.0	52.0	24.0
ADPA	Water & sewer lines laid	000000CM	724.1	690.0	646.2
AEPA	Farm acreage brought under irrigation	HA	72451.0	62924.0	87574.5
AFPA	Acreage protected against flood	HA	10906.0	3550.0	21346.0
AGPA	Unpaved roads	KM	1074.9	450.9	1215.8
AHPA	Paved roads	KM	1088.2	914.3	544.3
BAPA	Passengers transported (rail)	M.PAS-KM	1075.9	1571.5	1635.6
BBPA	Freight transported (rail)	M.MT-KM	2020.7	1904.4	2076.1
CAPA	Passengers transported (road)	000PAS	2195566.6	2218035.1	2201190.8
CBPA	Freight transported (road)	M.MT-KM	1188.6	1364.7	1399.7
DAPA	Passengers transported (maritime)	M.PAS-KM	91.9	82.7	74.9
DBPA	Freight transported (maritime)	M.MT-KM	45752.8	47945.7	54103.9
EAPA	Pass. transp. by natl. airline	M.PAS-KM	984.5	1161.0	1342.2
EBPA	Freight transp. by natl. airline	M.MT-KM	14.0	14.7	15.8
FAPA	Cargo loaded & unloaded	000000MT	28231.4	30293.4	33736.4
GAPA	Domestic mail sent	000U	73330.6	72265.5	70403.4
GBPA	International mail sent	000U	31.6	36.1	40.3
GCPA	International mail received	000U	58.7	57.1	53.7
GDPA	Telegrams sent	000U	15371.9	15441.8	15592.5
GEPA	Domestic telephone calls	000U	39494.9	44714.2	53558.9
HAPA	Workers in trade sector	000	281.6	296.1	303.8
IAPA	Workers in comm. svces. & housing	000	58.9	85.9	92.9
IBPA	Tourists lodged (dom. & intl.)	000	10819.6	11178.6	8040.8
JAPA	Students	U	3564435.0	3494859.0	3378282.0
JBPA	Scholarship students	U	550526.0	569382.0	582782.0
JCPA	Students graduating	U	722156.0	694889.0	725044.0
JDPA	Medical consultations	000	26846.3	28676.9	28803.8
JEPA	Patients admitted	U	1200248.0	1224988.0	1202657.0
JFPA	Emerg. rm. & polyclinic consult.	U	13475695.0	14182947.0	14400452.0
JGPA	Immunizations	U	3386705.0	4670019.0	4585796.0
KAPA	Patrons using library services	U	4854.8	5259.2	5326.9
KBPA	Books published	U	28743.8	33028.8	33611.7
KCPA	Newspapers run	000000	354.6	356.0	357.4
KDPA	Domestic radio broadcasting	HRS	42276.0	43056.0	48217.0
KEPA	Artistic performances	U	45410.0	32049.0	37898.0

158   Appendix A

Table A-2—Continued

Label	Product/Service	Unit	1977	1978	1979
KFPA	Particip. in organized sports	U	2206143.0	2294209.0	2354343.0
KGPA	Workers in var. soc. activ.	000	109.6	117.5	120.8
LAPA	Workers in public administration	000	134.1	140.4	150.5
NAPA	Workers in nonprod. activities	000	6.0	19.0	19.0

Label	Product/Service	Unit	1980	1981	1982
AAPY	Electric power	GwH	9895.5	10559.0	11069.7
BAPY	Crude oil	MT	273600.0	253200.0	541000.0
BCPY	Fuel oil	000MT	3025.6	3130.4	3197.8
BDPY	Diesel oil	000MT	1098.7	1118.1	1117.5
BEPY	Liquefied natural gas	MT	106800.0	103500.0	111500.0
BFPY	Gasoline	MT	807300.0	929200.0	846700.0
BGPY	Kerosene	MT	438000.0	428600.0	456700.0
BHPY	Motor oil & lubricants	MT	136845.0	119800.0	143200.0
BIPY	Natural gas	000CM	17755.1	13300.0	10700.0
BJPY	Manufactured gas	000CM	136016.3	138800.0	132800.0
CAPY	Refractory chromium	MT	28457.0	20500.0	27300.0
CBPY	Carbon steel	MT	303836.7	329700.0	301200.0
CCPY	Carbon steel bars	MT	260165.7	275000.0	203600.0
CDPY	Carbon steel rods	MT	248164.4	285500.0	254600.0
CEPY	Steel forgings	MT	1179.6	1351.8	1687.6
CFPY	Steel castings	MT	7035.1	10291.4	9630.8
CGPY	Cast-iron pipes (water supply)	MT	20460.9	19200.0	17400.0
CHPY	Cast-iron pipes	MT	1772.6	2402.4	2180.6
CIPY	Iron castings	MT	25239.7	24600.0	38500.0
CJPY	Barbed wire	MT	8234.1	7800.0	8700.0
DAPY	Nickel-cobalt oxide	MT	8019.2	8587.1	9107.4
DBPY	Nickel-cobalt sinter	MT	12000.9	12262.9	11894.3
DCPY	Nickel-cobalt sulfide	MT	18186.9	19409.9	16601.3
DDPY	Copper concentrate	MT	3304.8	2907.5	2645.2
DEPY	Aluminum shapes	MT	1995.6	3019.7	2915.6
EBPY	Ind. air cond. & refrig. equip.	U	1803.0	4870.0	4663.0
ECPY	Road levelers	U	0.0	81.0	2.0
EDPY	Road rollers	U	20.0	0.0	0.0
EEPY	Combines for sugarcane harvesting	U	501.0	605.0	602.0
EFPY	Sugarcane carts	U	3410.0	3207.0	3100.0
EGPY	Water pumps	U	3415.0	7249.0	6669.0
EHPY	Gas stoves	U	6852.0	21008.0	14702.0
EIPY	Kerosene stoves	U	107067.0	139500.0	124600.0
EJPY	Buses	U	1846.0	1665.0	1602.0
EKPY	Fishing boats	U	120.0	86.0	76.0
FAPY	Electrical cables & wire	MT	2547.2	2434.9	1424.0
FBPY	Insul. elec. cables & wires	000M	38006.4	53500.0	33500.0
FCPY	Elec. wire (for elec. motors)	MT	43.6	104.7	250.8
FDPY	Telephone wire	000M	6667.1	9184.2	7927.2
FEPY	Household refrigerators	U	25002.0	38628.0	15685.0
FFPY	Automobile batteries	U	301906.0	236700.0	220100.0
FGPY	Household radio receivers	U	200000.0	256000.0	239200.0

Table A-2—Continued

Label	Product/Service	Unit	1980	1981	1982
FHPY	Television receivers	U	40290.0	77800.0	50400.0
GAPY	Steel structures	MT	23938.1	32501.4	36277.7
GBPY	Stainless steel tanks	U	139.0	--	--
GCPY	Steel cans	000U	623.4	603.9	802.4
GDPY	Aluminum cans	000U	48540.2	57300.0	57200.0
GEPY	Electrodes (for welding)	MT	2404.3	2267.0	2171.6
GFPY	Bottle caps	000GRS	10983.0	10712.5	9410.2
GGPY	Pressure cookers	000U	112.1	151.6	182.9
GHPY	Nails	MT	8642.5	8250.7	8331.8
H1PY	Tire tubes	U	353983.0	358700.0	185400.0
H2PY	Rubber footwear	000PAIR	2738.3	3781.7	2624.5
H3PY	Plastic tubing (for elec. conn.)	000M	8819.2	9089.5	4875.8
H4PY	Matches	000000BX	383.4	466.0	417.6
H5PY	Refined glycerine	MT	1881.8	1832.9	1294.1
HAPY	Iron pyrites	MT	53401.8	33300.0	47600.0
HBPY	Salt	MT	130452.7	161100.0	198000.0
HCPY	Anhydrous ammonia	MT	165522.7	203000.0	119200.0
HDPY	Sulfuric acid (98%)	MT	402371.0	412800.0	332900.0
HEPY	Caustic soda (50%)	MT	3484.6	8029.0	11187.0
HFPY	Oxygen	000CM	11637.7	12031.2	12610.7
HGPY	Acetylene gas	000CM	2259.1	2436.9	2447.6
HHPY	Insecticides	MT	2354.0	1372.0	1517.0
HIPY	Superphosphates	MT	17781.0	28244.0	21815.0
HJPY	Ammonium nitrate	MT	312075.0	356500.0	206800.0
HKPY	Urea	MT	15789.0	49500.0	28200.0
HLPY	Complex fertilizers	MT	70160.4	62300.0	40000.0
HMPY	Mixed fertilizers	MT	891459.6	903900.0	897400.0
HNPY	Granulated fertilizers	MT	97532.4	101000.0	89000.0
HOPY	Rayon cord	MT	1647.6	1435.0	1306.0
HPPY	Rayon yarn	MT	0.0	0.0	0.0
HQPY	Oil-base paints	HL	42221.0	35400.0	10400.0
HRPY	Latex & acrylic paints	HL	67153.0	61800.0	36800.0
HSPY	Varnishes	HL	3726.0	800.0	1200.0
HTPY	Enamels	HL	36320.0	46500.0	18900.0
HUPY	Household detergent	MT	22747.0	27400.0	20500.0
HVPY	Laundry soap	MT	37706.7	40900.0	32400.0
HWPY	Hand soap	MT	14832.0	17200.0	16100.0
HXPY	Toothpaste	MT	3728.6	4011.0	4402.7
HYPY	Torula yeast	MT	40890.0	35600.0	40200.0
HZPY	Tires	U	386669.0	326500.0	218300.0
IAPY	Bagasse pulp	MT	29862.0	31600.0	33400.0
IBPY	Writing paper	MT	36713.0	40400.0	36500.0
ICPY	Gray cardboard	MT	13836.0	14700.0	14000.0
IDPY	Cardboard for corrugating	MT	7952.0	10500.0	12300.0
IEPY	Kraft cardboard	MT	--	--	--
IFPY	Bristol board	MT	9724.0	7400.0	16000.0
IGPY	Paper bags	000U	213843.8	208500.0	233900.0
IHPY	Corrugated boxes	000U	92829.1	103200.0	113200.0
IIPY	Waxed containers	000U	53037.2	58100.0	60500.0
IJPY	Multilayered paper bags	000U	74765.7	84800.0	94300.0
JAPY	Books	000U	26280.1	38300.0	32100.0
JBPY	Magazines	000U	72700.0	87700.0	78300.0
JCPY	Booklets	000U	23500.0	9000.0	57000.0
JDPY	Notebooks	000U	116159.7	101200.0	113200.0
JEPY	Cigarette labels	000000U	995.1	817.1	1023.4
KAPY	Sawn wood	CM	81240.0	83900.0	83800.0
KBPY	Wooden boxes	000U	7657.0	8393.8	11058.8
KCPY	Telephone poles	000CM	--	--	--

Table A-2—Continued

Label	Product/Service	Unit	1980	1981	1982
KDPY	Railroad ties	CM	31091.0	31300.0	29200.0
LAPY	Sand	CM	4002.6	4699.7	4652.4
LBPY	Crushed stone	CM	10027.1	9717.2	8886.5
LCPY	Cement	000MT	2830.8	3292.2	3163.3
LDPY	Terrazzo tiles	000SM	2081.9	2263.6	1887.7
LEPY	Floor tiles	000SM	2310.8	2239.3	2305.2
LFPY	Bricks	000U	108617.0	117500.0	111000.0
LGPY	Prefab. concrete blocks	000CM	737.3	762.2	779.8
LHPY	Refractory materials	MT	14673.5	16500.0	17900.0
LIPY	Concrete pipes (water supply)	000M	174.8	216.9	217.0
LJPY	Fiberglass roof panels	000SM	6094.2	5917.2	5993.3
LKPY	Fiberglass pipes (water supply)	000M	706.1	757.4	761.7
LLPY	Cinder blocks	000U	48027.2	51000.0	53100.0
MAPY	Flat glass	000SM	189.0	88.4	283.6
MBPY	Bottles	000000U	175.5	157.4	232.8
MCPY	Medicine vials	000000U	112.4	108.7	92.3
MDPY	Bathroom tiles	000U	66992.6	65800.0	49500.0
MEPY	Bathroom fixtures	000U	298.4	317.6	358.3
NBPY	Cotton textiles	000SM	157398.4	172271.2	--
NCPY	Wool textiles	000SM	300.6	262.4	283.9
NDPY	Rayon textiles	000SM	1107.5	1033.2	1010.9
NEPY	Sisal rope	MT	5647.0	3600.0	5800.0
NFPY	Socks	000U	27007.3	27900.0	25900.0
OAPY	Underwear (incl. nfants')	000U	64024.6	70300.0	69900.0
OBPY	Outerwear (incl infants')	000U	44053.5	46000.0	50900.0
OCPY	Blouses & gowns (excl. infants')	000U	1598.9	2700.0	1800.0
ODPY	Shirts (excl. infants')	000U	15621.6	16500.0	16400.0
OEPY	Pants (excl. infants')	000U	11835.8	13700.0	14500.0
OFPY	Skirts	000U	1324.7	2100.0	1500.0
OGPY	Sweaters (excl. infants')	000U	262.8	300.0	200.0
OHPY	Suits (excl. infants')	000U	71.0	0.0	100.0
OIPY	Dresses (excl. infants')	000U	361.2	500.0	500.0
OJPY	Cotton & rayon bags	000U	11655.0	11800.0	11000.0
OKPY	Kenaf bags	000U	11588.1	14400.0	18700.0
PAPY	Leather	000SM	2725.6	2903.7	2898.6
PBPY	Sole leather	MT	1711.9	1764.1	1336.2
PCPY	Cattle hides	000U	1212.5	--	--
PDPY	Leather footwear	000PAIR	12927.4	15500.0	13500.0
QAPY	Raw sugar	000MT	6554.4	7646.6	7777.6
QBPY	Refined sugar	000MT	871.6	944.5	945.0
QCPY	Final syrups	000MT	2268.8	2322.3	2493.9
QDPY	Bagasse for industrial uses	MT	311200.0	375600.0	--
RAPY	Deboned beef	MT	80317.8	84000.0	83400.0
RBPY	Pork	MT	34206.2	40400.0	42200.0
RCPY	Canned meats	MT	34807.6	41500.0	48800.0
RDPY	Fresh poultry	MT	34585.6	45900.0	45300.0
REPY	Wheat flour	MT	270968.8	354000.0	385700.0
RFPY	Lard	MT	831.5	887.2	979.9
RGPY	Tallow	MT	6531.6	6106.3	6347.7
RHPY	Hydrogenated fats	MT	17567.3	19184.5	19355.6
RIPY	Fresh & pasteurized milk	MT	670991.0	698200.0	687200.0
RJPY	Condensed milk	MT	37951.9	40000.0	34200.0
RKPY	Evaporated milk	MT	28344.6	25100.0	14500.0

Table A-2—Continued

Label	Product/Service	Unit	1980	1981	1982
RLPY	Powdered milk	MT	2502.8	2742.8	2357.0
RMPY	Cheeses	MT	11065.6	12000.0	9800.0
RNPY	Butter	MT	9518.8	9400.0	9600.0
ROPY	Yogurt	MT	49170.1	54000.0	53800.0
RPPY	Ice cream	000GAL	17095.2	18300.0	19400.0
RQPY	Refined vegetable oil	MT	60290.8	65000.0	65300.0
RRPY	Bread	MT	446800.0	462400.0	469600.0
RSPY	Crackers	MT	44077.2	47200.0	48200.0
RTPY	Cookies	MT	27742.5	29600.0	28000.0
RUPY	Pasta	MT	58875.1	59900.0	57200.0
RVPY	Nougats	MT	--	--	--
RWPY	Candies	MT	25100.0	25400.0	23800.0
RXPY	Canned fruits & vegetables	MT	121791.3	142600.0	131300.0
RYPY	Roasted coffee	MT	16723.0	17400.0	17700.0
R1PY	Fresh & frozen fish	MT	5819.8	--	--
R2PY	Fresh & frozen seafood	MT	10169.0	--	--
R3PY	Canned fish & seafood	MT	4510.3	4232.9	--
SAPY	Fish catch	MT	141560.0	127342.0	153276.0
TAPY	Denatured alcohol	000HL	841.2	781.5	867.2
TBPY	Anhydrous alcohol	HL	331181.1	--	--
TCPY	Alcoholic bev. (excl. wines)	000HL	401.9	384.7	570.3
TDPY	Wines	000HL	135.3	130.7	137.7
TEPY	Beer	000HL	2364.9	2243.2	2421.1
TFPY	Malts	000HL	232.9	207.5	199.3
TGPY	Soft drinks	000HL	1867.1	1307.6	2055.9
THPY	Mineral water	000HL	460.7	797.6	802.2
TIPY	Cigars	000U	166463.3	230300.0	358400.0
TJPY	Cigarettes	000000U	15108.9	15400.0	17000.0
TKPY	Pipe tobacco	MT	16.9	11.3	10.3
UAPY	Fodder	MT	1386679.9	1509600.0	1363600.0
UBPY	Lamps (industrial use)	U	9800.0	239700.0	66400.0
UCPY	Lamps (household use)	U	57900.0	401600.0	130000.0
VAPY	Unsawn wood (logs)	CM	132631.0	134300.0	136900.0
VBPY	Firewood	000CM	2425.9	2453.6	2495.7
WAPY	Sugarcane	000MT	66978.9	73567.8	74136.2
X1PY	Mangoes	MT	61577.0	56470.0	51807.7
X2PY	Guavas	MT	45667.8	42904.2	40987.1
X3PY	Avocados	MT	15030.3	10159.7	18090.4
X4PY	Papayas	MT	38690.0	31718.7	35216.8
X5PY	Coconuts	MT	18339.5	14357.3	17372.8
X6PY	Coffee	MT	19168.2	21609.2	25603.8
X7PY	Cocoa	MT	1447.9	1467.7	1599.0
X8PY	Tobacco	MT	6714.5	53926.6	44735.2
XAPY	Potatoes	MT	208540.8	245572.3	219701.0
XBPY	Sweet potatoes	MT	195162.5	159244.3	124986.1
XCPY	Malanga	MT	97105.5	68587.1	26434.1
XDPY	Yucca	MT	87246.1	132562.7	112682.6
XEPY	Yams	MT	9162.9	7615.9	4810.5
XFPY	Rice	MT	352197.0	328674.2	372232.7
XGPY	Corn	MT	1867.2	1251.8	1900.4
XHPY	Sweet corn	MT	13971.8	13606.8	11898.6
XIPY	Black beans	MT	3684.0	2646.3	4368.4
XJPY	Red beans	MT	196.6	305.7	351.2
XKPY	Black-eyed peas	MT	663.7	208.2	--
XLPY	Tomatoes	MT	217569.5	298477.2	206002.1
XMPY	Green peppers	MT	44583.5	34778.9	34608.4
XNPY	Onions	MT	9626.0	15686.0	13997.4
XOPY	Garlic	MT	195.0	173.9	611.3

Table A-2—Continued

Label	Product/Service	Unit	1980	1981	1982
XPPY	Squash	MT	40780.2	46684.7	53015.7
XQPY	Cucumbers	MT	24812.8	25037.5	26842.9
XRPY	Melons	MT	49839.8	58368.1	53410.2
XSPY	Cabbage	MT	16342.8	67063.8	38344.1
XTPY	Oranges	MT	193716.2	250617.5	347065.4
XUPY	Grapefruit	MT	19483.8	53703.3	46869.1
XVPY	Lemons	MT	21537.6	35070.5	47826.2
XWPY	Tangerines	MT	25980.0	33833.1	20055.7
XXPY	Plantains	MT	82146.5	75530.9	67267.5
XYPY	Bananas	MT	137585.4	162539.0	174036.9
XZPY	Pineapple	MT	17832.0	14345.3	15829.7
YAPY	Cattle	MT	279536.4	293000.0	267000.0
YBPY	Pigs	MT	53805.0	63000.0	65100.0
YCPY	Honey	MT	548.9	646.3	736.1
YDPY	Eggs	000U	1819329.4	2164100.0	2056900.0
YEPY	Milk	MT	725400.3	739400.0	752800.0
YFPY	Poultry	MT	58629.5	66500.0	56000.0
AAPA	Housing units	U	20378.0	25512.0	31094.0
ABPA	Cattle barns	U	56.0	54.0	32.0
ACPA	Fac. for scholars, students	U	13.0	6.0	4.0
ADPA	Water & sewer lines laid	000000CM	628.8	528.0	416.4
AEPA	Farm acreage brought under irrigation	HA	68609.3	78565.5	28438.5
AFPA	Acreage protected against flood	HA	10224.0	1140.7	--
AGPA	Unpaved roads	KM	1334.2	1696.0	2586.4
AHPA	Paved roads	KM	237.9	437.0	220.4
BAPA	Passengers transported rail)	M.PAS-KM	1801.8	1916.1	2073.3
BBPA	Freight transported (rail)	M.MT-KM	2358.1	2885.1	2668.9
CAPA	Passengers transported (road)	000PAS	2574502.3	2821900.0	2671300.0
CBPA	Freight transported (road)	M.MT-KM	1436.4	1425.9	1491.4
DAPA	Passengers transported (maritime)	M.PAS-KM	70.5	72.1	71.1
DBPA	Freight transported (maritime)	M.MT-KM	56843.4	49609.4	55332.9
EAPA	Pass. transp. by natl. airline	M.PAS-KM	1357.6	1642.8	1939.0
EBPA	Freight transp. by natl. airline	M.MT-KM	21.9	22.1	24.8
FAPA	Cargo loaded & unloaded	000000MT	35357.7	35743.0	34524.1
GAPA	Domestic mail sent	000U	83496.4	82674.5	85742.2
GBPA	International mail sent	000U	54.9	84.8	31.8
GCPA	International mail received	000U	76.1	178.6	229.2
GDPA	Telegrams sent	000U	15228.0	15662.7	16973.5
GEPA	Domestic telephone calls	000U	62934.3	77498.4	87419.0
HAPA	Workers in trade sector	000	302.0	310.7	324.1
IAPA	Workers in comm. svces. & housing	000	93.1	90.8	85.7
IBPA	Tourists lodged (dom. & intl.)	000	7941.0	8348.4	8804.4
JAPA	Students	U	3213014.0	3252321.0	3223452.0
JBPA	Scholarship students	U	580667.0	589542.0	583639.0
JCPA	Students graduating	U	636496.0	629786.0	702669.0

Table A-2—Continued

Label	Product/Service	Unit	1980	1981	1982
JDPA	Medical consultations	000	30000.2	31248.3	32016.8
JEPA	Patients admitted	U	1263599.0	1358547.0	1404687.0
JFPA	Emerg. rm. & polyclinic consult.	U	15165458.0	17743161.0	17397342.0
JGPA	Immunization	U	4734653.0	4481817.0	4464689.0
KAPA	Patrons using library services	U	5268.7	7222.0	8542.3
KBPA	Books published	U	33267.9	45392.2	43034.8
KCPA	Newspapers run	000000	360.8	361.7	349.4
KDPA	Domestic radio broadcasting	HRS	41313.0	36293.0	37309.0
KEPA	Artistic performances	U	32440.0	36036.0	44867.0
KFPA	Particip. in organized sports	U	2622169.0	3021500.0	3210600.0
KGPA	Workers in var. soc. activ.	000	126.7	138.2	153.7
LAPA	Workers in public administration	000	141.3	151.9	151.5
NAPA	Workers in nonprod. activities	000	14.6	23.4	27.3

Appendix B. United Nations International Standard Industrial Classification of All Economic Activities

List of Major Divisions, Divisions, and Major Groups

Division	Major Group	Group	

Major Division 1. Agriculture, Hunting, Forestry, and Fishing

11			Agriculture and hunting
	111	1110	Agricultural and livestock production
	112	1120	Agricultural services
	113	1130	Hunting, trapping, and game propagation
12			Forestry and logging
	121	1210	Forestry
	122	1220	Logging
13	130		Fishing
		1301	Ocean and coastal fishing
		1302	Fishing not elsewhere classified

Major Division 2. Mining and Quarrying

21	210	2100	Coal mining
22	220	2200	Crude petroleum and natural gas production
23	230		Metal ore mining
		2301	Iron ore mining
		2302	Nonferrous ore mining
29	290		Other mining
		2901	Stone quarrying, clay and sand pits
		2902	Chemical and fertilizer mineral mining
		2903	Salt mining
		2909	Mining and quarrying not elsewhere classified

Divi- sion	Major Group	Group

Major Division 3. Manufacturing

31			Manufacture of food, beverages and tobacco
	311-312		Food manufacturing
		3111	Slaughtering, preparing, and preserving meat
		3112	Manufacture of dairy products
		3113	Canning and preserving of fruits and vegetables
		3114	Canning, preserving, and processing of fish, crustacea, and similar foods
		3115	Manufacture of vegetable and animal oils and fats
		3116	Grain mill products
		3117	Manufacture of bakery products
		3118	Sugar factories and refineries
		3119	Manufacture of cocoa, chocolate, and sugar confectionery
		3121	Manufacture of food products not elsewhere classified
		3122	Manufacture of prepared animal feeds
	313		Beverage industries
		3131	Distilling, rectifying, and blending spirits
		3132	Wine industries
		3133	Malt liquors and malt
		3134	Soft drinks and carbonated waters industries
	314	3140	Tobacco manufactures
32			Textile, wearing apparel, and leather industries
	321		Manufacture of textiles
		3211	Spinning, weaving, and finishing textiles
		3212	Manufacture of made-up textile goods except wearing apparel
		3213	Knitting mills
		3214	Manufacture of carpets and rugs
		3215	Cordage, rope, and twine industries
		3219	Manufature of textiles not elsewhere classified
	322	3220	Manufacture of wearing apparel, except footwear
	323		Manufacture of leather and products of leather, leather substitutes, and fur, except footwear and wearing apparel
		3231	Tanneries and leather finishing
		3232	Fur dressing and dyeing industries
		3233	Manufacture of products of leather and leather substitutes, except footwear and wearing apparel
	324	3240	Manufacture of footwear, except vulcanized or molded rubber or plastic footwear
33			Manufacture of wood and wood products, including furniture

Divi-sion	Major Group	Group	
	331		Manufacture of wood and wood and cork products, except furniture
		3311	Sawmills, planing, and other wood mills
		3312	Manufacture of wooden and cane containers and small cane ware
		3319	Manufacture of wood and cork products not elsewhere classified
	332	3320	Manufacture of furniture and fixtures, except primarily of metal
34			Manufacture of paper and paper products; printing and publishing
	341		Manufacture of paper and paper products
		3411	Manufacture of pulp, paper, and paperboard
		3412	Manufacture of containers and boxes of paper and paperboard
		3419	Manufacture of pulp, paper, and paperboard articles not elsewhere classified
	342	3420	Printing, publishing, and allied industries
35			Manufacture of chemicals and of chemical, petroleum, coal, rubber, and plastic products
	351		Manufacture of industrial chemicals
		3511	Manufacture of basic industrial chemicals except fertilizers
		3512	Manufacture of fertilizers and pesticides
		3513	Manufacture of synthetic resins, plastic materials, and man-made fibers except glass
	352		Manufacture of other chemical products
		3521	Manufacture of paints, varnishes, and lacquers
		3522	Manufacture of drugs and medicines
		3523	Manufacture of soap and cleaning preparations, perfumes, cosmetics, and other toilet preparations
		3529	Manufacture of chemical products not elsewhere classified
	353	3530	Petroleum refineries
	354	3540	Manufacture of miscellaneous products of petroleum and coal
	355		Manufacture of rubber products not elsewhere classified
		3551	Tire and tube industries
		3559	Manufacture of rubber products not elsewhere classified
	356	3560	Manufacture of plastic products not elsewhere classified
36			Manufacture of nonmetallic mineral products, except products of petroleum and coal
	361	3610	Manufacture of pottery, china, and earthenware
	362	3620	Manufacture of glass and glass products

Divi-sion	Major Group	Group	
	369		Manufacture of other nonmetallic mineral products
		3691	Manufacture of structural clay products
		3692	Manufacture of cement, lime, and plaster
		3699	Manufacture of nonmetallic mineral products not elsewhere classified
37			Basic metal industries
	371	3710	Iron and steel basic industries
	372	3720	Nonferrous metal basic industries
38			Manufacture of fabricated metal products, machinery and equipment
	381		Manufacture of fabricated metal products, except machinery and equipment
		3811	Manufacture of cutlery, hand tools, and general hardware
		3812	Manufacture of furniture and fixtures primarily of metal
		3813	Manufacture of structural metal products
		3819	Manufacture of fabricated metal products except machinery and equipment not elsewhere classified
	382		Manufacture of machinery except electrical
		3821	Manufacture of engines and turbines
		3822	Manufacture of agricultural machinery and equipment
		3823	Manufacture of metal and woodworking machinery
		3824	Manufacture of special industrial machinery and equipment except metal and woodworking machinery
		3825	Manufacture of office, computing, and accounting machinery
		3829	Machinery and equipment except electrical not elsewhere classified
	383		Manufacture of electrical machinery apparatus, appliances, and supplies
		3831	Manufacture of electrical industrial machinery and apparatus
		3832	Manufacture of radio, television, and communication equipment and apparatus
		3833	Manufacture of electrial appliances and housewares
		3839	Manufacture of electrical apparatus and supplies not elsewhere classified
	384		Manufacture of transport equipment
		3841	Shipbuilding and repairing
		3842	Manufacture of railroad equipment
		3843	Manufacture of motor vehicles
		3844	Manufacture of motorcycles and bicycles
		3845	Manufacture of aircraft
		3849	Manufacture of transport equipment not elsewhere classified

Divi-sion	Major Group	Group	

	385		Manufacture of professional and scientific and measuring and controlling equipment not elsewhere classified, and of photographic and optical goods
		3851	Manufacture of professional and scientific, and measuring and controlling equipment, not elsewhere classified
		3852	Manufacture of photographic and optical goods
		3853	Manufacture of watches and clocks
39	390		Other manufacturing industries
		3901	Manufacture of jewelry and related articles
		3902	Manufacture of musical instruments
		3903	Manufacture of sporting and athletic goods
		3909	Manufacturing industries not elsewhere classified

Major Division 4. Electricity, Gas, and Water

41	410		Electricity, gas, and steam
		4101	Electric light and power
		4102	Gas manufacture and distribution
		4103	Steam and hot water supply
42	420	4200	Water works and supply

Major Division 5. Construction

50	500	5000	Construction

Major Division 6. Wholesale and Retail Trade and Restaurants and Hotels

61	610	6100	Wholesale trade
62	620	6200	Retail trade
63			Restaurants and hotels
	631	6310	Restaurants, cafés, and other eating and drinking places
	632	6320	Hotels, rooming houses, camps, and other lodging places

Major Division 7. Transport, Storage and Communication

71			Transport and storage
	711		Land transport
		7112	Urban, suburban, and interurban highway passenger transport
		7113	Other passenger land transport
		7114	Freight transport by road
		7115	Pipeline transport
		7116	Supporting services to land transport

Divi- sion	Major Group	Group	
	712		Water transport
		7121	Ocean and coastal water transport
		7122	Inland water transport
		7123	Supporting services to water transport
	713		Air transport
		7131	Air transport carriers
		7132	Supporting services to air transport
	719		Services allied to transport
		7191	Services allied to transport
		7192	Storage and warehousing
72	720	7200	Communication

Major Division 8. *Financing, Insurance, Real Estate, and Business Services*

81	810		Financial institutions
		8101	Monetary institutions
		8102	Other financial institutions
		8103	Financial services
82	820	8200	Insurance
83			Real estate and business services
	831	8310	Real estate
	832		Business services except machinery and equipment rental and leasing
		8321	Legal services
		8322	Accounting, auditing, and bookkeeping services
		8323	Data processing and tabulating services
		8324	Engineering, architectural, and technical services
		8325	Advertising services
		8329	Business services, except machinery and equipment rental and leasing, not elsewhere classified
	833	8330	Machinery and equipment rental and leasing

Major Division 9. *Community, Social, and Personal Services*

91	910	9100	Public administration and defense
92	920	9200	Sanitary and similar services
93			Social and related community services
	931	9310	Education services
	932	9320	Research and scientific institutes
	933		Medical, dental, other health and veterinary services
		9331	Medical, dental, and other health services
		9332	Veterinary services
	934	9340	Welfare institutions

Divi-sion	Major Group	Group	
	935	9350	Business, professional, and labor associations
	939		Other social and related community services
		9391	Religious organizations
		9399	Social and related community services not elsewhere classified
94			Recreational and cultural services
	941		Motion picture and other entertainment services
		9411	Motion picture production
		9412	Motion picture distribution and projection
		9413	Radio and television broadcasting
		9414	Theatrical producers and entertainment services
		9415	Authors, music composers, and other independent artists not elsewhere classified
	942	9420	Libraries, museums, botanical and zoological gardens, and other cultural services not elsewhere classified
	949	9490	Amusement and recreational services not elsewhere classified
95			Personal and household services
	951		Repair services not elsewhere classified
		9511	Repair of footwear and other leather goods
		9512	Electrical repair shops
		9513	Repair of motor vehicles and motorcycles
		9514	Watch, clock, and jewelry repair
		9519	Other repair shops not elsewhere classified
	952	9520	Laundries, laundry services, and cleaning and dyeing plants
	953	9530	Domestic services
	959		Miscellaneous personal serives
		9591	Barber and beauty shops
		9592	Photographic studies, including commercial photography
		9599	Personal services not elsewhere classified
96	960	9600	International and other extraterritorial bodies

Major Division 0. Activities Not Adequately Defined

0	000	0000	Activities not adequately defined

Sources: United Nations, Statistical Office, *International Standard Industrial Classification of All Economic Activities.*

Appendix C. Estimating Total Agricultural Output from *Acopio* Data

For each agricultural commodity, the relationships among total production (T), *acopio* (A), and state (S) and private farmers' (P) production can be expressed as follows:

$$(1) \qquad T = S + KP + (1 - K)\, P\,, \qquad K <= 1$$

$$(2) \qquad A = S + KP$$

where K and $1-K$ are the shares of private farmers' production going to *acopio* and self-consumption, respectively. Typically, time-series data exist for A, S, and KP. As indicated in the text, data are also available for T for selected commodities and years; in cases where T is available $(1-K)$, P can be obtained from equation (1) by substitution:

$$(3) \qquad (1 - K)\, P = T - A$$

so that
$$1 - K = \frac{T - A}{P}$$

and
$$K = \frac{P + A - T}{P}$$

Estimates for K and 1-K for rice and beans derived using the approach described above are given in table C-1 and C-2.

The relationships between the rates of change over time in total production, *acopio*, and state production can be obtained by combining equations (1) and (2) and taking the derivative with respect to time. Thus,

$$\frac{dT}{dt} = \frac{dS}{dt} + \frac{A-S}{K}\frac{dA}{dt} - \frac{A-S}{K}\frac{dS}{dt}$$

which can be simplified as

$$\frac{dT}{dt} = \frac{dS}{dt} + \frac{A-S}{K}\left(\frac{dA}{dt} - \frac{dS}{dt}\right)$$

Table C-1. Private Production of Rice Distributed between *Acopio* and Self-Consumption (thousands of metric tons)

Year	Production	*Acopio*	Distribution Self-Consumption	*Acopio* as Share of Production (%)	Self-Consumption as Share of Production (%)
1970	82.2	7.2	75.0	8.8	91.2
1974	143.1	15.8	127.4	11.0	89.0
1975	130.6	21.9	108.7	16.8	83.2
1976	140.2	24.2	116.0	17.3	82.7
1977	142.5	20.9	121.6	14.7	85.3
1978	133.0	19.6	113.4	14.7	85.3
1979	130.7	17.4	113.3	13.3	86.7
1980	148.5	22.9	125.6	15.4	84.6

Source: Calculated from table 6.

Table C-2.   Private Production of Beans Distributed between *Acopio*
and Self-Consumption (thousands of metric tons)

Year	Production	Distribution *Acopio*	Self-Consumption	*Acopio* as Share of Production (%)	Self-Consumption as Share of Production (%)
1970	-0.6	2.5	-3.1	--	--
1974	0.6	2.0	-1.4	--	--
1975	1.0	3.0	-2.0	--	--
1976	1.1	1.8	-0.7	--	--
1977	2.2	1.4	0.8	63.6	36.4
1978	3.4	1.5	1.9	44.1	55.9
1979	3.5	1.6	1.9	45.7	54.3
1980	6.9	1.9	5.0	27.5	72.5

Source: Calculated from table 6.

Appendix D. Stability of Shares of GSP Components across Valuation Methodologies

Data on the value of output of the productive sphere (GSP) and its components through 1976 were calculated by CEE on the basis of *"circulación completa"* (complete circulation), an output valuation procedure reportedly akin to the gross turnover valuation method. Beginning with 1977, valuation was changed to *"a salida de empresa"* (at enterprise exit) and since then data are only available on the latter basis.[1] However, the CEE recalculated GSP for 1975 and 1976, originally released on the basis of complete circulation, to conform to the enterprise-exit methodology and published these data (GSP and component of GSP) in recent statistical yearbooks (table D-1). Neither data for earlier time periods nor a general method for bridging the differences in the two sets of data has been published.

In the special publication prepared for the 1982 seminar on conversion from MPS to SNA, CEE converted GSP for 1974 from complete circulation (CC) to enterprise exit (EE) valuation, but did not provide a similar conversion for the components of GSP.[2] Since, for the purpose of developing value-added weights, disaggregated value of output data are required, a method has been developed to convert value of output data at the sector level from one valuation methodology to the other.

It was hypothesized that, since the only change between the two sets of data was a valuation change, it might be possible to make a conversion through a simple transformation. The share of the value of total output (GSP) produced by each of eight sectors (P_i, i=1, . . . ,8) in the productive sphere was calculated separately from CC and EE data from 1975 and 1976. For each of the two years, the ratio of the shares for a given sector (r_i) was constructed:

$$r_{i,t} = \frac{P_{i,CC,t}}{P_{i,EE,t}} , \, t = 75,76$$

Table D-1.   GSP Based on Complete Circulation and Enterprise Exit Valuation (million pesos)

Sector	Complete Circulation					
	1974		1975		1976	
	Pesos	%	Pesos	%	Pesos	%
GSP	13,423.5	100.0	15,799.3	100.0	15,860.5	100.0
Industry	5,393.1	40.2	6,067.2	38.4	6,250.4	39.4
Construction	1,178.8	8.8	1,407.0	8.9	1,491.8	9.4
Agriculture	1,220.7	9.1	1,296.8	8.2	1,352.9	8.5
Fishing	68.6	0.5	61.7	0.4	80.2	0.5
Forestry	38.3	0.3	35.6	0.2	34.5	0.2
Transportation	851.3	6.3	1,011.3	6.4	1,039.1	6.6
Communications	73.2	0.6	78.0	0.5	82.1*	0.5
Trade	4,599.5	34.3	5,841.7	37.0	5,529.5	34.9
Others	--	--	--	--	--	--

	Enterprise Exit					
	1974		1975		1976	
	Pesos	%	Pesos	%	Pesos	%
GSP	12,479.0	100.0	13,913.1	100.0	14,086.1	100.0
Industry	6,210.8	49.8	6,638.6	47.7	6,909.0	49.1
Construction	1,086.9	8.7	1,250.3	9.0	1,320.1	9.4
Agriculture	1,507.5	12.1	1,537.7	11.1	1,595.3	11.3
Fishing	93.6	0.8	85.6	0.6	106.2	0.8
Forestry	77.4	0.6	69.4	0.5	70.1	0.5
Transportation	891.0	7.1	1,006.3	7.2	1,035.9	7.4
Communications	76.1	0.6	78.1	0.6	82.1	0.6
Trade	2,535.7	20.3	3,218.8	23.1	2,935.9	20.8
Others	--	--	28.3	0.2	31.1	0.2

Sources: Complete circulation: *Anuario estadístico de Cuba 1976*.
Enterprise exit: *Anuario estadístico de Cuba 1980*.
*Erroneously reported as 32.1 million pesos in original source.

where

$P_{i,CC,t}$ is the share of output of the ith sector under the complete circulation method for year t, and

$P_{i,EE,t}$ is the share of output of the ith
sector under the enterprise-exit
method for year t.

The calculated values for r_{it} are given in table D-2.

It was observed from data in table D-2 that the values of $r_{i,75}$ and $r_{i,76}$ are relatively close, suggesting that the two sets of data could be readily transformed. Thus, it was assumed that

$$r_{i,74} = \frac{r_{i,75} + r_{i,76}}{2}$$

that is, that the ratio of the shares of value produced by each sector under the two valuation methodologies in 1974 could be approximated by the average of the corresponding ratios for 1975 and 1976. (Since the sum of the $r_{i,74}$ added up to more than 100, they were readjusted so that they summed to 100.0, using a procedure that made larger adjustments to sectors that had greater differences in $r_{i,t}$ between 1975 and 1976 and greater value of $p_{i,t}$ under the CC method.) The estimated $r_{i,74}$ (also included in table D-2) were then applied to the reported value for GSP in 1974 calculated on the enterprise exit method (12,479.0 million pesos) to obtain the value of output produced by each sector. The estimates of the value of the components of GSP in 1974 are reported in the last column of table D-1.

Table D-2.   Calculated $r_{i,t}$ for 1975 and 1976 and Estimated for 1974

Sector	t=1975	t=1976	t=1974
Industry	1.2425	1.2446	1.24
Construction	1.0091	0.9964	1.00
Agriculture	1.3465	1.3277	1.34
Fishing	1.5754	1.4910	1.53
Forestry	2.2137	2.2878	2.25
Transportation	1.1300	1.1225	1.13
Communications	1.1370	1.1260	1.13
Trade	0.6257	0.5978	0.61

Source: Calculated from data in table D-1.

Appendix E. Activity Index Aggregation Formulae

The aggregate value of an economy's output changes over time as a result of the variability in two factors: the physical volume of output (goods and services) produced, and the prices these outputs command. A measure that purports to reflect the *real* growth rate of the economy should be concerned only with variations in the value of total output that result from changes in physical output. For an economy that produces a single output i (either a product or a service), this can be accomplished by computing the growth rate over time of physical output of i. This approach is not suitable for a multiproduct economy, where it is reasonable to expect that the rate of change over time of physical production will vary across products or services. In this case, it is necessary to combine changes in each individual output series into a single measure that can be interpreted as representing the average change in real output for the entire economy.

One common approach, and the one I have adopted, is to construct constant-price quantity index numbers for branches of the economy and to combine these indexes into measures of activity at the level of economic sectors and, ultimately, of the entire economy. The first step in the process is to calculate Laspeyres-type quantity indexes of the form

$$I_h = \frac{\sum P_{io} \times Q_{it}}{\sum P_{io} \times Q_{io}} \qquad (1)$$

where Q_{io} is the physical output of product i in the base year, Q_{it} is the corresponding physical output in year t, P_{io} is the base-period price for the ith product in branch h, and I_h is the output index for the hth branch of the economy.

I imputed missing values in the output series using one of two approaches: (a) for a single missing value between two data points, by a simple arithmetic interpolation; and (b) for two or more consecutive missing observations (either surrounded by other observations or at the beginning or end of a series), by using the average weighted growth rate of other series within the branch. Only output series for which a price from the price set is available in the base period can enter into the calculations; indexes were not calculated for multioutput branches for which no price data at all or only a price for a single commodity was available. As noted in chapter 3, for services sectors output series were equally weighted, since no adequate price data were available.

The individual branch indexes I_h from equation (1) are aggregated into activity indexes for each of the economic sectors using

$$I_j = \frac{\sum_h I_h \times W_h}{\sum_h W_h} \qquad (2)$$

where W_h is the relative importance (weight) assigned to the hth branch within sector j and I_j is the activity index for sector j. For those sectors that were not subdivided into branches, sector output indexes were obtained directly from equation (1).

Finally, the indexes for each of the sectors of the economy, I_j, are combined into the index of overall economic activity growth using a weighting system that reflects the relative importance of the various sectors. The aggregation formula is

$$I = \frac{\sum_j I_j \times W_j}{\sum_j W_j} \qquad (3)$$

where I_j is the output index for each sector of the economy obtained from equation (2), W_j is the weight assigned to the jth sector, and I is the aggregate index of economic activity.

Abbreviations

AEC	Anuario estadístico de Cuba
AFC	Adjusted factor cost
BE	Boletín estadístico de Cuba
BNC	Banco Nacional de Cuba (Cuban National Bank)
CAE	Clasificador de Actividades Económicas (Classification of Economic Activities)
CEE	Comité Estatal de Estadísticas (State Statisctics Committee)
CEP	Comité Estatal de Precios (State Price Committee)
CMEA	Council for Mutual Economic Assistance
CPE	Centrally planned economy
ECE	Economic Commission for Europe
ECIEL	Programa de Estudios Conjuntos sobre Integración Económica Latinoamericana (Program of Joint Studies on Latin American Integration)
ECLA	Economic Commission for Latin America (United Nations)
GDP	Gross Domestic Product
GMP	Gross Material Product
GNP	Gross National Product
GSP	Global Social Product
GVO	Gross Value of Output
ICIODI	Instituto Cubano de Investigaciones y Orientación de la Demanda Interna (Cuban Institute for Research and Orientation of Domestic Demand)
I-O	Input-Output
ISIC	International Standard Industrial Classification of All Economic Activities
JUCEPLAN	Junta Central de Planificación (Central Planning Board)
MPS	Material Product System
NMP	Net Material Product
NMS	Nonproductive (or nonmaterial) services
NNP	Net National Product
PI	Physical indicator
SBEN	Sistema de Balances de la Economía Nacional (Material Product System)
SCN	Sistema de Cuentas Nacionales (National Accounts System)

SDPE	Sistema de Dirección y Planificación de la Economía (Economic Management and Planning System)
SNA	System of National Accounts

Notes

1. Introduction

1. The national income accounting system used by centrally planned economies is formally called the System of Balances of the National Economy (MPS); market economies use the System of National Accounts (SNA). See United Nations, *Basic Principles of the System of Balances of the National Economy*; and idem, *A System of National Accounts*.

2. For a succinct description of the main concepts of the MPS, see Central Intelligence Agency, National Foreign Assessment Center, *USSR: Toward a Reconciliation of Marxist and Western Measures of National Income*, p. 3

3. For a comprehensive study of the relationship between the MPS and the SNA, including a discussion of the difficulties in converting from one system to the other, see United Nations, *Comparison of the System of National Accounts and the System of Balances of the National Economy*, Pt. 1: *Conceptual Relationships*; idem, Pt. 2, *Conversion of Aggregates of SNA to MPS and Vice-Versa for Selected Countries*.

4. United Nations, Economic Commission for Latin America (ECLA), *Comparabilidad de los sistemas de cuentas nacionales y del producto material en América Latina*.

5. Seminario Latinoamericano de Cuentas Nacionales y Balances de la Economía, *Cuba: Conversión de los principales indicadores macroeconómicos del sistema de balances de la economía nacional (SBEN) al sistema de cuentas nacionales (SCN)*.

6. In a report issued in mid-1982, the Banco Nacional de Cuba (Cuban National Bank, BNC) presented a time series for Cuban GDP spanning the period 1971–80. There is no explanation in the text of the report as to how the GDP estimates were made or any reference to the 1974 MPS/SNA conversion. However, the reported GDP estimate for 1974 in the BNC report does correspond to the one obtained from the MPS/SNA conversion exercise. See Banco Nacional de Cuba, *Economic Report*, p. 30. The GDP series in this BNC report is presented in chapter 5 of this study.

7. For a description of the scaling-up procedure, see, e.g., Paul Marer, "Alternative Estimates of the Dollar GNP and Growth Rates of CMEA Countries," in U.S. Congress, Joint Economic Committee, *European Economies: Slow Growth in the 1980s*, vol. I (Washington, D.C.: GPO, 1985).

8. An evaluation of the feasibility of using the scaling-up procedure for estimating Cuban GDP is contained in Carmelo Mesa-Lago and Jorge Pérez-López, *A Study of Cuba's Material Product System, Its Conversion to the System of National Accounts, and Estimation of Gross Domestic Product Per Capita and Growth Rates*, World Bank Staff Working Paper, no. 770 (1985).

9. For a detailed description of the two output valuation methods, see ibid.

10. Eva Ehrlich, "An Examination of the Inter-Relation between Consumption Indicators Expressed in Physical Indicators and Per Capita National Income," *Czechoslovak Economic Papers* 7 (October 1966):109–135. For estimates of GDP per capita in dollars for the Soviet Union and Eastern European CPEs using this methodology, see Economic Commission for Europe (ECE), "International Comparisons of Real Incomes, Capital Formation and Consumption"; and idem, "Comparative GDP Levels," *Economic Bulletin for Europe* 31, no. 2 (1980):1–56; World Bank, "International Comparisons of Estimated Real Per Caput Income Levels—the ECE's Physical Indicators Approach Updated for 1973."

11. Carmelo Mesa-Lago and Jorge Pérez-López, "Estimating Cuban Gross Domestic Product Per Capita in Dollars Using Physical Indicators," *Social Indicators Research* 16 (1985):275–300.

12. Ibid.: 298–299.

13. Abram Bergson, "Soviet National Income and Product in 1937," *Quarterly Journal of Economics* 1, 65 (May 1950):208–241, and 2, 65 (August 1950):408–441. This approach is cogently presented in idem, *The Real National Income of Soviet Russia since 1928*.

14. See, e.g., the large number of studies on the Soviet Union cited in U.S. Congress, Joint Economic Committee, *USSR: Measures of Economic Growth and Development, 1950–80*. Regarding the application of this methodology to countries other than the Soviet Union, see, e.g., John K. Chang, *Industrial Development in Pre-Communist China*; Pong Lee and John Montias, "Indices of Rumanian Industrial Production"; and George J. Staller, "Czechoslovak Industrial Growth: 1948–1959," *American Economic Review* 52 (June 1962):385–407. For examples of applications of the methodology to Cuba, see Jorge F. Pérez-López, "An Index of Cuban Industrial Output, 1930–58"; and Claes Brundenius, *Revolutionary Cuba: The Challenge of Growth with Equity*.

1. Physical Output Data

1. Issues of the *Boletín* for 1964–71 were published by the Junta Central de Planificación (Central Planning Board, JUCEPLAN). According to Carmelo Mesa-Lago, "Cuban Statistics Revisited," *Cuban Studies/Estudios Cubanos* 9, no. 2 (July 1979):60–61, the issue of the *Boletín* corresponding to 1969 was not published.

2. The 1972–74 issues of the *Anuario* were published by JUCEPLAN. Beginning with the issue for 1975, the *Anuario* has been published by CEE. The most recent issue available is for 1982.

3. For example, CEE, *Cifras estadísticas*; idem, *Estadísticas quinquenales de Cuba 1965–1980*; idem, *Desarrollo económico y social de Cuba durante el período 1958–1980*; and idem, *Cuba en cifras*, issues for 1980 and 1981.

4. For example, BNC, *Development and Prospects of the Cuban Economy*; idem, *Cuba: Economic Development and Prospects*; and idem, *Cuba: Economic and Social Development 1976–80 and First Half 1981*. Especially important is a report published in mid-1982 for Cuba's attempt to renegotiate its hard currency debt: idem, *Economic Report*.

5. CMEA, *Statisticheskii ezhegodnik (Statistical Yearbook)*.

6. For example, United Nations, *Statistical Bulletin, Statistical Yearbook*, and *Yearbook of National Accounts*; United Nations, ECLA, *Economic Survey of Latin America*; United Nations Conference on Trade and Development, *Cuba: Recent Economic Developments and Future Prospects*.

7. The classic qualitative analysis of Cuban statistics during the first decade of the revolution is Carmelo Mesa-Lago, "Availability and Reliability of Statistics in Socialist Cuba," *Latin American Research Review (LARR)*, Pt. 1, 4, no. 1 (Spring 1969):53–91, and Pt. 2, 4, no. 2 (Summer 1969):47–81. Mesa-Lago has continued his critical assessment of Cuban statistics. See, e.g., *The Economy of Socialist Cuba: A Two-Decade Appraisal*; and his occasional reviews of Cuban statistical publications in *Cuban Studies/Estudios Cubanos*.

8. Héctor Ayala Castro, "Transformaciones de propiedad, control obrero e intervención de empresas en Cuba," *Economía y Desarrollo*, no. 47 (May–June 1978):49–50.

9. The official text of the Agrarian Reform Law is given in *Gaceta Oficial* (3 June 1959), special issue. It also appears in Leonel-Antonio de la Cuesta, comp. *Constituciones cubanas*, pp. 475–495.

10. Michel Gutelman, *La agricultura socializada en Cuba*, p. 68.

11. A useful chronology of the nationalization of U.S.-owned investments in Cuba can be found in Paul E. Sigmund, *Multinationals in Latin America: The Politics of Nationalization*, chap. 4.

12. The official text of the law appears in *Gaceta Oficial* (17 July 1960).

13. The official text of the resolution is given in *Gaceta Oficial* (6 August 1960), special issue.

14. Carlos Rafael Rodríguez, *Cuba en el tránsito al socialismo*, p. 123.

15. The official text of the law appears in *Gaceta Oficial* (15 October 1960).

16. Other sources indicate that the state's share of agriculture in 1961 was closer to 40 percent. See, e.g., transcript of a speech by the Cuban delegate to the thirty-ninth session of the Food and Agriculture Organization in October 1962, printed in *El Mundo* (25 October 1962), p. 5; and Héctor Ayala Castro, "Los cambios en las relaciones de propiedad, 1961–1963," *Economía y Desarrollo*, no. 65 (November–December 1961): 183.

17. The text of the law is reproduced in de la Cuesta, *Constituciones cubanas*.

18. Carmelo Mesa-Lago, "The Revolutionary Offensive," *Transaction* 6, no. 6 (April 1969):22. See also idem, "Ideological Radicalization and Economic Policy in Cuba," *Studies in Comparative International Development* 5, no. 10 (1969–70):204.

19. Mesa-Lago, "The Revolutionary Offensive."

20. Article 24 of the Socialist Constitution of 1976 provides that "land owned by small farmers can only be inherited by descendants who will work the land personally, except where permitted by law." The official text of the Socialist

Constitution is given in *Gaceta Oficial* (24 February 1976), Special issue. The intent of the drafters seems to have been to prevent the further division of private farms. An article-by-article commentary on the Constitution does not elaborate on what exceptions to this rule might have been contemplated: see Fernando Alvarez Tabío, *Comentarios a la Constitución Socialista*, pp. 113–116.

21. Juan Valdés Paz. "La pequeña producción agrícola en Cuba," *Revista del México Agrario* 12, no. 1 (January–March 1982):130.

22. "Resolución sobre la cuestión agraria y las relaciones con el campesinado," *Economía y Desarrollo*, no. 36 (July–August 1976):164–165.

23. CEE, *Desarrollo económico y social*, p. 66; Héctor Ayala Castro, "Transformación de la propiedad en el período 1964–80," *Economía y Desarrollo*, no. 68 (May–June 1982):24–25.

24. Some of the problems associated with the employment data are addressed in chapter 2.

25. For example, I am aware of a systematic survey of 10,000 families (1 in 220 families nationwide) using a stratified sample that permits reliable (95 percent confidence) expenditure estimates at the national and provincial levels. See Eugenio R. Balari and Luis C. Ramírez, "Eficiencia y calidad en la investigación económica en el Instituto de la Interna Demanda [*sic*]," *Areíto* 6, no 23 (1980):28; Eugenio R. Balari, "Cinco años de trabajo del Instituto Cubano de Investigaciones y Orientación de la Demanda Interna," *Investigaciones Científicas de la Demanda en Cuba*.

26. For example, ICIODI, *Normas racionales de consumo para alimentos, vestuarios y calzado y equipamiento para la vivienda*, and other works published by ICIODI cited in Gustavo San Pedro "Las normas racionales de consumo."

27. Oscar Duyos, "Los problemas actuales del acopio y los precios de compra de los productos estatales," *Cuba Socialista* 9, no 33 (May 1964):67. See also Antero Regalado, "Las funciones del ANAP," *Cuba Socialista* 9, no 35 (July 1964):16, 19.

28. For instance, a provocative analysis of agricultural yields in Cuba in the state and private sectors by Forster uses *acopio* data. See Nancy Forster, "Cuban Agricultural Productivity: A Comparison of State and Private Farm Sectors," *Cuban Studies/Estudios Cubanos* 11, no. 2/12, no 1 (July 1981–January 1982):112–113, esp.

29. *Anuario estadístico de Cuba 1980*, table V. 15, p. 74. This table has been included in more recent issues of the *Anuario*.

2. Value-Added Weights

1. ECLA, "The Cuban Economy in the Period 1959–63," pp. 259–289.

2. Some of these changes were reported in *Economic Survey of Latin America 1965*, pp. 284 ff.

3. It should be recalled that the first statistical yearbook for revolutionary Cuba published by JUCEPLAN, *Boletín estadístico de Cuba 1964*, was not released until 1966.

4. ECLA, "The Cuban Economy," p. 268, footnote.

5. Exceptions to this methodology are given in ibid.

6. The Cuban submission was published as a two-part article under the title "El esarrollo industrial de Cuba," *Cuba Socialista*, Pt. 1, 6, no. 56 (April 1966):128–

183, and Pt. 2, 6, no. 57 (May 1966):94–127. The reference to value added in the industrial sector appears in Pt. 2, p. 98.

7. One researcher has pointed out that there are at least two errors in the value-added data reported for 1962: (1) value added by the forestry sector is three times larger than GVO; and (2) the wage bill in the construction materials sector is larger than value added. See Brundenius, *Revolutionary Cuba*, p. 26. Contrary to Brundenius's analysis, these two situations are not impossible (for example, forestry activities may be operating at a loss), but do suggest that there may be errors in the data.

8. The discussion ignores the military sector because of the lack of information. Some tentative estimates of the size of the armed forces have been made by Mesa-Lago. According to him, military personnel averaged 374,500 in 1962–65; 302,000 in 1966–70; 193,000 in 1971–75; and 225,000 in 1976–78. See Mesa-Lago, *The Economy of Socialist Cuba*, p. 111. The estimates are in line with estimates in Claes Brundenius, "Notes on the Development of the Cuban Labor Force," *Cuban Studies/Estudios Cubanos* 13, no. 2 (Summer 1983):76. Brundenius estimates the Cuban military labor force at 285,000 in 1979 and 319,000 in 1980.

9. "El desarrollo industrial de Cuba," 2: 113.

10. The seminar, its objectives, and attendees received considerable publicity in the Cuban press. See, e.g., articles in *Granma* (5, 7, 8, and 11 May 1982); and "Clausura y punto de partida," *Bohemia* 74, no. 28 (9 July 1982):32.

11. ECLA, *Comparabilidad de los sistemas de cuentas nacionales y del producto material en América Latina*.

12. *Cuba: Conversión de los principales indicadores macroeconómicos del Sistema de Balances de la Economía Nacional (SBEN) al Sistema de Cuentas Nacionales (SCN) 1974*.

13. On this point see ibid., p. 6.

14. Ibid, table 1, p. 15.

15. Annual state budgets for 1982–85 do exist and data are available but are not included in the table.

16. Partial budget data for 1977 are presented in BNC, *Economic Report*, p. 31, suggesting that a state budget for 1977 did exist.

17. For example, Zoila González Maicas, "La matriz de insumo-producto: un nuevo instrumento de planificación industrial," *Nuestra Industria. Revista Económica* 2, no. 8 (August 1964):64–75; Enrique González Romero and Zoila González Maicas, "Algunas contribuciones al análisis y utilización de la matriz de insumo-producto," *Nuestra Industria. Revista Económica* 3, no. 12 (April 1965):3–25. See also Ricardo Rodas, "Una aplicación de las tablas de insumo-producto al sector industrial cubano," *Comercio Exterior* 2, no. 3 (July–September 1964):5–45.

18. The direct-requirements matrix is included in González Maicas, "La matriz."

19. The final-requirements matrix appears in González Romero and González Maicas, "Algunas contribuciones."

3. Product/Services Weights

1. This thesis is developed, e.g., by James M. Malloy, "Generation of Political Support and Allocation of Costs," pp. 23–42.

2. This section relies heavily on Miguel Angel Araque, "Antecedentes en Cuba de la formación de precios," *Bohemia* 71, no. 2 (12 January 1979):16–23; and "Proposición de un sistema de precios utilizando los costos planificados como precios de entregas dentro del sector estatal," *Nuestra Industria. Revista Económica* 5 (June 1967).

3. Although the movement has been toward progressive reduction in the number of rationed products, there have been instances in which products that were removed from the rationing system were returned to it. For example, in May 1982, the Domestic Trade Ministry reported that because of shortages of raw materials and reductions in imports, the following products would again be subject to the rationing system: men's trousers, bras, bedspreads, imported hose, yarns, ballpoint pens, bicycle tires, lipstick, nail polish, and bobby pins (radio broadcast over the Cuban Domestic Service on 28 May 1982, as reported in Foreign Broadcast Information Service, *Daily Report—Latin America* 6, no. 105 (1 June 1982):Q3.

4. "De la economía cubana de hoy: reponde Humberto Pérez," *Bohemia* 75, no. 10 (11 March 1983):32. See also Medea Benjamin, Joseph Collins, and Michael Scott, *No Free Lunch*, esp. chap. 3.

5. Publication of the data required 129 volumes of three hundred pages each. See "¿Qué son las listas oficiales de precios y de tarifas?" *Granma* (4 August 1977):3.

6. Brundenius, *Revolutionary Cuba*, pp. 166–167, quoting data from the *Lista oficial de precios*.

7. "Sobre la reforma de precios minoristas y las gratuidades indebidas," *Granma* (14 December 1981):2–3.

8. For dairy products, conversions from volume to weight units were based on data in Milk Industry Association, *Milk Facts 1982*. For textiles and apparel, conversions from units of weight to specific units were made using the relationship for the United States in 1981 from National Cotton Council of America, *Cotton Counts Its Customers*. For energy products, conversion from volume to weight units is based on factors in United States, Federal Energy Administration, *Energy Interrelationships*.

9. "De la economía cubana de hoy."

10. Jesús Abascal López, "Consumo y nivel de vida," *Cuba Internacional*, no. 12 (December 1984):33, quoting Domestic Trade Minister Manual Vila Sosa.

11. See, e.g., Nancy Forster and Howard Handelman, "Government Policy and Nutrition in Revolutionary Cuba," *University Field Staff International Reports*, no. 19 (1982): pp. 12–13.

12. "Satisfacen las necesidades," *Prisma Latinoamericano* 10, no. 145 (September 1984):24; interview with then–JUCEPLAN President Humberto Pérez, "Lo que el pueblo debe saber," *Bohemia* 71, no. 7 (16 February 1979):75–78; José M. Norniella Rodríguez, "El mercado paralelo: una vía del sistema de Dirección y Planificación de la Economía para eliminar el racionamiento," *Cuestiones de la Economía Planificada* 3, no. 6 (November–December 1980):48–65.

13. Jesús Abascal López, "Dime lo que comes," *Cuba Internacional*, no. 9 (September 1984):24; Alfonso Chardy, "Open Market Lets Resurgent Havana Dress for Success," *Miami Herald* (25 March 1985).

14. Law-Decree 77, approved by the Executive Committee of the Council of Ministers on 5 April 1980. For a brief description of the law-decree, see

"Establecido el mercado libre campesino," *Legalidad Socialista*, no. 8 (1980):1, 4.

15. See, e.g., the discussion in Benjamin, Collins, and Scott, *No Free Lunch*, esp. pp. 64–80.

16. Speech by Fidel Castro at the Fourth Congress of the Union of Communist Youth, 4 April 1982, as reproduced in *Granma* (6 April 1982):4.

17. Benjamin, Collins, and Scott, *No Free Lunch*, p. 75.

18. Law-Decree 106 of 30 September 1982, *Gaceta Oficial* (22 October 1982):223–226.

19. Morris Bornstein, "The Soviet Price System," *American Economic Review* 52, no. 1 (March 1962):64. See also idem, "Soviet Price Theory and Policy," in United States, Congress, Joint Economic Committee, *New Directions in the Soviet Economy*, Pt. 1.

20. For example, Antonio Jorge and Jorge Salazar-Carrillo, "Economic Measurement in an Open, Non-Market Economy: The Use of Prices for Estimation in Cuba."

21. See Bergson, *The Real National Income*, chap. 8.

22. For further information on the price collection procedures, see Jorge Salazar-Carrillo, *Prices and Purchasing Power Parities in Latin America 1960-1972*; and idem and Jorge Bortscheff, "The Comparison of Prices, Purchasing Power and Real Products in Central America."

23. U.S. Bureau of Mines, *Minerals Yearbook*, various issues, and U.S. Bureau of Labor Statistics, *Wholesale Prices and Price Indexes*, various issues.

24. See, e.g., Peter Isard, "How Far Can We Push the 'Law of One Price'?" *American Economic Review* 67, no. 5 (December 1977):942–948; and Irving Kravis and Robert E. Lipsey, "Export Prices and the Transmission of Inflation," *American Economic Review* 67, no. 1 (February 1977):155–163.

4. Results

1. Despite considerable research, I have not found a satisfactory explanation of the employment category shifts that occurred between 1976 and 1977. I can hypothesize that they are the result of a reorganization of certain activities within enterprises and may be related to the implementation of the SDPE. For example, a shift to consider cafeteria workers in bus stations as employees of the trade sector rather than of the transportation sector would be consistent with the observed changes in the data.

5. Comparisons with Other Measures

1. BNC, *Economic Report*, p. 31.

2. "Cuba: Conversión de los principales indicadores macroeconómicos," p. 15.

3. Brundenius, *Revolutionary Cuba*.

4. Claes Brundenius and Andrew Zimbalist, "Recent Studies on Cuban Economic Growth: A Review," *Comparative Economic Studies* 27, no. 1 (Spring 1985):34.

5. Brundenius, *Revolutionary Cuba*, p. 29. The basic needs index is described in his chap. 4.

6. Conclusions

1. Mesa-Lago, *The Economy of Socialist Cuba*.

Appendix D
1. According to the methodological notes in recent statistical yearbooks (e.g., *Anuario estadístico de Cuba 1980*, p. 49), the shift to the enterprise-exit valuation methodology did not extend to agriculture (which continues under the complete circulation method) and construction (which uses a special valuation method called "branch exit"). Despite this, in this appendix I have assumed that the valuation changes were effected for all economic sectors, since it can be readily observed from table D-1 that the value of output of the agricultural and construction sector for 1975 and 1976 on the two bases also differs.
2. *Cuba: conversión de los principales indicadores*, table 1, p. 15.

Bibliography

Abascal López, Jesús. "Consumo y nivel de vida." *Cuba Internacional*, no.12 (December 1984):28–33.

————. "Dime lo que comes." *Cuba Internacional*, no. 9 (September 1984):21–27.

Acosta, José. "Cuba: de la neocolonia a la construcción del socialismo." *Economía y Desarrollo*, no. 20 (November-December 1973):59–117.

Alvarez Tabío, Fernando. *Comentarios a la constitución socialista*. Havana: Editorial de Ciencias Sociales, 1981.

Araque, Miguel Angel. "Antecedentes en Cuba de la formación de precios." *Bohemia* 71, no. 2 (12 January 1979):16–23.

Ayala Castro, Héctor. "Los cambios en las relaciones de propiedad, 1961–1963." *Economía y Desarrollo*, no. 65 (November-December 1981):181–197.

————. "Transformaciones de la propiedad en el período 1964–80." *Economía y Desarrollo*, no. 68 (May-June 1982):11–25.

————. "Transformaciones de propiedad, control obrero e intervención de empresas en Cuba." *Economía y Desarrollo*, no. 47 (May-June 1978):45–69.

Balari, Eugenio R. "Cinco años de trabajo del Instituto Cubano de Investigaciones y Orientación de la Demanda Interna." *Investigaciones Científicas de la Demanda en Cuba*. Havana: Editorial Orbe, 1979.

Balari, Eugenio R., and Luis C. Ramírez. "Eficiencia y calidad en la investigación económica en el Instituto de la Interna Demanda." *Areito* 6, no. 23 (1980):28–34.

Banco Nacional de Cuba (BNC). *Cuba: Economic Development and Prospects*. Havana, 1978.

————. *Cuba: Economic and Social Development 1976–80 and First Half 1981*. Havana, 1981.

————. *Development and Prospects of the Cuban Economy*. Havana, 1975.

————. *Economic Report*. Havana, August 1982.

Benjamin, Medea; Joseph Collins; Michael Scott. *No Free Lunch*. San Francisco: Institute for Food Development Policy, 1984.

Bergson, Abram. *The Real National Income of Soviet Russia since 1928*. Cambridge: Harvard University Press, 1961.

————. "Soviet National Income and Production in 1937." *Quarterly Journal of Economics*, Pt. 1, 65 (May 1950):208–241; Pt. 2, 65 (August 1950):408–441.

Bornstein, Morris "The Soviet Price System." *American Economic Review*

52, no. 1 (March 1962):64–103.

————. "Soviet Price Theory and Policy." In U.S. Congress, Joint Economic Committee, *New Directions in the Soviet Economy*, Pt. 1, pp. 65–98. Washington, D.C.: GPO, 1966.

Brundenius, Claes. "Notes on the Development of the Cuban Labor Force." *Cuban Studies/Estudios Cubanos* 13, no. 2 (Summer 1983):65–77.

————. *Revolutionary Cuba: The Challenge of Growth with Equity*. Boulder, Colo.: Westview, 1984.

Brundenius, Claes, and Andrew Zimbalist. "Recent Studies on Cuban Economic Growth: A Review." *Comparative Economic Studies* 22, no. 1 (Spring 1985):21–45.

Central Intelligence Agency. National Foreign Assessment Center. *USSR: Toward a Reconciliation of Marxist and Western Measures of National Income*. ER 78-10505. Washington, D.C., October 1978.

Chang, John K. *Industrial Development in Pre-Communist China*. Chicago: Aldine, 1969.

Chardy, Alfonso. "Open Market Lets Resurgent Havana Dress for Success." *Miami Herald*, 25 March 1985.

"Clausura y punto de partida." *Bohemia* 74, no. 28 (9 July 1982):32.

Comité Estatal de Estadísticas (CEE). *Anuario Estadístico de Cuba*. Various years.

————. *Cifras estadísticas*. Havana, 1980.

————. "Cuba: Conversión de los principales indicadores macroeconómicos del Sistema de Balances de la Economía Nacional (SBEN) al Sistema de Cuentas Nacionales (SCN) 1974." Mimeographed. Havana, March 1982.

————. *Cuba en cifras*. Havana, 1980, 1981.

————. *Desarrollo económico y social de Cuba durante el período 1958–1980*. Havana, 1981.

————. *Estadísticas quinquenales de Cuba, 1965–1980*. Havana, 1982.

————. Dirección de Demografía. *Encuesta demográfica nacional 1979*. Havana, 1981.

Comité Estatal de Precios (CEP). *Lista oficial de precios*. 2 vols. Havana, 1981.

Council for Mutual Economic Assistance (CMEA). *Statisticheskii ezhegodnik*. Moscow, various years.

De la Cuesta, Leonel-Antonio, comp. *Constituciones cubanas*. Miami: Ediciones Exilio, 1974.

"El desarrollo industrial de Cuba." *Cuba Socialista*, Pt. 1, 6, no. 56 (April 1966):128–183; Pt. 2, 6, no. 57 (May 1966):94–127.

Duyos, Oscar. "Los problemas actuales del acopio y los precios de compra de los productos estatales." *Cuba Socialista* 9, no. 33 (May 1964):66–78.

Economic Commission for Europe (ECE). "Comparative GDP Levels." *Economic Bulletin for Europe* 31, no. 2 (1980):1–56.

————. "International Comparisons of Real Incomes, Capital Formation and Consumption." *Economic Survey of Europe in 1969*, Pt. 1, pp. 139–152. New York: United Nations, 1970.

Ehrlich, Eva. "An Examination of the Inter-Relation between Consumption Indicators Expressed in Physical Indicators and Per Capita National Income." *Czechoslovak Economic Papers* 7 (October 1966):109–135.

"Establecido el mercado libre campesino." *Legalidad Socialista*, no. 8 (1980):1, 4.

Forster, Nancy. "Cuban Agricultural Productivity: A Comparison of State and Private Farm Sectors." *Cuban Studies/Estudios Cubanos* 11, no. 2, 12, no. 1 (July 1981–January 1982):105–125.

Forster, Nancy, and Howard Handelman. "Government Policy and Nutrition in Revolutionary Cuba." *University Field Staff International Reports*, no. 19 (1982).

González Maicas, Zoila. "La matriz de insumo-producto: un nuevo instrumento de planificación industrial." *Nuestra Industria. Revista Económica* 2, no. 8 (August 1964):68–75.

González Romero, Enrique, and Zoila González Maicas. "Algunas contribuciones al análisis y utilización de la matriz de insumo-producto." *Nuestra Industria. Revista Económica* 3, no. 12 (April 1965):3–25.

Gutelman, Michel. *La agricultura socializada en Cuba.* Mexico City: Editorial Era, 1970.

Instituto Cubano de Investigaciones y Orientación de la Demanda Interna (ICIODI). *Normas racionales de consumo para alimentos, vestuarios y calzado y equipamiento para la vivienda.* Havana, 1974.

Isard, Peter. "How Far Can We Push the 'Law of One Price'?" *American Economic Review* 67, no. 5 (December 1977):942–948.

Jorge, Antonio, and Jorge Salazar-Carrillo. "Economic Measurement in an Open, Non-Market Economy: The Use of Prices for Estimation in Cuba." Discussion Paper no. 14, Department of Economics, Florida International University. Mimeographed, February 1984.

Junta Central de Planificación. *Censo de población y viviendas 1970.* Havana: Editorial Orbe, 1975.

———. Dirección Central de Estadística. *Boletín Estadístico.* Various years.

Kravis, Irving, and Robert E. Lipsey. "Export Prices and the Transmission of Inflation." *American Economic Review* 67, no. 1 (February 1977):155–163.

Lee, Pong, and John M. Montias. "Indices of Rumanian Industrial Production." In John M. Montias, ed., *Economic Development in Communist Rumania*, pp. 248–266. Cambridge: MIT Press, 1967.

Malloy, James M. "Generation of Political Support and Allocation of Costs." In Carmelo Mesa-Lago, ed., *Revolutionary Change in Cuba*, pp. 23–42. Pittsburgh, Pa.: University of Pittsburgh Press, 1971.

Marer, Paul. "Alternative Estimates of the Dollar GNP and Growth Rates of CMEA Countries." In U.S. Congress. Joint Economic Committee. *East European Economies: Slow Growth in the 1980s.* Washington, D.C., US Government Printing Office, 1985, pp. 1:133–193.

Mesa-Lago, Carmelo. "Availability and Reliability of Statistics in Socialist Cuba." *LARR*, Pt. 1, 4, no. 1 (Spring 1969):53–91; Pt. 2, 4, no. 2 (Summer 1969):47–81.

———. "The economy: Caution, Frugality, and Resilient Ideology." In Jorge I. Domínguez, ed., *Cuba: Internal and International Affairs*, pp. 113–166. Beverly Hills: Sage, 1982.

———. *The Economy of Socialist Cuba: A Two-Decade Appraisal.* Albuquerque:

University of New Mexico Press, 1981.

———. "Ideological Radicalization and Economic Policy in Cuba." *Studies in Comparative International Development* 5, no. 10 (1969–70):203–216.

———. "The Revolutionary Offensive." *Transaction* 6, no. 6 (April 1969):22–29.

Mesa-Lago, Carmelo, and Jorge Pérez-López. "Estimating Cuban Gross Domestic Product Per Capita in Dollars Using Physical Indicators." *Social Indicators Research* 16 (1985):275–300.

———. *A Study of Cuba's Material Product System, Its Conversion to the System of National Accounts, and Estimation of Gross Domestic Product Per Capita and Growth Rates.* World Bank Staff Working Paper, no. 770. Washington, D.C.: World Bank, 1985.

Milk Industry Association. *Milk Facts 1982.* Washington, D.C., 1982.

National Cotton Council of America. *Cotton Counts Its Customers.* Memphis, 1982.

Norniello Rodríguez, José M. "El mercado paralelo: una vía del sistema de dirección y planificación de la economía para eliminar el racionamiento." *Cuestiones de la Economía Planificada* 3, no. 6 (November–December 1980):48–65.

Pérez, Humberto. "Lo que el pueblo debe saber." *Bohemia* 71, no. 7 (16 February 1979):75–78.

Pérez-López, Jorge. "An Index of Cuban Industrial Output, 1930–1958." In James W. Wilkie and Kenneth Ruddle, *Quantitative Latin American Studies: Methods and Findings*, pp. 37–72. Los Angeles: UCLA Latin American Center, 1977.

"Proposición de un sistema de precios utilizando los costos planificados como precios de entregas dentro del sector estatal." *Nuestra Industria. Revista Económica* 5 (June 1967).

"¿Qué son las listas oficiales de precios y de tarifas?" *Granma* (4 August 1977):3.

Regalado, Antero. "Las funciones del ANAP." *Cuba Socialista* 9, no. 35 (July 1964):9–24.

"Resolución sobre la cuestión agraria y las relaciones con el campesinado." *Economía y Desarrollo*, no. 36 (July–August 1976):16–167.

Rodas, Ricardo. "Una aplicación de las tablas de insumo-producto al sector industrial cubano." *Comercio Exterior* 2, no. 3 (July–September 1964):5–45.

Rodríguez, Carlos Rafael. *Cuba en el tránsito al socialismo.* Mexico City: Siglo XXI, 1978.

Salazar-Carrillo, Jorge. *Prices and Purchasing Power Parities in Latin America 1960–1972.* Washington, D.C.: OAS, 1979.

Salazar-Carrillo, Jorge, and Jorge Bortscheff. "The Comparison of Prices, Purchasing Power and Real Products in Central America." In William R. Cline and Enrique Delgado, eds., *Economic Integration in Central America*, pp. 371–392. Washington, D.C.: The Brookings Institution, 1978.

San Pedro, Gustavo, et al. "La normas racionales del consumo." In ICIODI, *Investigaciones científicas de la demanda en Cuba*, pp. 58–78. Havana: Editorial Orbe, 1979.

"Satisfacen las necesidades." *Prisma Latinoamericana* 10, no. 145 (September 1984):23–24.

Seminario Latinoamericano de Cuentas Nacionales y Balances de la Economía. *Cuba: Conversión de los principales indicadores macroeconómicos del Sistema de Balances de la Economía Nacional (SBEN) al Sistema de Cuentas Nacionales (SCN).* Havana, March 1982.

Sigmund, Paul E. *Multinationals in Latin America: The Politics of Nationalization.* Madison: University of Wisconsin Press, 1980.

"Sobre la reforma de precios minoristas y las gratuidades indebidas." *Granma* (14 December 1981):2-3.

Staller, George J. "Czechoslovak Industrial Growth: 1948-1959." *American Economic Review* 52 (June 1962):385-407.

Tribunal de Cuentas, Dirección de Fiscalización Preventiva y Control de Presupuestos del Estado. "Análisis de los sectores económicos en Cuba y su tributación." Havana: mimeographed, 22 July 1957.

United Nations. Statistical Office. *Basic Principles of the System of Balance of the National Economy.* Ser. F, no. 17. New York, 1971.

––––––. *Comparison of the System of National Accounts and the System of Balances of the National Economy.* Pt. 1: *Conceptual Relationships.* Ser. F, no. 20: Pt. 2: *Conversion of Aggregates of SNA to MPS and Vice Versa for Selected Countries.* Ser. F, no. 20. New York, 1981.

––––––. *International Standard Industrial Classification of All Economic Activities.* Ser. M, no. 4, rev. 2. New York, 1968.

––––––. *Statistical Bulletin.* Various years.

––––––. *Statistical Yearbook.* Various years.

––––––. *A System of National Account.* Ser. F, 2, rev. 3. New York, 1968.

––––––. Conference on Trade and Development. *Cuba: Recent Economic Developments and Future Prospects.* UNCTAD/MFD/TA/21. New York, 1982.

––––––. Economic Commission for Latin America (ECLA). "Comparabilidad de los sistemas de cuentas nacionales y del producto material de América Latina." E/CEPAL/SEM.5/L.2. Mimeographed, New York, 13 April 1982.

––––––. "The Cuban Economy in the Period 1959-63." *Economic Survey of Latin America 1963,* pp. 259-289. New York, 1965.

––––––. *Economic Survey of Latin America.* New York, various years.

United States. Bureau of Labor Statistics. *Wholesale Prices and Price Indexes.* Washington, D.C., various years.

––––––. Bureau of Mines. *Minerals Yearbook.* Washington, D.C., various years

––––––. Congress. Joint Economic Committee. *USSR: Measures of Economic Growth and Development, 1950-1980.* Washington, D.C., GPO, 1982.

––––––. Federal Energy Administration. *Energy Interrelationships.* Washington, D.C.: GPO, 1977

––––––. Joint Economic Committee. *East European Economies: Slow Growth in the 1980s.* Washington, D.C.: GPO, 1985, pp. 1:133-193.

Valdés Paz, Juan. "La pequeña producción agrícola en Cuba." *Revista del México Agrario* 12, no. 1 (January-March 1982):125-155.

World Bank. "International Comparisons of Estimated Real Per Capita Income Levels—the ECE's Physical Indicators Approach Updated for 1973." Mimeographed, 19 March 1978.

Index

"*Acopio*" system, 23–31, 93; relationship between, and total agricultural production, 24, 30–31
Activity indexes, estimated, 97–113
Agriculture: comparison of growth rates in, 119–126; estimated activity indexes of, 97–103; growth estimates for, based on official data, 119; growth estimates for, by Brundenius, 119
Air transportation, estimated activity index of, 104
Apparel, estimated activity index of, 110

Banco Nacional de Cuba (BNC): estimates of Cuban gross domestic product by, 117, 126; publication of economic statistics by, 7
Bergson, Abram, 4, 92
Beverages and tobacco, estimated activity index of, 97, 110
Black market, 24, 86; prices in, 86, 89
BNC (Banco Nacional de Cuba): estimates of Cuban gross domestic product by, 117, 126; publication of economic statistics by, 7
Bottom-up method (of estimating gross domestic product): applied to Cuba, 4–5, 127; criticisms of, 4; defined, 4; and index categories, 47
Brundenius, Claes, 84, 117–128
Budget, state, 59–60

CAE. *See* Clasificador de Actividades Económicas

Capital stock, 38; changes in (*see* Investment)
CEE. *See* Comité Estatal de Estadísticas
CEP (Comité Estatal de Precios), 84
Chemicals, estimated activity index of, 97
Circulación completa, 2, 53
Clasificador de Actividades Económicas (CAE), 11; correlation of, with International Standard Industrial Classification of All Economic Activities, 11, 23
CMEA. *See* Council for Mutual Economic Assistance
Collectivization, 8–11, 83; in agriculture, 8–11; in foreign investments, 9; in industry, 8–11; in services, 8–11, 83
Comité Estatal de Estadísticas (CEE): conversion from Material Product System of National Accounts, 2; data published by, 7, 24, 47, 57, 117; estimates of gross domestic product (1974), 2, 117
Comité Estatal de Precios (CEP), 84
Complete circulation valuation method, defined, 2, 53
Construction, estimated activity index of, 104
Construction materials, estimated activity index of, 97
Council for Mutual Economic Assistance (CMEA), and publication of Cuban economic statistics, 7, 24–25, 39

ECIEL (Programa de Estudios Conjuntos sobre Integración Económica Latinoamericana), 92
ECLA (Economic Commission for Latin America), 2, 33–34
Economically active population, 38
Education and public health, estimated activity index of, 104
Ehrlich, Eva, 3
Electricity, estimated activity index of, 97
Electronics, estimated activity index of, 97, 110
Employment, 35–38; anomaly in series for the trade sector, 103–104; discontinuities in data for civilian state, 35; estimates of private sector, 36
Enterprise-exit valuation method, 2, 53
Enterprise valuation method. *See* Enterprise-exit valuation method

Factor-cost standard (for prices), 91; adjusting prevailing prices to approximate, 92
Fishing, estimated activity index of, 97, 110
Forestry, estimated activity index of, 101
Free peasant markets, 24, 86; prices in, 91

GDP. *See* Gross domestic product
Global social product: comparison of growth rates in, 126–128; estimated activity index of, 110–113; growth rates in, based on official data, 126
GMP. *See* Material product
GNP (Gross national product), 2
Goods and services for accumulation: defined, 110; estimated activity index of, 110
Goods and services for consumption: defined, 110; estimated activity index of, 110
Goods for accumulation: defined, 110; estimated activity index of, 104–110
Goods for consumption: defined, 110;

estimated activity index of, 104–110
Goods-producing sectors, estimated activity index of, 97, 103
Gross domestic product: comparison of growth rates in, 126–128; estimated activity index of, 113; estimates of, by Banco Nacional de Cuba, 117; estimates of, by Brundenius, 117–119
Gross material product. *See* Material product
Gross national product (GNP), 2
Gross turnover valuation method, 2, 53
Gross value of output (GVO), 34; estimated (for 1961) from GSP data, 34; methods for disaggregating official data for 1974, 47–60; official data for 1974, 47, 57; using state budget allocations for financing nonproductive sphere as disaggregating scheme, 59
GSP. *See* Global social product
GVO. *See* Gross value of output

Industry: comparison of growth rates in, 119–126; estimated activity index of, 97–103; growth estimates in, based on official data, 119; growth estimates in, by Brundenius, 119
Input-output table (1963), 60–65; direct requirements matrix in, 62–63; final requirements matrix in, 62; industry coverage in, 62; sensitivity to economic changes in Cuba in, 65; as source of value-added/gross value of output coefficients, 65–72
International Standard Industrial Classification of All Economic Activities (ISIC), 11; correlation with Cuba's Clasificador de Actividades Económicas, 11, 23
Investment, 34; data by type and use, 39–46
I-O. *See* Input-output table
ISIC. *See* International Standard Industrial Classification of All Economic Activities.

Janossy, Ferenc, 3
JUCEPLAN (Junta Central de Planificación), 33, 84

Leather products, estimated activity index of, 97, 110
Livestock, estimated activity index of, 101

Maritime transportation, estimated activity index of, 104
Material product: comparison of growth rates in, 126–128; estimated activity index of, 110–113; estimates of, by Brundenius, 117–118; index of, based on official data, 117
Material Product System (MPS): bottom-up method of conversion from, to System of National Accounts, 4–5; CEE/ECLA conversion of, 2, 41; contrasted with System of National Accounts, 2; conversion from, to System of National Accounts, 2; defined, 1; macroeconomic measures, 1–2; physical indicators method of conversion of, 3–4; scaling-up method of conversion of, 2–3; United Nations conversion of, 2
Mercados libres campesinos. See Free peasant markets
Mesa-Lago, Carmelo, 3, 127
Metal products, estimated activity index of, 97
Mining and metallurgy, ferrous, estimated activity index of, 97
Ministry of Industries, 60, 62

Nationalization. *See* Collectivization
Net material product (NMP), 2
Net national product (NNP), 2
NMP (Net material product), 2
NMS. *See* Nonmaterial services
NNP (Net national product), 2
Nonelectrical machinery, estimated activity index of, 110
Nonmaterial services (NMS): data availability, 3, 47; defined, 2; excluded in macroeconomic indicators in Material Product System, 2; included in macroeconomic indicators in System of National Accounts, 2
Nonproductive services, estimated activity index of, 104
Nonsugar agriculture, estimated activity index of, 101

Paper and paper products, estimated activity index of, 97
Parallel market, 86; prices in, 89–91
Physical indicators method: applied to Eastern Europe and the Soviet Union, 4; defined, 3; problems in applying, to Cuba, 3–4
Physical output data, 7–31; for agriculture, 23–31; for industry, 11; lack of, for certain services sectors, 21–22; for services, 11, 21–23; sources of, 7; use of employment, as proxies for activity in certain services sectors, 21–22, 103–104
Prices, official (Cuba): general freeze of, 84; lack of, for services activities, 104; and rationing, 84; reductions in (1959), 83–84; reform of retail (1981), 84
Prices, proxy, 91–92; as approximations of adjusted factor cost, 92; caveats concerning, 93; Guatemalan, 92; lack of, for services activities, 104; U.S., 92–93
Price system (Cuba), 83–91; government tampering with (1959), 83. *See also* Black market; Free peasant market; Prices, official; Prices, proxy
Printing, estimated activity index of, 97
Processed foods, estimated activity index of, 97, 110
Production factors, returns to: in capital, 38–46; in labor, 35–38; lack of data on, 46
Productive services, estimated activity index of, 104

Programa de Estudios Conjuntos sobre Integración Económica Latinoamericana (ECIEL), 92

Rationing system, 84
Reform, agrarian, 8–9

A salida de empresa (enterprise-exit valuation method), 2, 53
Scaling-up method (of converting from Material Product System to System of National Accounts): defined, 2; unfeasibility of applying to Cuba, 2–3
SDPE (Sistema de Dirección y Planificación de la Economía), 84
Services for accumulation: defined, 110; estimated activity index of, 104–110
Services for consumption: defined, 110; estimated activity index of, 104–110
Services sectors, estimated activity index of, 103–110
Sistema de Dirección y Planificación de la Economía (SDPE), 84
SNA. See System of National Accounts
Social security, welfare, cultural, and scientific activities, estimated activity index of, 104
Statistics, economic, 1, 2, 3, 7, 47, 72, 103, 127

Sugar, estimated activity index of, 97
System of Balances of the National Economy. See Material Product System
System of National Accounts (SNA), 1; contrasted with Material Product System, 2; macroeconomic measures in, 2

Textiles, estimated activity index of, 97, 110
Trade, estimated activity index of, 103

United Nations, 2, 7

Value-added data: inadequacy of official, 35; for industrial sectors, 35; by labor, 38; by labor and nonlabor inputs from input-output table, 60–65; official (for 1961–1963), 33–34
Value-added weights, 33–72; estimated from gross value of output data and value-added/gross value of output coefficients, 47–72; estimated from returns to factors data, 35–46

Wage bill, 35; discontinuities in data for civilian state, 35; as proxy for value added by labor, 38